W9-BBI-968

JOHN JONES PETTUS

JOHN JONES PETTUS

Mississippi Fire-Eater:
His Life and Times
1813-1867

Robert W. Dubay

UNIVERSITY PRESS OF MISSISSIPPI

JACKSON

Copyright © 1975 by the
University Press of Mississippi
Library of Congress Catalog Card Number 74-33923
ISBN 0-87805-066-3
Manufactured in the United States of America

THIS VOLUME IS AUTHORIZED
AND SPONSORED BY THE
UNIVERSITY OF SOUTHERN MISSISSIPPI

GADSDEN
PUBLIC
LIBRARY

For
J. G., Alvina,
and Linda Dubay

B
Pettus

173478

Contents

Acknowledgments

THE PAGES THAT FOLLOW were initially inspired by Professor William K. Scarborough of the University of Southern Mississippi. As one of his students, I came to benefit from his high counsel, advice, and accomplished craftsmanship in more ways than I have space to enumerate. Similarly, Professors John E. Gonzales and Kenneth G. McCarty of the same institution also contributed their share of sage commentary and gentle wisdom during difficult periods.

Of the many historical depositories visited along the way, none earned my indebtedness more than the Mississippi Department of Archives and History. New and modern quarters now house that organization, but somehow the old, slightly shabby, accommodations of yesteryear are still fondest in my mind. With uncommon skill and dispatch, the members of that department made my path a little easier to traverse.

I also wish to express appreciation to the respective staffs of the Duke University Library, the University of North Carolina Library, and the Alabama Department of Archives and History.

Finally, a word of gratitude must be accorded Mr. John Weedon of Denver, Colorado, who allowed me access to relevant private correspondence; to the Foundation of Dalton Junior College, Dalton, Georgia, for financial assistance; to Derrell C. Roberts, who lent a kind hand on my behalf; and the two Lindas who spent those long hours in typing—Linda Dubay and Linda Phillips.

R. W. D.

Bainbridge, Georgia

Introduction

WITH THE EXCEPTION of South Carolina and Virginia, few southern states played a more significant role in secessionist and Civil War history than did Mississippi. One might reasonably assume that by now such a subject would have been so thoroughly canvassed as to permit little margin for further comment. Yet the bulk of existing studies relating to these topics is sometimes limited in scope, application, or approach.[1] The passage of time, the appearance of fresh evidence, and the shifting of perspective have combined to render previous scholarship a little less useful. New questions are always at hand, the answers to which are essential to a more comprehensive understanding of Mississippi's affairs and their respective relationship to other states and the ill-fated Confederate States of America.

The present study focuses on a somewhat lesser-known political figure, John Jones Pettus—a man whose life and career parallel the all important latter stages of the sectional controversy and the greater portion of the Civil War. Although occupying some form of public station almost continuously for twenty years, he has been viewed superficially and, on occasion, inaccurately by certain historians, or his contributions to the affairs of the day have been minimized.[2] This situation can probably be attributed to the fact that Pettus' activities were often over-

[1] Few monographs concerning the period of Mississippi history presently under consideration have appeared in recent years, and those which have been published are largely confined to military affairs. See Edwin C. Bearss, *Decision In Mississippi: Mississippi's Important Role in the War Between the States* (Jackson, 1962) and Peter F. Walker, *Vicksburg: A People at War, 1860–1865* (Chapel Hill, 1960). The two standard sources of an indispensable nature are Percy L. Rainwater, *Mississippi: Storm Center of Secession, 1856–1861* (Baton Rouge, 1938) and John K. Bettersworth, *Confederate Mississippi: The People and Policies of a Cotton State in Wartime* (Baton Rouge, 1943).

[2] One monograph of recent vintage, for example, consistently refers incorrectly to Pettus as John "Pettis." See Benjamin Quarles, *The Negro In the Civil War* (New York, 1968), 274. Another study inaccurately describes Pettus as the governor of Arkansas. See Jonathan T. Dorris, *Pardon and Amnesty Under Lincoln and Johnson: The Restoration of the Confederates to Their Rights and Privileges, 1861–1898* (Chapel Hill, 1953), 277.

shadowed by other, more prominent, contemporary Mississippians, such as William Barksdale, Albert Gallatin Brown, Jefferson Davis, Henry Stuart Foote, and John J. McRae. In all likelihood this is as it should be; but it may equally be argued that "lesser" men are sometimes of more than passing value when assessing more familiar personalities or events.

John Pettus ascended his state's political structure in rather rapid fashion. The capstone of his career came at a critical juncture in sectional affairs (October, 1859) when he was elected governor. As a champion of the fire-eater wing of the Democratic party he labored long and hard for the cause of secession, and played no small role in the eventual achievement of that objective.

In many respects Pettus personified the thinking of a majority of his constituents when he undertook the duties of Mississippi's chief executive in late 1859. However, once war became a reality his leadership assumed the proportions of a paradox. On certain occasions he displayed an uncommon cautiousness, prudence, and foresight not always found in a man of his ideological temperament. At other times Pettus was naïve, unprepared, unimaginative, and wholly impractical. In any event, the sum of his day to day activities should hopefully provide a clearer picture of both Mississippi and the embattled South during a turbulent era. For if, as historian Ulrich B. Phillips once observed, "intelligence is to be gauged in political programmes, the conditions of life which gave them origin must first be known."[3]

[3] Ulrich B. Phillips, *Life and Labor In The Old South* (Boston, 1929), vii.

JOHN JONES PETTUS

I

Growing up
in the Old South

THIS STUDY RIGHTLY BEGINS with John Pettus of Fluvanna County, Virginia. Born in September, 1782, Pettus resided on his parents' small Virginia plantation until some time in 1805, when he moved to Davidson County, Tennessee, in order to resume his courtship of a certain Alice Taylor Winston. Alice was the daughter of Anthony and Kezia Jones Winston, who had previously maintained a farm in Virginia near the Pettus holdings. The Winston family was one of good social standing, several Winston relatives having served with distinction as colonial officers in the Revolutionary War and others being connected by marriage to such well known Virginia families as the Taylors and the Madisons. Anthony Winston's decision to seek economic advancement in Tennessee was apparently responsible for disrupting the matrimonial plans of John and Alice. But Pettus was persistent and his eventual renewed relationship with Alice Winston culminated in their marriage on December 21, 1807. Since both parties owned farms within a mile of Andrew Jackson's palatial Hermitage, Jackson was naturally invited to attend the ceremony and reportedly "danced at the wedding."[1]

---

[1] Edmund W. Pettus to Ira P. Jones, April 23, 1900, in Edmund Winston Pettus Papers, Alabama Department of Archives and History, Montgomery, Ala.; John P. Weedon to Elizabeth S. Roberts, March 27, 1932, in William Pettus Weedon Collection, Denver, Colo.; Pocahontas Hutchinson Stacy, "The Pettus Family of Virginia" (Typescript in Mississippi Department of Archives and History, Jackson, Mississippi), 23; "Pettus Family *Bible* Records" (Typescript

3

Over the next few years the Pettus and Winston households remained closely associated, but for some unknown reason continuously alternated their respective residences within the Tennessee counties of Madison, Davidson, Franklin, and Wilson. While they were living in the latter district, the first of John and Alice Pettus' children was born on September 22, 1808, and christened Mary Kezia. Two more infants, Anthony Winston and Martha Walker, entered the family in 1810 and 1812, respectively.

Sometime during 1811, Kezia Winston returned to Virginia for the purpose of administering to ill relatives and apparently remained there far beyond the emergency. Alice Pettus' attachment to her mother was evidently quite strong and she soon began to insist "that she could not remember her mother's face." When the burden of loneliness became too hard to bear, Alice "rode all the way back home to Virginia with a baby in her arms to see her mother."[2]

In the spring of 1813, while dwelling in Madison County, Tennessee, John Pettus temporarily left his farm and family in order to join the forces of Andrew Jackson, then engaged in the Creek Indian War. Pettus held the rank of ensign and, according to Jackson, performed his duties with merit and dispatch.[3] Alice, meanwhile, was expecting the couple's fourth child and went to stay with her parents in Wilson County. There, on October 9, 1813, a second son was born and named John Jones in honor of his father and maternal grandmother.

Realizing the farming potential of new lands he had seen during the Creek War, John Pettus returned to Tennessee and immediately transferred his family to Madison County, Alabama. Another daughter, Harriett Overton, was born there on June 1, 1815. The restless father, however, was not yet content and within a year the Pettuses were found in neighboring Limestone

---

copy in Weedon Collection), n.d.; Edmund W. Pettus to Mrs. A. P. Hall, August 20, 1902, in Weedon Collection.

[2] Bessie S. Roberts to John Weedon, March 27, 1931, in E. W. Pettus Papers.

[3] Willie Pettus Lapsby to John L. Powers, November 20, 1897, in John L. Powers Papers, Mississippi Archives.

County. The birth of three additional children, William (August, 1817), Judith (August, 1819), and Edmund Winston (July 6, 1821) completed the family circle. The latter was also destined to become a prominent figure in southern history.[4]

In the fall of 1822 John Pettus died. Although Pettus was semiliterate and comparatively poor, possessing only two quarter sections of land, his will dictated that his children receive "a good English Education."[5] Afterward, the family continued to remain in Limestone County and with the aid of friends and relatives devoted considerable time to routine farm labor. As requested, the education of the children was not neglected and Alice saw to it that they learned to read and write, with lessons conducted during evening hours. The mother's efforts were supplemented by those of daughter Harriett. Harriett, although badly burned in early childhood, managed to learn to read with the "partial use of one eye," and in turn diligently instructed her brothers and sisters in the fundamentals of education.[6]

At about the age of twenty-two John Jones Pettus moved to Sumner County, Mississippi. Although he had received little in the way of formal schooling, it was his intention to practice law while continuing plantation agriculture. The rest of the family soon followed him, but promise of more lucrative economic advancement lured him to Kemper County, and it was at Scooba, Mississippi, that he established a permanent home.[7]

The Mississippi of the 1830s could well be described as "lively." With a population of scarcely more than 70,000 white inhabitants and an equal number of Negro slaves, financial pros-

[4] For material concerning Edmund Pettus, see William Brewer, *Alabama: Her History, Resources, War Record, and Public Men from 1540 to 1872* (Montgomery, 1872), 324; "Edmund Winston Pettus," *Dictionary of American Biography*, eds. Allen Johnson and Dumas Malone (New York, 1928–37), XIV, 519–20; "Edmund Winston Pettus," *The New Century Cyclopedia of Names*, ed. Clarence L. Barnhart (New York, 1954), III, 3157; Ezra J. Warner, *Generals In Gray: Lives of the Confederate Commanders* (Baton Rouge, 1959), 238–39.
[5] John Pettus Will, September 4, 1822, in E. W. Pettus Papers.
[6] Bessie S. Roberts comments in "Pettus Family *Bible* Records," August 24, 1928.
[7] Dunbar Rowland, *The Official and Statistical Register of the State of Mississippi* (Nashville, 1908), 147.

pects for the future looked bright. "Millions of acres of rich lands [were] ready for occupation, and the stimulus of sudden wealth promised by the ever-increasing demand for cotton" could hardly have made the times anything other than exciting. A new constitution was adopted by the state in 1832, according to which document the voice of the common man was furthered and the institution of slavery was viewed as "a positive good."[8] John Pettus knew these things and it was within such an atmosphere that he cast his lot for the future.

A short time after his arrival in Kemper County Pettus married a cousin, Permelia Virginia Winston. By 1843 cotton planting had yielded rewards enough to enable him to pay for nine slaves and 1,600 acres of land. His prosperity continued to accelerate at a steady pace and by 1850 he was recorded as having twenty-four bondsmen.[9] Pettus was a kind and gentle master, according to the testimony of one of his slaves many years later.[10]

Alice, John's widowed mother, eventually established herself in the same county, becoming a planter and slaveowner with at least nine chattels and nearly as much land as her son. The transplanted Pettus clan indeed shared the good fortune of Mississippi's economic abundance in the 1840s and 1850s.[11]

Although daily plantation life was demanding, John Pettus managed to find delight and relaxation in hunting and fishing

[8] William E. Dodd, *Robert J. Walker, Imperialist* (Chicago, 1914), 10; Edwin A. Miles, *Jacksonian Democracy in Mississippi* (Chapel Hill, 1960), 163–65.

[9] *Personal Tax Rolls, Kemper County, Mississippi, 1843* (Microfilm copy in Mississippi Archives), roll 337; *1850 Population Census Schedules, Kemper County, Mississippi* (Microfilm copy in Mississippi Archives), roll 374.

[10] Mrs. G. C. Boyd, "Personal Interview with ex-slave Joe Pettus" (Typescript in personal possession of Mrs. G. C. Boyd, DeKalb, Mississippi), 1936. Such attitudes concerning chattels were not uncommon. See John Q. Anderson, "Dr. James Green Carson Ante-Bellum Planter of Mississippi and Louisiana," *Journal of Mississippi History*, XVIII (October, 1956), 261–62; Horace S. Fulkerson, *Random Recollections of Early Days in Mississippi* (Vicksburg, 1885), 128; Frederick Law Olmsted, *A Journey in the Back Country in the Winter of 1853–1854* (New York, 1907), I, vi.

[11] *1850 Population Census Schedules, Kemper County, Mississippi* (Microfilm copy in Mississippi Archives), roll 374; Alice Taylor Pettus Land Certificates, February 27, 1841, in E. W. Pettus Papers; John H. Moore and Margaret D. Moore, *Mississippi: A Student's Guide to Localized History* (New York, 1969), 14.

expeditions, on which occasions his brothers and sisters often accompanied him. A young neighbor, John Jackson, was once invited to such a Pettus deer hunt. Jackson later recalled that the two of them, riding double, had left early one summer morning. Since the hunters agreed not to eat until a deer had been slain, the boy had to be given an apple every little while in order to satisfy his mounting hunger. Instructed to pinch his older companion if a deer was sighted, Jackson gladly complied when the illusive prey finally came into view. Pettus, an expert marksman, "raised his rifle and counted dinner, dinner, dinner and fired. The deer fell dead." [12]

One of the Pettus flock who was not always present to enjoy such experiences was younger brother Edmund. In order to wed his sweetheart, Mary Chapman, he first had to meet her stipulation of acquiring a college education. In pursuit of this objective Edmund enrolled at Clinton College in Smith County, Tennessee, in 1836 and did not return home once during his four years at that institution. While in college Edmund grew a full beard, and, upon successful completion of a law program, he returned incognito to his brother's Mississippi home with humor on his mind. Arriving at John's residence late one afternoon, Edmund portrayed himself as a traveler and requested permission to spend the night. In keeping with the custom of the period, John answered affirmatively and indicated that supper would soon be ready. While serving the meal an old female slave suddenly recognized the long absent Edmund, "dropped a plate of biscuits and threw up her hands, exclaiming, 'Fore Gawd, it's Marse Ed, it's Marse Ed!' " [13]

While wit had its place in John Pettus' life, so did more serious matters—namely, governmental affairs. In those days Mississippi politics boasted an array of outstanding personalities, Albert Gallatin Brown, John Quitman, John McRae, and

[12] Mrs. G. C. Boyd, "Personal Interview with John Jackson" (Typescript in personal possession of Mrs. G. C. Boyd, DeKalb,), 1937.
[13] Will T. Hale and Dixon L. Merritt, *A History of Tennessee and Tennesseans* (Chicago, 1913), II, 285; Bessie S. Roberts comments in "Pettus Family *Bible* Records," August 24, 1928.

Henry Stuart Foote being among the more notable figures. But there were other men who would soon begin their ascent toward political immortality, two of whom were John Pettus and Jefferson Davis. Distantly related by marriage,[14] these two future partisans were to develop a lasting and important friendship which would ultimately find each of them in the eye of the greatest political storm the nation had ever seen.

[14] This relationship is traceable in the Taylor family. See Walter L. Fleming, "Jefferson Davis' First Marriage," in Franklin L. Riley (ed.), *Publications of the Mississippi Historical Society* (Oxford, Miss., 1912), XII, 21–36; Walter L. Zorn, *The Descendants of the Presidents of the United States of America* (2nd. ed.; Monroe, Mich., 1955), 98.

II

Politics:
The Formative Years

KEMPER COUNTY was established in 1823 and named in honor of Colonel Reuben Kemper, a Virginia soldier who had spent a portion of his career in Mississippi during its territorial period. At the time of its formation, the county encompassed 752 square miles and maintained a rural, sparsely populated identity. Negro slavery was both extensive and deep-rooted from the beginning, and by 1850 nearly 40 percent of Kemper's total inhabitants were bondsmen, with only one black in the entire county able to boast of being free.[1]

In the early days of Kemper County's history, social and political leadership was provided by such locally prominent personalities as author Joseph Baldwyn, Judge W. G. Gibbs, and lawyers Abel Key and Benjamin C. Opeef.[2] Another name was soon added to the list, that of John Jones Pettus.

Friends and associates urged Pettus to allow his name to be placed in contention for a seat in the lower house of the state legislature during the late 1830s. Pettus agreed and suggested that the campaign of 1841 might be an ideal time. However, as his aspirations appeared to be reaching a climax, the state legislature combined Kemper County with neighboring Neshoba

---

[1] Robert Lowry and William H. McCardle, *A History of Mississippi* (Jackson, 1891), 509; Mississippi State Planning Commission, *A Summary of Statistical Data Relating to the Growth and Distribution of Mississippi Population* (Typescript in Miss. Arch.), 29.

[2] Lowry and McCardle, *A History of Mississippi*, 509.

County in order to create a more balanced electoral district with respect to population. This change of events kept Pettus out of the running until early 1843 when the two counties were again separated. As called for by the state constitution of 1832, elections were held on the first Monday and Tuesday in November. In the 1843 contest, the slaveholding cotton planter John Pettus outpolled rivals Edward Mosby and John J. Cocke by more votes than the total cast for both opponents. Democrat Pettus thereby became the seventh man in Kemper history to serve in the Mississippi House of Representatives, in which body he took his seat on January 1, 1844.[3]

Pettus undertook the duties and responsibilities of his two-year term almost immediately by presenting a monetary claim against the state on behalf of constituent Joseph Pearce. During this legislative session Pettus' daily routine was filled with those numerous and often monotonous events which accompany any such political office. Although he probably passed through the halls of the capitol scarcely noticed, several personality traits were nonetheless manifested in his character at that time. A clear record for promptness, exactness, and attention to detail highlighted his activities, and his consistent voting pattern displayed a firm devotion to principle, even if it meant upholding a lost cause. On one occasion, for example, when the contest for the election of a United States senator was particularly close, Pettus steadfastly supported the eventual loser.[4]

Pettus' Kemper constituents were apparently satisfied with their public servant, for he was reelected to a second term in 1845 by what amounted to a landslide victory over rival Peter H. C. Jennings.[5] When Pettus returned to Jackson he was appointed to the House Committee on Elections. The 1846 session

[3] Returns of the General Election of the State of Mississippi, Kemper County, 1843, in Records of the Secretary of State, Ser. F, LVIII, Miss. Archives; Lowry and McCardle, A History of Mississippi, 510; State of Mississippi, Journal of the House of Representatives of the State of Mississippi (1844), 4.

[4] Mississippi House Journal (1844), 127. State legislatures elected United States Senators in this period. See Mississippi House Journal (1844), 188–89.

[5] Returns of the General Election of the State of Mississippi, Kemper County, 1845, in Records of the Secretary of State, Ser. F, LXI, Miss. Arch.

added one new ingredient to Pettus' political personality—
strong advocation of public-sponsored internal improvements
and favorable railroad legislation.[6]

In November, 1847, Pettus' second term in the house expired.
Instead of standing for reelection he cast an eye toward the
recently vacated state senate seat of Emmanuel A. Durr and
subsequently conducted a triumphant campaign for the post by
outpolling opponent Robert J. Love by the incredible margin of
911 to 6. Pettus thus became the fifth man in history to represent
Kemper County in that position, and on January 3, 1848, appeared in the senate chamber to take the oath prescribed by the
constitution.[7]

Although John Pettus was now a junior senator he proceeded
at once to assume an active lead in that body's deliberations. At
this stage of his political evolution he became a passionate sup-
porter of state-sponsored education and on January 28 introduced a resolution calling for the "preservation of liberty and
the happiness of mankind" through further appropriations for
public schools. The resolution was not worded in particularly
convincing fashion, but must have reflected the majority outlook
of his colleagues; it was passed by a vote of 18 to 11.[8]

An item of particular note, which evinced a generous attitude
toward state sovereignty, was the Kemper Countian's support
for a bill to provide for increased regulation of bank notes from
other states which circulated within Mississippi. Before the
senate adjourned in March, Pettus had also successfully aided
in the passage of a bill to charter a railroad and assisted in another measure concerning internal improvements on rivers within the state.[9]

When the legislature reconvened in January of the following

[6] Mississippi *House Journal* (1846), 4. See index of Mississippi *House Journal*
(1846) for votes on related bills.

[7] Lowry and McCardle, *A History of Mississippi*, 510; Returns of the General
Election of the State of Mississippi, 1847, in Records of the Secretary of State,
Ser. F, LXV, Miss. Arch; State of Mississippi, *Journal of the Senate of the State of
Mississippi* (1848), 7.

[8] Mississippi *Senate Journal* (1848), 537.

[9] *Ibid.*, 561, 675, 905, 933.

year, Pettus lost little time in renewing his drive for increased railroad mileage.[10] However, in 1850 there were far greater issues brought into focus than those devoted exclusively to the internal affairs of Mississippi. An approaching collision of sectional interests brought most other business to a standstill.

Broadly speaking, the western gold rush of 1848–49 had thrust California into a situation never before encountered in the history of the American republic. For with a sudden influx of population the prospect existed that California might be admitted to statehood without having to undergo territorial status. Such circumstances threatened to destroy the national balance between slave and free states and thus created the framework for North–South antagonism, the possible outcome of which was unclear. The floors of Congress soon rang with bitter oratory as the underlying issues of slavery, political equality, and constitutional interpretations were aired in fiery fashion. In many parts of the South, in particular, the concept of secession was discussed and debated, and good and reasonable men on both sides of the Mason–Dixon line feared the outcome of such unconventional talk.

Mississippians responded to the political scene with excitement, though disagreeing as to what alternatives might be employed in dealing with the issues. Congressman Jefferson Davis, for instance, held the opinion that Daniel Webster would "take Southern ground" in order "to avoid the danger of disunion" and thereby see to it that some kind of compromise was effected.[11] Others, however, favored more positive steps. Especially revealing was the action undertaken by the state senate's Committee on Federal and State Relations, which brought forth a resolution calling for the southern states to meet at Nashville, Tennessee, in June for the purpose of counseling "together for their common safety." State senator John Pettus exhibited his first recorded feelings of sectional chauvinism by announcing his support for

[10] Mississippi *Senate Journal* (1850), 365.
[11] Jefferson Davis to William Cannon, March 6, 1850, in William R. Cannon Papers, Library of Congress, Washington, D.C.

the project, a position that undoubtedly his lionhearted idol, John C. Calhoun, would have applauded.[12]

In Mississippi the crisis of 1850 continued to flourish proportionate to the activities of local politicians, dividing the two dominant parties along opposing lines. On March 6 the legislature selected twelve delegates—six Whigs and six Democrats—to represent the state at the proposed Nashville convention. A lengthy resolution was also adopted at that time which pledged a strong states' rights stand and called upon the delegation to be unified in the face of northern antagonism. The state senate went on record as offering the city of Jackson and the facilities of the Mississippi capitol for an alternative meeting site, in the event Nashville proved unfavorable. Among the delegates selected to go to Nashville was John Pettus.[13]

In the meantime Pettus occupied his time with an investigation of the Southern Railroad Company. The purpose of the inquiry was to determine whether or not the railroad would be granted permission to expand its facilities. A highly favorable Pettus-authored report of February 21 was laced with a touch of southern nationalism. While insisting that eastern Mississippi would benefit economically by such expansion, the document indicated that additional rail mileage would serve "as a means of drawing more closely the southern states of this confederacy" by greatly facilitating "their commerce and friendly intercourse." The future military needs of the South might also be enhanced "should protection and defense be needed from insurrection within or invasion from without."[14] Clearly, Pettus was affected by the times.

The summer of 1850 saw a number of meetings held throughout the state for the purpose of adopting resolutions to be presented at the Nashville convention. A growing sense of radical-

---

[12] Mississippi *Senate Journal* (1850), 357; Gerald M. Capers, *John C. Calhoun—Opportunist: A Reappraisal* (Gainesville, Fla., 1960), 253.
[13] Mississippi *Senate Journal* (1850), 712–13; State of Mississippi, *Laws of the State of Mississippi* (1850), 521–26; Natchez *Weekly Courier*, March 20, 1850; Mississippi *Senate Journal* (1850), 710.
[14] Mississippi *Senate Journal* (1850), 565, 712–13.

ism was in evidence among certain states' rights Democrats; the slavery issue in particular was an absorbing one. In like fashion state newspapers split along party lines and argued both for and against Henry Clay's congressional compromise proposals. More radical sheets took the view that compromise was tantamount to concession, thereby giving "a strong impetus to the secession movement in Mississippi." Seldom before in the history of the state had passions risen to such heights. As one paper put it: "We are not afraid to meet the raw head and bloody bones of disunion, face to face."[15]

Ultimately, as the settlements of 1850 were forged on the floors of Congress, interest in a meeting of southern states to discuss such questions waned correspondingly. But men like John Pettus and others of growing secessionist stripe were not in the market to promote sectional harmony.

When a convention did assemble at Nashville in June, 1850, it lacked both the total number of delegates initially designated and the national attention that such a gathering might have attracted had it transpired earlier. The atmosphere emanating from the proceedings was more conservative than originally expected. For his part, Pettus declined to attend, believing that moderation and compromise were signs of weakness. Nevertheless, the Nashville delegates did address themselves to the issues of the day and went on record as supporting a states' rights position in national affairs.[16]

The events that transpired as a result of the 1850 crisis were important for Mississippi. The twin forces of southern nationalism and secession had been clearly identified and articulated, but the hotspurs had to bide their time for a while longer. Men of moderate persuasion carried the day, and once the fervor of the

---

[15] James W. Garner, "The First Struggle Over Secession in Mississippi," in Franklin L. Riley (ed.), *Publications of the Mississippi Historical Society* (Oxford, Miss., 1901), IV, 93; Holman Hamilton, *Prologue to Conflict: The Crisis and Compromise of 1850* (Lexington, 1964), 93–94, 133–34; Jackson *Semi-Weekly Mississippian*, August 16, 1850.

[16] M. W. Cluskey (ed.), *The Political Text-Book, 1858* (Philadelphia, 1860), 597. See also Joseph H. Parks, "John Bell and the Compromise of 1850," *Journal of Southern History*, IX (August, 1943), 345.

moment had subsided many Mississippians breathed a sigh of relief. Whigs championed the compromise measures, and as one of their number put it: "We have passed through a severe contest, and achieved a signal victory. It was an American contest, and a constitutional victory."[17]

But all was not politically quiet in the wake of the 1850 political excitement. Moderate Democrats resented Whig charges that they were unreasonable disunionists and radicals. Although further rancor was diffused to some extent by economic prosperity, such individuals as John Quitman were highly displeased that "no man or set of men" had come forward to give "particular direction" to a disunion movement.[18]

John Pettus, an ardent opponent of all compromise solutions to sectional differences, sulked at home and spent considerable energy attending to plantation affairs. But the wounds left by late developments ran deep and would never heal. Pettus personified a small but growing new breed of Mississippian—the secessionist.[19]

Except for continued sponsorship of railroads, the 1852 legislative session produced little in the way of note as far as John Pettus was concerned. However, when the Kemper County senator offered himself as a candidate for reelection the follow-

[17] The best study of Mississippi's role in the Nashville convention is Cleo Hearon, "Mississippi and the Compromise of 1850," in Franklin L. Riley (ed.), *Publications of the Mississippi Historical Society* (Oxford, Miss., 1914), XIV, 7–227. For further analysis pertaining to other aspects of the subject see Lewy Dorman, *Party Politics in Alabama From 1850 Through 1860* (Wetumpka, Ala., 1935), 44; Arthur C. Cole, "The South and the Right of Secession in the Early Fifties," *Mississippi Valley Historical Review*, I (December, 1914), 398; Howard C. Perkins, "A Neglected Phase of the Movement for Southern Unity, 1847–1852," *Journal of Southern History*, XII (May, 1946), 158; "Wiley Harris," in Dunbar Rowland, *Courts, Judges and Lawyers of Mississippi, 1798–1935* (Jackson, 1935), I, 320; Samuel S. Boyd, *Speech of Hon. Samuel S. Boyd, Delivered at the Great Union Festival Held at Jackson, Mississippi, On the 10th Day of October, 1851* (Natchez, 1851) 1.
[18] Aberdeen *Monroe Democrat*, January 16, 1851; J. F. H. Claiborne, *Life and Correspondence of John A. Quitman* (New York, 1860), II, 123.
[19] Hearon, "Mississippi and the Compromise of 1850," 211–20; R. S. Cotterill, *The Old South: The Geographic, Economic, Social, Political and Cultural Expansion, Institutions and Nationalism of the Ante-Bellum South* (Glendale, Calif., 1937), 215.

ing year, his margin of victory over lawyer opponent Robert H. Cole was much slimmer than that of previous campaigns. A hard-line stand involving the issues of 1850 had cost him support. Cole tallied 492 votes, as compared with 606 for Pettus.[20]

When the Mississippi legislature convened in early January, 1854, Pettus was among seven men nominated for the powerful and revered position of president of the senate. On the first ballot Pettus received the largest number of votes but failed to obtain a required majority, and a second round of balloting was neces-sary to achieve a decision in his favor. The second most respected senate post was that of secretary, which went to Theodore Bunch. Both men were described by local newspapers as "States' Rights Democrats."[21]

The lame duck governor of Mississippi at this particular junc-ture was Henry Stuart Foote, a member of the Unionist party who had won the post during the aftermath of the compromise of 1850. The governor-elect, due to be inaugurated on January 11, 1854, was a "humorous and fascinating" Democrat, John J. McRae. Governor Foote apparently suffered from a profound sense of disgust over recent political affairs, especially those concerning state and national elections. He expressed specific aversion to Jefferson Davis' support of Franklin Pierce in the last presidential election. Pierce's policies, according to Foote, "were ruining both the country and the Democratic party."[22]

Realizing full well that he could no longer control the political climate in Mississippi nor play as decisive a role as he had earlier in his career, Foote addressed the opening session of the legisla-ture in extremely bitter terms. He declared that he had pondered the idea of resigning his office in protest as soon as the recent gu-bernatorial election returns had become available. Foote further underscored his opposition to increased triumphs by the Missis-

---

[20] Returns of the General Election of the State of Mississippi, Kemper County, 1853.

[21] Mississippi Senate Journal (1854), 4–5; Yazoo City Weekly Whig, January 13, 1854.

[22] Reuben Davis, Recollections of Mississippi and Mississippians (Boston, 1890), 325; John E. Gonzales, "Henry Stuart Foote: A Forgotten Unionist of the Fifties," The Southern Quarterly, I (January, 1963), 135.

sippi Democratic party by announcing his intention of moving to California.[23]

Undoubtedly the governor's original notion of renouncing his post appealed to him more and more in the days that followed. At noon on January 6, 1854, Foote's resignation was received by the state senate. Since the Constitution of 1832 had, "for reasons of economy," abolished the office of lieutenant governor, the line of executive succession passed to the president of the senate. John Pettus, presently occupying that position, was sworn in as governor before noon on January 7. J. M. Acker of Monroe County ascended to the job of president pro tempore of the senate.[24]

Little of significance could transpire during Pettus' brief tenure as governor ad interim. Chief executive for only 120 hours, Pettus served the shortest gubernatorial term in the state's history. His only recorded act was to order a special election in Noxubee County to fill the office of deceased state representative Francis M. Irby.[25]

On the appointed date, January 11, John McRae was inaugurated governor, and Pettus returned to his duties as senate president. As presiding officer, he did not engage in floor debate throughout the remainder of the session. Pettus was again unanimously accorded the same honor at the next convening of the senate, which body characterized his actions as fair and equitable.[26]

Between 1854 and 1857 other issues of prominence unfolded in Mississippi and in no small way played a role in the often heated and confused political atmosphere of the state. The activities of the nativist American party in Mississippi as well as

[23] Mississippi *Senate Journal* (1854), 11; Dunbar Rowland, *History of Mississippi: The Heart of the South* (Jackson, 1925), I, 745–46; Gonzales, "Henry Stuart Foote," 135.

[24] Mississippi *Senate Journal* (1854), 4–5, 118, 122; Winbourne M. Drake, "The Mississippi Constitutional Convention of 1832," *Journal of Southern History*, XXIII (August, 1957), 365; Yazoo City *Democrat*, January 8, 1854.

[25] Jackson *Clarion-Ledger*, January 14, 1968; Governor's Executive Journal: Governors Foote, Pettus, McRae, 1852–1857.

[26] Mississippi *Senate Journal* (1854), 137, (1856), 6, 596.

the rapid progress of the newly created Republican party and the national response it attracted in the presidential election of 1856 caused much apprehension among state Democrats. Although James Buchanan carried the Democratic standard to victory in 1856, many Mississippians, including Governor Mc-Rae, felt threatened and feared for the "safety and perpetuity" of the Union if the Republicans ever succeeded in capturing the White House.[27]

In January, 1857, the Mississippi legislature was called into special session for the purpose of discussing legislative reapportionment. The gathering would have remained insignificant had it not corresponded with the "bleeding Kansas" crisis—an event of some magnitude for several of Mississippi's political leaders. Old sectional wounds were reopened and those disunion men of longstanding were once again outspoken. Pettus, already a convert to secession principles, introduced a senate resolution calling for the "unqualified condemnation" of Governor Robert J. Walker of Kansas and President Buchanan, both of whom were accused of being "unfaithful to the principles of the Kansas–Nebraska bill and the cherished constitutional rights of the Southern States."[28]

Newspapers, in a fashion reminiscent of the events of 1850, took up the new set of circumstances with full vigor and placed the issues before their readers. One important Natchez publication contained a "prophecy of a sectional convulsion" and called for the realignment of political parties along sectional lines. But it was the Fayette *Jefferson Journal* that probably got to the heart of the matter best, reminding its subscribers that the anti-slavery forces were at one time only "a faint, clear, and gurgling rill" that had now become a powerful and dangerous

---

[27] Hinds County *Gazette*, December 10, 1856.
[28] Rowland, *History of Mississippi*, I, 764; Mississippi *Senate Journal*, Called Session (1857), 110–11. Although Pettus' resolution did not pass, a similar concept had been incorporated into the state Democratic platform the previous summer. See the Pontotoc *Examiner*, November 27, 1857. Robert J. Walker was a former United States senator from Mississippi and the first member of a presidential cabinet from that state. See James P. Shenton, *Robert John Walker: A Politician from Jackson to Lincoln* (New York, 1961), 150–61.

torrent. "The Southern Democracy cannot and will not succumb to the flagrant and unprecedented tyranny of Robert J. Walker and his associates," opined another Fayette tabloid. Clearly, many Mississippians believed that southern interests with respect to slavery were not being adequately safeguarded in the federal territories. "The banner of the State Rights Democracy," wrote state attorney general David Glenn, "will again be given to the breeze" and it must be looked to "as our surest refuge in the day of trial and danger."[29]

By state election day, 1857, the passionate heat of the times was still in evidence in Mississippi, as it had been in previous crises involving federal–state relations. The newly elected Democratic governor, William McWillie, reminded constituents during the course of his inaugural address that he believed the "overthrow of the social institutions of the South" was uppermost in the minds of many northerners. Abolitionist activities would not cease and "the expectation that this fanaticism will die out or recede from its purpose" was sheer folly. McWillie stated that all thoughtful Mississippians should "by a thorough arming and organization convince our assailants that we cannot be attacked with impunity" and thereby serve notice "that we are full ready, and willing and able to take care of ourselves in the Union if we can; out of it if we must."[30]

Throughout the political furor, other matters, often far removed from the legislative arena, also occupied the attention of John Pettus. He, along with such other notable contemporary Mississippians as Ethelbert Barksdale, William S. Barry, and J. F. H. Claiborne, had founded the Historical Society of Mississippi. A charter defining the organization's purpose as one of collecting, preserving and perpetuating "by publication . . . the scattered and perishable memorials, both written and traditional of our social and political history," was granted by the legislature in November, 1858. Although Pettus became a vice

---

[29] Natchez *Mississippi Free Trader*, February 6, April 28, 1857; Fayette *Jefferson Journal*, November 20, 1857; Fayette *Watch Tower*, August, 7, 1856.
[30] Natchez *Mississippi Free Trader*, November 20, 1857.

president of the society, renewed sectional aggravation soon syphoned off his energies.[31]

John Pettus did not seek another senate term in 1857. His farewell address to that body gave no hint of what additional political aspirations he might have had in mind. Instead, he spoke of his years of legislative service and noted that "continued expressions of friendship and esteem" had made the years pleasant. Such kindnesses filled his heart "with the emotions of deep and abiding gratitude."[32]

When the following session of the state legislature convened, lawyer Isaac Enloe represented Kemper County in the senate. John Pettus had other things to do. Political conditions in Mississippi seemed to beckon to a spokesman of Pettus' temperament and perspective. He, like the entire South, had an appointment with destiny—a time when flesh and theory would become one in both action and direction, offering convincing evidence that the last act in sectional affairs had yet to be played. For better or worse, Pettus would offer himself as a candidate in the next gubernatorial election.

[31] Z. T. Leavell, "The Ante-Bellum Historical Society of Mississippi," in Franklin L. Riley (ed.), *Publications of the Mississippi Historical Society* (Oxford, Miss., 1904), VIII, 321; Charles S. Sydnor, "Historical Activities in Mississippi in the Nineteenth Century," *Journal of Southern History*, III (May, 1937), 139–60; John Pettus to Alice Pettus, October 27, 1856, in E. W. Pettus Papers.
[32] Dunbar Rowland, *Encyclopedia of Mississippi History* (Madison, Wisc., 1907), II, 410.

III

The Day of the Fire-eater:
The Gubernatorial Election
of 1859

THROUGHOUT THE 1850s the political climate of Mississippi underwent momentous change. Before the close of the decade one
party would dominate the political apparatus so thoroughly, and
with such determinism, that the freedom necessary to debate the
vital questions of the day was severely limited. Under such conditions it was nearly impossible for the twin voices of reason
and moderation to be heard, let alone heeded.

After the presidential election of 1852, the national Whig
party and its Mississippi counterpart declined steadily in influence. The frequent failure of Whigs to unite on candidates,
issues, or platforms served no cause other than that of Democratic politicians, many of whom were of the states' rights
variety.

Response to the never-ending aggravation of sectional affairs
ebbed and flowed among Democratic leaders in proportion to
support offered by constituents. Following the 1850 compromise
period, a tide of unionism temporarily silenced those Mississippians who advocated a firm stand on any dispute which
threatened southern institutions. However, each new volley of
sectional excitement carried with it a backwash of doctrinaire se-
cessionists. But the time for complete surrender to such a radical
alternative was not yet at hand, and for a while longer the future
course of Mississippi politics remained uncertain.

Following the decay of the national Whig party, the American or Know-Nothing party made advances in Mississippi. Really little more than a loose coalition, the Know-Nothing banner attracted a sprinkling of Democrats and a sizeable number of former Whigs. In the gubernatorial election of 1855 the American–Whig alliance put forth Pontotoc lawyer and "agreeable speaker" Charles D. Fontaine as its candidate, while incumbent John J. McRae carried the Democratic standard. When the ballots were tallied, McRae had muddled through with 32,666 votes to 27,579 for Fontaine. The anti-Democratic forces might have done even better had they offered the voters anything other than the questionable promise of wresting "political control of the state from the Fire Eater elements of the Democratic Party."[1]

After the election Know-Nothingism rapidly disintegrated and by the state political contest of 1857 was no longer a major factor in Mississippi politics. The anti-slavery stand of the party's northern wing undoubtedly played no small role in its southern downfall. While the Democratic ticket, led by William McWillie, had no difficulty in capturing the governor's chair again in 1857, all opposition to the increased fire-eating tendencies of the party did not vanish. Although sometimes split and disorganized, die-hard Whigs were determined to continue the struggle, within the Mississippi political scene at least, and to attempt to hold the American Republic together at any cost.[2]

The national events of the mid-1850s, however, provided additional heat for the secessionist fever raging among hard-core Mississippi Democrats. The Kansas question, abolitionist agitation, northern nullification of the fugitive slave laws, conflict

[1] Davis, *Recollections of Mississippi*, 347; Rowland, *History of Mississippi*, I, 752; Donald M. Rawson, "Party Politics in Mississippi, 1850–1860" (Unpublished Ph.D. Dissertation, Department of History, Vanderbilt University, 1964), 148. See also Vicksburg *Weekly Whig*, November 1, 1854.

[2] W. Darrell Overdyke, *The Know-Nothing Party in the South* (Baton Rouge, 1950), 278. The appeal of the Know-Nothing philosophy in Mississippi has mistakenly been traced to the party's negative stands on Catholicism, federal land policies, and foreign immigration. As far as Mississippi was concerned, however, the American party's all-encompassing program of unionism represented the chief attraction. Whigs naturally gravitated to the new organization since they no longer had a national party of their own.

over slavery in the territories, and the rapid growth of the Republican party combined to force all categories of Mississippians to reexamine more closely than ever their relationship to the federal Union. By 1859 political alternatives within the state were greatly narrowed and middle ground was scarce; the upcoming local elections promised to be both significant and decisive.

The Democratic nominating convention was scheduled to meet in Jackson on July 5, 1859, to select a slate of candidates for the fall contest. The prevailing tone under which the delegates would gather had been apparent for several months. The various county caucuses which nominated deputies to the state convention produced memorials laced with fire-eater sentiment and resolutions embracing the doctrine of secession. In Lawrence County concern over sectional affairs reached an acute stage, and a body of constituents called for the reopening of the overseas slave trade, the acquisition of Cuba as a slave state, and disunion in the event a Republican ever became president of the United States.[3]

Nowhere was the existing political atmosphere of the day brought into sharper focus than at the Southern Commercial Convention held in Vicksburg May 9–13, 1859. Economic considerations relating to the South fell by the wayside when Mississippians John McRae and Charles Clark and Alabama's William Lowndes Yancey assumed control of the meeting and converted it into a forum for political agitation. Resolutions similar to those of Lawrence County were brought forward.[4]

Moderate men, however, stood opposed to the more extreme points of view and did not give way easily, denying "that the delegates at the convention were representative or aware of the

[3] Jackson Semi-Weekly Mississippian, May–June, 1859; Natchez Mississippi Free Trader, May 28, 1859.
[4] "Proceedings of the Southern Convention Held At Vicksburg, Mississippi," DeBow's Review, XXVII (July, 1859), 99; Vicksburg Weekly Whig, May 13, 1859. For a running account of the convention consult the Port Gibson Daily Southern Reveille, May 12–May 18, 1859.

true Southern sentiment." In any event, the activities at Vicksburg were widely reported throughout Mississippi and served
to bolster the ambitions of individuals already dedicated to reap-
ing a harvest of radicalism. Disturbed by the temper of the times,
cautious men of moderate persuasion took every available occasion to warn of the dangers of disunion talk. Speaking at an Independence Day rally, J. F. H. Claiborne, an outspoken critic of
extreme solutions to sectional problems, told his audience that
the bond of national union would last forever, "if agitators and
fanatics will let it alone."[5] Such words met but faint response.

Prior to the convening of the Democratic convention there
was much conjecture concerning prospective gubernatorial candidates. One name was mentioned more frequently than any
other—John Jones Pettus. Editorials and testimonials endorsing
Mississippian printed a public letter affirming that no one would
find Pettus obnoxious. The paper noted that during his years in
the legislature, Pettus had favored internal improvements and
him were carried in state newspapers. The Jackson *Semi-Weekly*
railroad expansion and, most important, "in Federal politics
[had] always stood with the Mississippian. No prospects of sudden promotion have availed to draw him off from devotion
to State Rights Democracy." Other messages of support represented Pettus as an agricultural reformer and an industrious
planter who exercised good business judgment.[6]

On July 5, 1859, by far the largest Democratic state convention ever to assemble in Mississippi convened at Jackson under
the dominance of the fire-eater wing of the party. Most of the
state's brightest political stars were in attendance and left little
margin for doubt concerning the issue of federal–state relations.
United States Senator Albert Gallatin Brown brought his feelings
into focus on the eve of the gathering when he declared that if
slavery was not protected by the national government "he would

[5] Herbert Wender, *Southern Commercial Conventions, 1837–1859* (Baltimore, 1930), 235; July 4, 1859, Speech, in J. F. H. Claiborne Papers, Library of Congress, Washington, D.C.
[6] Jackson *Semi-Weekly Mississipian,* July 2, 10, 1859.

see the Union destroyed . . . so deep into the sea of oblivion that
no plummet could ever fathom its depths."[7] Brown's remarks
might have served as the convention's keynote address. Men of
economic means and drastic political conviction occupied the
seats of power in the assembly hall. Railroad executive George
H. Gordon was elected to preside over the proceedings, and the
important post of chairman of the Platform Committee was occupied by doctrinaire secessionist and newspaper publisher
Ethelbert Barksdale.

The first item of convention business was that of adopting
resolutions which would jointly serve as platform planks and as
a guideline in selecting candidates. Several motions were submitted for consideration, most of which bore the fire-eater stamp.
But before any decision could be rendered, United States Senator Jefferson Davis took the floor and urged cautious moderation.
Davis' comments fell on deaf ears; that same afternoon six resolutions dealing with the vital issues of the day were passed without much difficulty. The first resolution reaffirmed the principles
laid down by the National Democratic party in 1856 and held
that slavery in the territories was not to be interfered with. A
second motion also dealt with slavery and contended that the
"right of property in slaves is distinctly and expressly affirmed in
the Constitution—the only power over it conferred upon Congress, is the power . . . of guarding and protecting the owners in
their rights." But by far the most significant plank was that
concerning the next national election and the possibility that a
member of the "Black" Republican party might be elected president. Under such circumstances Mississippi would "regard it as
a declaration of hostility, and will hold herself in readiness, to
cooperate with her sister States of the South, in whatever measures she may deem necessary for the maintenance of their rights
as co-equal members of the Confederacy." The remainder of the
platform called for the acquisition of Cuba, endorsed most of

[7] Rowland, *Official and Statistical Register*, 302; Natchez *Mississippi Free
Trader*, June 24, 1859.

the policies of President Buchanan's administration, and insisted that southern rights be enforced "by all departments of the federal government."[8]

Early on the morning of July 6, nominations were opened for the office of governor. Among those placed in contention were Thomas J. Hudson, George R. Fall, Madison M. McAfee, Albert K. Blythe, John F. Cushman, and John Pettus, all of whom were prominent in state and local politics. Voting began at noon. On the first roll call, after some nominees had withdrawn their names, the results read: Pettus 35, Hudson 28, Cushman 26, and Fall 6. Pettus continued to acquire additional support on subsequent ballots and on the sixth round was unanimously nominated by acclamation. In John Pettus, "a disunion man of the most unmitigated order," rested the party's chances for victory.[9] More important was the fact that fire-eaters, not just states' righters, had for the first time won a highly coveted prize.

Three other men were also selected to accompany Pettus on the ticket. Pontotoc County's state senator, Benjamin R. Webb, was chosen as the Democratic candidate for secretary of state. Although he was in poor health, it was reported that his party devotion was "equalled only by his strict integrity, high-toned feelings, and a peculiar fitness for the office." Webb was "honest, capable and faithful—coming up to the true Jeffersonian standard." Edward B. Burt, selected to run for the office of auditor of public accounts, was described as a "democrat of the Calhoun, Jackson and Polk school." The "bold, fearless, manly working democrat" M. D. Haynes of Yazoo County filled the state treasurer slot.[10]

Reaction to the announced slate of candidates was mixed, with newspapers among the first to reflect popular sentiment. The Natchez *Mississippi Free Trader* called Pettus the "drummond light" of his party and predicted that he would "be elected

[8] Jackson *Semi-Weekly Mississippian*, July 26, 1859; Natchez *Weekly Courier*, July 9, 1859; Natchez *Mississippi Free Trader*, July 8, 1859.
[9] Jackson *Semi-Weekly Mississippian*, July 8, 1859; Davis, *Recollections of Mississippi*, 378.
[10] Natchez *Mississippi Free Trader*, July 18, 1859.

by a larger majority than any preceding Executive." While similar enthusiasm made up the preponderance of opinion, there were a few dissenting editors, such as Fleet T. Cooper of the Monticello *Journal* who declared that Pettus was "too slow a cock for a Mississippi Governor. . . . He has not fire and brimstone enough in his composition to meet the combustible present and ominous future." In rebuttal the Okolona *Prairie News* retorted that it did not matter whether or not the candidate had the "nerve for crises, he will be voted for, as a Mississippi matter of course."[11]

Dissatisfaction with the Democratic nominees also surfaced in other, more obvious, quarters and involved the archrivals of the Mississippi Democrats, the Whigs. As early as May, 1859, a mass meeting was held at Apollo Hall in Vicksburg. Former governor Henry Foote, the local mayor, and other noteworthy figures in state politics were in attendance when plans were charted for the purpose of opposing their political foes in fall elections.[12] In pursuit of this objective, Whigs and a smattering of moderate Democrats held a rival political convention in the senate chamber of the capitol building on July 11. Isaac M. Patridge, editor of the Vicksburg *Weekly Whig*, presided over the gathering.

From all indications, the Whig convention was an empty spectacle. No slate of candidates was announced. Instead, a steering committee, chaired by William A. Lake, was appointed to urge upon its "friends throughout the State, the necessity of perfecting their organizations in the several counties, with the view of future action."[13] The decision to defer the presentation of an opposition ticket would later prove to be a costly blunder, once again underscoring the long-standing lack of agreement among moderates throughout the state.

Meanwhile, Democrats plunged headlong into a well-oiled electioneering effort. On July 12 the Jackson *Semi-Weekly*

---

[11] *Ibid.*; Monticello *Journal*, July 15, 1859; Okolona *Prairie News*, July 21, 1859.
[12] Natchez *Weekly Courier*, May 27, 1859.
[13] Jackson *Semi-Weekly Mississippian*, July 12, 1859.

Mississippian announced that John Pettus would soon publish
a schedule of personal appearances for addressing the people in
order "to make a thorough canvass of the State between now and
the elections, and to discuss at the hustings the important political questions of the day." Pettus began his campaign on July
8 with a speech at Cooper's Well and before long the nominee,
a slaveholder himself, was airing his views on that peculiar
institution. According to the Jackson newspaper, he believed
slavery to be the "only proper status" for the African. To free the
Negro from the "humane labor system of the South" would be
at "war with the true interests of both white and black races."
An address at Macon saw the language of caution and statesmanship thrown to the wind when it was declared that the Democratic candidate would favor a splitting of the Union if a Republican became president of the United States. A tour of Houston
produced much the same theme; it was there that Pettus promised to turn the arts of peace into the science of war in order
to resist the "inauguration of a Black Republican." Further, the
state legislature would be asked "to fill the arsenal with arms,
that we might be ready for the worst [if] William H. Seward
or some member of his clan, is elected by one portion of the
union to rule over the whole United States."[14]

In early August, Pettus returned to speak before his constituents in Kemper County. The Paulding *Eastern Clarion* reported
that over two thousand civic-minded persons attended a barbe-
cue in his honor, an account undoubtedly exaggerated, especially in view of the fact that the area was in the grip of a rainstorm.
But another correspondent who braved the inclement weather
recorded a revealing description of Pettus' speech, the text of
which strengthened his stand on slavery and clarified his attitudes toward the federal union. The protection of slaves, said
the candidate, was the responsibility of Congress. The defense of
private property was one of the primary functions of government and absolute safeguarding of Negro bondage in the territories was "in accordance with the constitution." The speeches at

[14] *Ibid.*, August 2, 1859.

the Scooba rally closed amid a salvo of applause and everyone seemed highly pleased, having "listened throughout the day to volley after volley of first rate specimens of stump oratory [concerning those] grave questions which are agitating our political fabric to its base."[15]

On September 2 several Democratic candidates appeared in Jackson and addressed a convocation gathered in their honor. The featured speaker was the gubernatorial nominee, and he compared the abolitionist movement to a landslide—"thundering on . . . carrying everything before it." The South was about to be overcome by an avalanche of such sentiment. Since the Republicans and their fellow travelers were obviously to blame for this state of affairs it was now necessary to seek permanent remedies. Reading the crowd a portion of William Seward's famous Rochester speech concerning slavery, Pettus contended that the nation was in the midst of a crossfire between the forces of unrestricted freedom and those of servitude. If the battle was lost, the South would be forced to abandon its system of labor and "set up in its stead the Yankee hireling system." The audience needed no convincing and response to the nominee's remarks was punctuated with expressions of enthusiasm. The harangue went on, reaching new heights of frenzy. Southerners, Pettus assured his listeners, could not permit the liberation of slaves, for once freed they would undoubtedly rise up against whites in much the same fashion as those had on the island of Jamaica. "We must oppose . . . or perish," he roared, urging the entire South to speedily unite in defense of her interests and institutions.

Two days later Pettus stumped Vicksburg. That city, like much of the Mississippi River region, contained strong pro-Union sentiment and was traditionally Whig in political affiliation. Not one to shy away from opposition, Pettus took his message to the throng that gathered to hear him and in the language of cold fury told his listeners that Mississippi should "adopt a policy of

---

[15] DeKalb *Democrat*, August 10, 1859; Jackson *Semi-Weekly Mississippian*, August 19, 1859.

armed neutrality in the face of Northern opposition to slavery."[16]

With the fall elections scarcely a month away, the Whigs (or the Oppositionists, as they were now known) finally agreed upon a slate of candidates to refute the stands already articulated by the Democrats. On September 7, 1859, the Opposition ticket was announced, representing at best a patchwork coalition. The nominees included Harvey W. Walter for governor, Joseph Regan for state treasurer, A. E. Reynolds for auditor of public accounts, and W. W. Walter for secretary of state. Foremost hopes for victory rested on the shoulders of gubernatorial nominee Walter. A prominent lawyer, Mason, and railroad promoter from Holly Springs, Walter's chief claim to fame lay in his active support for constructing the Mississippi Central Railroad. He, like his Democratic counterpart, was interested in public education and internal improvement projects. However, Walter drew verbal abuse for aspiring not only to the governor's chair, but the White House.[17]

Opposition forces, having already lost much precious time by not fielding a ticket sooner, still persisted in squabbling among themselves over a suitable platform. The end result was virtually no platform at all. Instead, an attempt was made to solicit votes from anyone opposed to acquiring Cuba and reopening the slave trade. However, a moderate approach to the issues of a congressional slave code for the territories and of avoiding secession in the event of a Republican president did not constitute a sufficient base upon which to forge a spirited campaign. Even though they robbed themselves of the most attractive issues of the day and were far out of tune with the charged political atmosphere, Oppositionists could hardly have offered much more, short of committing ideological suicide.

Conversely, while their foes were confused and disorganized, Democrats pressed the campaign in earnest. With opposition

[16] Vicksburg *Weekly Whig*, September 7, 1859.
[17] Vicksburg *Weekly Sun*, September 7, 1859; John F. Stover, "Colonel Henry S. McComb, Mississippi Railroad Adventurer," *Journal of Mississippi History,* XVIII (July, 1955), 177; George H. Ethridge and Walter N. Taylor (eds.), *Mississippi, A History* (Hopkinsville, Ky., 1939), 265–66.

other than an imaginary Republican menace now in the field, the contest generated last minute momentum. Mid-September found John Pettus entering Hancock County for the finale of his bid for the executive mansion. Despite rain and high winds he spoke at the Gainesville courthouse, declaring that Democrats were solid on the issues, and "found a response in the hearts of the people." After Gainesville, there was a hurried stop at Shieldsboro for which "men of every race" turned out.[18]

The campaign trail had been long and rigorous. Pettus, although "not an eloquent or pretty speaker," had fulfilled his pledge to visit all areas of the state and discuss the platform with the people. This accomplished, he returned to his plantation to await the verdict of an electorate who coveted a "genuine participation in community affairs" and the political consequences which might be in the offing for all Mississippians.[19]

On the first Monday and Tuesday of October, as required by amended election statutes, Mississippians went to the polls to decide the fate of the candidates. The outcome of the balloting was a foregone conclusion, but the end product surprised even the most optimistic of observers. The Opposition was crushed by a margin of better than three to one, with the lesser posts graphically illustrated thus:

SECRETARY OF STATE

B. R. Webb (D) 34,949
W. W. Walter (O) 9,897

AUDITOR OF PUBLIC ACCOUNTS

E. R. Burt (D) 34,928
A. E. Reynolds (O) 9,748

STATE TREASURER

M. D. Haynes (D) 35,022
Joseph Regan (O) 9,618[20]

[18] Vicksburg Weekly Whig, September 23, 1859.
[19] Jackson Weekly Mississippian, August 31, 1859; Frank L. Owsley, Plain Folk of the Old South (Baton Rouge, 1949), 129; Charles S. Sydnor, Slavery In Mississippi (New York, 1933), 192–93.
[20] Natchez Mississippi Free Trader, October 22, 1859.

In the all-important race for governor, John Pettus, running slightly behind the rest of the ticket, tabulated 34,559 votes, as opposed to 10,308 for Walter. Only fifteen ballots were cast for any other contender, thus indicating the clarity of choice between the two rival camps. Pettus carried every county but three. In fact, Walter did not receive a single vote in Franklin, Jackson, Marion, or Rankin counties. Elsewhere, Walter's most resounding defeat came in Pontotoc County where he pocketed but 22 votes as compared with 1,913 for the Democrat. John Jones Pettus was at last elected governor of Mississippi. That the fire-eater doctrine had triumphed was unmistakable; the day of the demagogue had arrived.

Commentary on the election varied widely according to party affiliation. Even before the official results were known, the Vicksburg *Weekly Whig* reminded its readers that Harvey Walter had taken a bold stand and predicted that he would "poll the largest vote of any man on the opposition ticket." This prognosis was indeed correct, but the final news brought small comfort. Another pro-Opposition writer was worried by the fire-eater victory, which he labled "an evident mass of approaching disaster." But if the losers were somber, the Democrats were jubilant. The Jackson *Semi-Weekly Mississippian* compared the Democratic canvass to "a fire in the woods" that had "swept everything before them," and the victorious Pettus was elated by the outcome.[21]

If the gubernatorial election of 1859 can serve as a measuring device, it should reveal, with reasonable accuracy, that a fair portion of public opinion had become responsive to the fire-eater point of view. If, on the basis of the respective platforms, the Whigs can be labeled "compromisers" or "conservatives" and the Democrats "hard-liners," it would appear evident that a good portion of the electorate going to the polls was committed

[21] Vicksburg *Weekly Whig*, November 2, 1859; J. W. R. Taylor to J. F. H. Claiborne, August 30, 1860, in J. F. H. Claiborne Papers, University of North Carolina Library, Chapel Hill, N.C.; Jackson *Semi-Weekly Mississippian*, October 12, 1859.

to finding some solution to the sectional questions of the day.

Oppositionists had injured their own cause in several ways. On the one hand, they had failed to come to grips with a suitable platform and at the same time had quarrelled over the merits of their own candidates, managing to circulate a ticket in only twenty-five of sixty counties. As compared with the gubernatorial election of just four years earlier, the 1859 contest witnessed a 30 percent drop in voter participation. Hence, the Democrats had apparently gained little real strength between 1855 and 1859, and the Whig–Opposition forces lost nearly half of their following at the polls. At least 20,000 voters either simply did not take the trouble to vote, disliked one or both candidates, were waiting for the presidential contest of the following year, or believed that the end result of the election was already decided. In so doing, such persons may have aided in the creation of a false show of support for the Democratic party. Had the absent voters gone to the polls it is interesting to speculate on the possible outcome.

The Whig–Opposition party not only lacked energy but singleness of purpose. An important contributor to the final 1859 verdict was the fact that the Democrats controlled the overwhelming portion of the state's newspapers. The power and influence of the press was a decisive factor, at least in terms of making the contest appear to be an inescapable conclusion. Typical of the newspaper support enjoyed by the Democrats was that offered by the Jackson *Semi-Weekly Mississippian*. This sheet had the largest state-wide circulation and was under the "caustic and severe" editorship of Ethelbert Barksdale.[22] In any event, the Mississippi Democratic party of late 1859 was hard-core, dedicated, able, and potentially dangerous.

Pettus' gubernatorial term did not begin until late November. During this post-election interim period, John Brown's infamous

---

[22] I. M. Patridge, "The Press of Mississippi—Historical Sketch," *DeBow's Review*, XXIX (October, 1860), 509; R. H. Henry, *Editors I Have Known* (New Orleans, 1922), 93; Davis *Recollections of Mississippi*, 352.

raid on Harper's Ferry, Virginia, transpired on October 16, 1859. Repercussions shook Mississippi to its foundations. Brown's overt and untimely act radically altered the temperament of many hitherto moderates and pushed them toward the arms of radicalism. No better testimony regarding such change of direction exists than that recorded by a typical Whig planter from Bolivar County, who affirmed: "Until the John Brown raid I never for a moment lost my loyalty to the union, but after that I became a secessionist."[23] Thus it was that amid fear of slave rebellion and rumors of similar violence John Pettus took office.

On Monday, November 21, 1859, the governor-elect was inaugurated with much pomp and ceremony. At an early hour the floor and galleries of the hall of the house of representatives were filled with ladies who had come to witness the important event. A parade, consisting of a band, a local militia unit, numerous state officials and private citizens, made its way from the executive mansion to the capitol building. Outgoing Governor McWillie escorted Pettus, and the two men rode in an open carriage driven by Pettus' black coachman, Pleas. Upon their arrival in the house chamber, the chief justice of the state supreme court administered the oath of office and Mississippi had a new governor for the coming two years.

Since the inauguration took place little more than a month after John Brown's raid, it was almost inevitable that Pettus would devote much of his address to the sectional controversy. Slavery, abolitionism, and the "Black" Republican party were dealt harsh words, while the "scene at Harper's Ferry" was termed "only the beginning of the end of this conflict." Pettus reviewed the origin, history, and progress of the "anti-slavery party," reminding his listeners that northern state governments had been actively aiding those churches, societies, and individuals who resisted the return of fugitive slaves. The sum of these lessons was that the federal government "to which we formerly looked for protection of our rights beyond the limits of our own

---

[23] Frank A. Montgomery, *Reminiscences of a Mississippian in Peace and War* (Cincinnati, 1901), 35.

State, seems to either be unwilling or unable to guard the rights or redress the wrongs of slaveholders."[24]

Pettus went on to note that past compromise efforts had been ignored by the North and that to look for salvation in the "Black" Republican party would be "as vain as the prayer of the heathen to his wooden idol." The answer to William Seward's Republican "dogma of equality of the negro to the white man" was for the South to unfurl a banner "inscribed 'Superiority and Supremacy of the White Race.'" The new Mississippi chief executive then called for southerners to demonstrate to the people of the North that such a dastardly course as abolition would deprive the latter of lucrative commercial advantages with residents below the Mason–Dixon line. Economic pressure would not politically endanger the Union, but appeared to be the "only course remaining to the South by which she . . . [could] preserve her rights and the Union." In any case, Pettus said, southerners must procede to adopt vigorous defense measures for the purpose of protecting the existing political order. Indeed, if the stronghold of slavery was not garrisoned by men who considered safeguards necessary, then the South's fate would be self-sealed. Energetic preparations were necessary to meet a seemingly "irrepressible" situation.

To achieve the ends of which he spoke, Pettus recommended that a convention of southern states be summoned to share ideas and propose workable alternatives to deal with sectional issues. To such a meeting the governor pledged to send Mississippi's "truest and best" men. If, after a display of solidarity, northerners persisted in their efforts to undermine southern institutions, a final solution to sectional differences might materialize. In the event of armed conflict the South would emerge victorious, said Pettus, sustained by the knowledge that she had "a better cause, double the population and twenty times the resources of the [original] thirteen colonies."

In closing his soul-stirring address, Pettus sought the help of God in resolving both present and future crises and affirmed that

[24] Mississippi *Senate Journal* (1859), 105–109.

if the South held fast to traditional principles, it "might yet remain free." Thus, with singular clarity the governor put the state's official position on record in unmistakable terms. Those around him, including many men of elective office, were of like opinion in sounding a strong note of warning and discord.[25]

Both the Mississippi gubernatorial election of 1859 and its aftermath must be viewed as significant. There could be no doubt that the electorate had brought forth a fire-eating champion of southern rights to lead the state during the critical times that lay ahead. Clear and cool minds had defaulted by not conducting a more rigorous opposition at this crucial juncture, and the subsequent selection of an increasingly inflexible person to speak for all Mississippians has to be viewed as unfortunate. Pettus was only a notch above the average in terms of age, property holdings, and slave ownership;[26] he related to the common man and won office by capitalizing on his concerns and fears. The home-grown alarmists within the Democratic ranks could now march boldly into the headwinds of sectional strife, believing that the recent election had given them a mandate to do so.

By late 1859 the personalities and ideological ingredients necessary for arriving at some sort of final solution to national issues were present and poised for action, at least in Mississippi. No one, even the most casual observer, could fail to realize that existing leadership was determined to protect the state at all hazards. Clear-eyed men were too few and too silent, while a growing number of individuals adopted the opinion that the chief glory of society resided in its achievements in arms. In short, the state election of 1859 was but the vanguard of a small breeze that would soon turn into a political whirlwind when the ultimate test of crisis came the following year.

[25] Natchez *Weekly Courier*, November 29, 1859.
[26] 1860 Population Census Schedules, Hinds County, Mississippi (Microfilm copy in Miss. Arch.), roll 374; 1860 Population Census Schedules, Kemper County, Mississippi (Microfilm copy in Miss. Arch.), roll 129.

IV

The Question
of Southern Unity

WHEN JOHN PETTUS took office as the sixteenth governor of Mississippi, the state legislature had several more weeks of work to complete before the Christmas recess. The normal spirit of good will accompanying the holiday season failed to materialize that year, largely because of overtones arising from John Brown's raid, which had stirred intense conflicting emotions throughout the nation. Many Mississippians, including the governor, were not oblivious to the vast array of rumors which flew in every direction. Reports that abolitionists had secretly invaded the state and were planning a servile slave insurrection to coincide with Christmas festivities were commonplace. Although such hearsay proved groundless, a great degree of vigilance was exercised and the legislature was asked to pass a law ordering the arrest of all free Negroes who failed to remove themselves from the state before July 1 of the following year.[1]

Meanwhile, Governor Pettus, who had called for a tangible display of southern solidarity against the North, proceeded to act. Evidence of unity would take the form of a convention where representatives of the slaveholding states would have the opportunity to agree upon a common course of action. At Pettus' request, state senator Raymond Neill undertook the task of setting up the legislative machinery for such a project. While the

---

[1] Yazoo City *Democrat*, December 10, 1859; Jackson *Semi-Weekly Mississippian*, December 7, 1859.

issue of a convention was being debated in late 1859, Pettus made a concerted effort to secure a united political front at home by announcing appointments to his staff, some of whom were members of the late Opposition party. Those designated as close associates included Nathaniel Barksdale, C. G. Armstead, Henry Muldow, V. T. Terrel, G. M. Gowler, W. A. Barbour, John Russell and Samuel Terral.[2]

Throughout December, Mississippians kept posted on events transpiring in Virginia relative to the aftermath of John Brown's raid. Particular focus was accorded Virginia Governor John Letcher, who went on record as recommending that there be no more compromises with northern abolitionists. The South, he reportedly said, must first organize and arm, then demand security for its position in the Union. According to Letcher such precautions were now necessary since insurrection was the "lesson of the hour" and virtually anyone was "free to rise up against fixed government." But in view of Letcher's stand, the Mississippi legislature took no such action prior to Christmas adjournment, other than recommending that Congress compensate citizens whose slaves were freed by virtue of "escaping to the non slaveholding States."[3]

Not all Mississippians welcomed such harsh words and several individuals took special pains to say so. The Vicksburg Weekly Whig of December 21 advised its readers to maintain perspective and not let "a few fanatics at the North and a few alarmists" in the South lead the nation toward ruin. Still, the preponderance of statements made elsewhere in the slave states were of such caliber as to add further fuel to the disunion cause.

Illustrative of the growing feeling of radicalism was the concern that many persons had for access to weapons. Typical of these inquiries was a letter to Governor Pettus from a Mississippi hot-spur residing in New Orleans. The latter, a friend of state

---

[2] Rowland, *Encyclopedia of Mississippi History*, II, 411.
[3] Jackson *Semi-Weekly Mississippian*, December 15, 1859; Vicksburg *Weekly Whig*, December 14, 1859.

treasurer Haynes, offered to deliver 3,000 rifles and muskets to the governor.[4] But to Pettus' way of thinking, the need for military supplies was not yet of paramount concern; rather, developments on the political front needed to be pursued.

Much of the sense of crisis and discontent that colored the southern political landscape throughout late 1859 and early 1860 was directly traceable to John Brown's raid. Those who desired to disrupt the Union saw the incident as a device that could be useful in drumming up separationist feeling. Especially to the hot-bloods of Mississippi, the events of October 16, 1859, "meant much more than a mere isolated insurrection on the periphery of the Upper South. Rather, Harper's Ferry appeared as both a precedent and a premonition." With state newspapers packed with "reports of suspected servile revolts, violence or incendiary activity" and daily pleas "for increased vigilance against the ubiquitous enemy," it became almost impossible to avoid the temper of the times.[5]

In the back of the minds of several Mississippi radicals was the concept of secession. But the accomplishment of that objective would be no easy task, and it was doubtful that enough support could be mustered at this stage to carry it through to fruition. However, the Brown incident and its location did furnish fuel for the disunion fires. Virginia enjoyed the most sophisticated position among slaveholding states. If nothing more could be gained by southern hot-spurs than to obtain Virginia's participation and acceptance of a program of common unity, the road to possible secession would be made clearer and more respectable. Time and conditions in the Old Dominion appeared ripe for such an approach, for surely Virginians must now realize that their interests needed concrete programs of defense.[6]

[4] R. W. James to John J. Pettus, December 24, 1859, in John J. Pettus Papers, Mississippi Department of Archives and History, Jackson.
[5] Donald B. Kelley, "Harper's Ferry: Prelude to Crisis in Mississippi," *Journal of Mississippi History*, XXVII (November, 1965), 369–70.
[6] Avery O. Craven, *The Growth of Southern Nationalism, 1848–1861* (Baton Rouge, 1953), 308–309.

Governor Pettus' convention plan had received a certain amount of favorable response, both among constituents and certain newspapers. Yet the Mississippi legislature remained passive and the initiative for such a gathering passed to South Carolina. South Carolinians had also been studying recent developments in Virginia and had arrived at the conclusion that the circumstances necessary to stimulate that key state were at hand. A convention to devise some policy for concurrent action was deemed appropriate. Virginia's participation was almost mandatory in order to insure success.

In December, 1859, a joint committee of the South Carolina legislature charted plans for a meeting of the slaveholding states. Resolutions to that effect were approved along with a drastic increase in state military expenditures. A delegation was ordered sent to the Old Dominion to officially convey South Carolina's indignation at Brown's incursion and to invite Virginia to attend a southern convention. If their mission proved successful, the role of leadership would probably rest somewhere other than with South Carolina, as that state "had a reputation for ultraism."[7]

In late December it was announced that Christopher G. Memminger had been appointed as commissioner to personally transmit South Carolina's message to Virginia. The decision to send the German-born Memminger as an envoy was no accident. By this stage of his public career, he had made the transition from unionist to secessionist. A personification of the changing times, Memminger was ideal for the job of imbuing Virginians with "South Carolina doctrine." Amid speculation as to the true nature of his assignment, Memminger arrived in Richmond early in January. Only a few days before, it had been reported that Virginia's Governor Letcher personally supported a southern convention. Futher likelihood that approval of the project would be forthcoming was sustained by knowledge that an organization known as the Central Southern Rights Association of Virginia

---

[7] Charleston *Daily Courier*, December 23, 1859; Clement Eaton, *A History of the Southern Confederacy* (New York, 1958), 5.

had been active along similar lines for several weeks in that state.[8]

On January 20, Memminger addressed the Virginia legislature and clarified his reasons for appearing. The text of his remarks was carefully prepared so as to discount radicalism as an immediate objective. He reviewed the entire sweep of sectional controversy, underscoring the need for common defense preparations. "Must we," Memminger inquired, "accept the alternative of unconditional submission because there is risk of revolution?" Accordingly, southern institutions could "only be maintained by constant and untiring effort."[9]

Reaction to Memminger's address proved favorable, at least in some quarters. The Richmond *Semi-Weekly Examiner* editorialized that "immediate . . . disunion, rash and suicidal from want of concert of action among the Southern States, is not what South Carolina desires at the hands of Virginia." Instead, this initiative was one of "chivalrous desire to share the dangers which environ Virginia as a frontier State."[10]

A joint committee of eighteen was appointed by the host legislature to prepare a suitable reply to the South Carolina overture. In a few days three brief motions were framed, advocating that Virginia not participate in any conference. But before any official action was taken, an alternative resolution was brought forward proposing that three delegates be appointed to attend a convention scheduled for the summer of 1860 in Atlanta, Georgia.[11]

The struggle between those in favor and those opposed to the convention was made more complicated by an underlying po-

[8] Ollinger Grenshaw, "Christopher G. Memminger's Mission to Virginia, 1860," *Journal of Southern History*, VIII (August, 1942), 338; Harold S. Schultz, *Nationalism and Sectionalism in South Carolina, 1852–1860* (Durham, 1950), 202; New York *Times*, January 9, 1860; "Southern Rights Association of Virginia," *DeBow's Review*, XXVII (February, 1860), 173–82.

[9] Henry D. Capers, *The Life and Times of C. G. Memminger* (Richmond, 1893), 278.

[10] Richmond *Semi-Weekly Examiner*, January 24, 1860, quoted in Dwight L. Dumond (ed.), *Southern Editorials on Secession* (New York, 1931), 16–17.

[11] New York *Times*, January 25, 31, 1860; Jackson *Semi-Weekly Mississippian*, February 2, 1860.

litical ferment within the Old Dominion. While awaiting an
official response from the legislature, Memminger proceeded to
poll both public and private opinion concerning the matter and
soon learned that "even the most extreme leaders were reluctant
to give public endorsement to a Southern Conference." Presidential aspirations on the part of some factions dictated that they
"avoid taking any action which might react to the disadvantage
of their candidates." Among those mentioned as possible compromise choices in national politics were Robert M. T. Hunter
and Henry A. Wise.[12]

Local newspapers served as voices for the two major political
forces in Virginia and exhibited differing points of view on the
utility of a slave states convention. The Democratic Richmond
Enquirer ardently favored the conference scheme, labeling it
as the "great pivot" around which to plant a Virginian in the
White House. The Richmond *Whig and Public Advertiser*, however, took issue with this line of reasoning and believed that
an Atlanta meeting would be tantamount to secession.[13] This
type of rivalry and power struggle generated a stalemate on the
issue at hand. In disgust, commissioner Memminger penned a
letter to South Carolina newspaper editor Robert Barnwell
Rhett summing up the situation. With patience worn thin, Memminger affirmed that political conditions in Virginia were deplorable, making that state comparatively powerless. His mission an apparent failure, the frustrated deputy took leave of
Virginia in early February.

On February 13 a series of resolutions were again formally introduced before the Virginia legislature. These proposals expressed the view that it was inexpedient to send any representatives to an Atlanta conclave. Governor Letcher was instructed

---

[12] Schultz, *Nationalism and Sectionalism in South Carolina*, 202; Martha T.
Hunter, *A Memoir of Robert M. T. Hunter* (Washington, D.C., 1903), 113–14;
Charles H. Ambler, *Sectionalism in Virginia from 1776 to 1861* (Chicago, 1910),
327; Barton H. Wise, *The Life of Henry A. Wise of Virginia, 1806–1876* (New
York, 1899), 263.
[13] Richmond *Enquirer*, March 31, 1860; Richmond *Whig and Public Advertiser*,
March 25, 1860.

to make this decision known to his counterparts in the other slave states. This cool response to South Carolina's endeavors was not totally unexpected. Memminger himself was aware of it, and had notified his governor, William P. Miles, that the Deep South states would have to take the lead and "drag after us those divided States."[14]

A contemporary observer might have concluded that Virginia's unsatisfactory reply would end any further conference preparations. But the state of Mississippi had been acting simultaneously and when the legislature convened in January, 1860, the political and sectional issues of the day once again held center stage. News of the South Carolina resolutions, combined with Governor Pettus' earlier recommendations, brought legislative deliberation into the forefront. Clearly, now as in the past, the "interests of Mississippi identified her with South Carolina."[15]

On January 18, thirteen Resolutions on Federal Relations were introduced in the Mississippi senate. These motions dealt with the essential questions of slavery, property rights, and the Republican party, promising no quarter for those individuals who "assumed a revolutionary position toward the South." Two days later, state senator Peter B. Starke offered a motion to send commissioners to Virginia for a repeat of the Memminger mission. As Starke put it, the "danger impending over the Union" must be emphasized.[16]

A few days later, Governor Pettus threw his weight behind South Carolina's actions and recommended that Mississippi "respond favorably to the invitation, and that measures be adopted . . . to have [the] State fully represented in the Convention." Prior to the convening of such an assembly, Mississippi lawmakers must see to it that commercial relations were made less profitable to those who would make war on southern rights.

[14] New York *Times*, February 14, 1860; Memminger to Miles, January 3, 1860, in Miles Papers, Southern Historical Collection, University of North Carolina.
[15] Cleo Hearon, "Nullification In Mississippi," in Franklin L. Riley (ed.), *Publications of the Mississippi Historical Society* (Oxford, Miss., 1912), XII, 41.
[16] Mississippi *Senate Journal* (1859), 227–80, 293–94.

A tax of from 5 to 10 percent on goods brought into the South was suggested as a "mode of awakening the attention of the Northern people to the injuries done."[17]

The first attempt to have Mississippi represented at the Atlanta convention was made by legislator Livingston Mims. But a Mims proposal of early January was not accepted because of a conflict over dates. Instead, five Joint Resolutions on Federal Relations were passed by the state legislature on February 10. These resolutions dealt with slavery, Republican presidential aspirations, the Atlanta convention, the need for other states to fall into step on the issue of common defense, and the sending of a commissioner to Virginia.[18]

There was some opposition to the resolutions which called for an Atlanta meeting and for the dispatching of an envoy to the Old Dominion. Although approved by respective margins of 70 to 15 and 48 to 35, debate on the topics became heated at times. One Whig observer, Benjamin L. C. Wailes, concluded that such devices were designed by "insane politicians" who were "determined to drive us into a state of anarchy and civil war." Such a "disastrous condition of things" appeared "inevitable unless the sound Northern statesmen should interfere to save the country."[19]

On February 11 Governor Pettus appointed Peter B. Starke of Bolivar County to undertake the delicate and responsible duties of Mississippi's commissioner to Virginia. Three days later a joint session of the legislature elected Samuel S. Boyd (Adams County), Wiley P. Harris (Hinds County), A. M. Clayton (Marshall County), Samuel J. Gholson (Monroe County), W. R. Hill

[17] Jackson *Semi-Weekly Mississippian*, January 25, 1860; Mississippi *Senate Journal* (1859), 301–302; Brandon *Herald of the South*, December 21, 1859.
[18] Jackson *Semi-Weekly Mississippian*, January 21, 1860; Joint Resolutions on Federal Relations, February 10, 1860, in Vol. XLIX of Governor's Correspondence, Ser. E, Mississippi Department of Archives and History, Jackson, hereinafter cited as Governor's Correspondence.
[19] Rainwater, *Mississippi: Storm Center of Secession*, 105; Charles S. Sydnor, *A Gentleman of the Old Natchez Region: Benjamin L. C. Wailes* (Durham, 1938), 295.

(Yazoo County), Henry Dickerson (Lowndes County), and Hiram Cassedy (Franklin County) to represent the Magnolia State at the Atlanta conference.[20]

Governor Pettus' choice of Peter Starke was one well thought out. Starke, a one-time resident of Virginia, was a former Whig. At the time of his appointment, the forty-six-year-old politician represented a four-county district in the state senate. Starke's mission began amid an air of confidence, bolstered by the knowledge that Mississippi actions had already found fertile ground in other states. The Florida legislature, for example, had recently resolved to abide by, and cooperate with, "any course" that the southern states deemed necessary in "their united wisdom." Alabama politicians were calling for a boycott of northern goods, while Louisiana's governor, Thomas Overton Moore, pledged that his state would "never separate herself from her sister slaveholding States."[21]

Even so, certain opposition to the conference plan and the envoy to Virginia was still apparent in Mississippi. Whigs once more formed the core of discontent. A meeting of southern fire-eaters, according to the Vicksburg *Weekly Whig*, of February 10, 1860, was neither probable nor desirable and "would weaken the bonds of the nation as [much as] the crazy fanatics of New England." On the other hand, it was Virginia Whigs who welcomed the suggestion of Starke's visit, hoping it would further the political confusion among Democrats in the state.

News of the Mississippi commissioner's impending arrival preceded him. Viewed as a true conservative and "devoted follower of Henry Clay," Starke was reported to be for the maintenance of the Union by means of compromise. Armed with instructions from Governor Pettus, with resolutions, and with the

[20] State of Mississippi, *Communications From the Hon. Peter B. Starke as Commissioner to Virginia, to His Excellency J. J. Pettus, With Accompanying Documents* (Jackson, 1860), 21; Natchez *Weekly Courier*, February 14, 1860.
[21] Rowland, *Official and Statistical Register*, 882; Jackson *Semi-Weekly Mississippian*, January 10, February 2, 1860; Van D. Odom, "The Political Career of Thomas Overton Moore, Secession Governor of Louisiana," *Louisiana Historical Quarterly*, XXVI (October, 1943), 993.

assurance of a cordial reception at journey's end, Starke set out for Richmond. A traveling companion, William A. Lake, a Whig lawyer from Vicksburg and a member of the Mississippi legislature, accompanied Starke. They arrived in the Virginia capital on Sunday, February 18, less than a week and a half after the departure of South Carolina's Memminger.[22]

That same evening the Virginia State Democratic Convention completed its business and adjourned. Shortly after the close of the formal gathering another meeting was held, attended by members of the late convention. Although acting on its own, the rump assembly adopted, by "a very large majority," a resolution favoring the proposed Atlanta convention. The delegation then proceeded to Peter Starke's hotel, got him out of bed, and prevailed upon him to deliver "a very good though short speech." The Mississippian vigorously declared that he had been sent to Virginia "for the Union and not for disunion . . . . The South would not go out of the Union, but if she were not protected by Federal authority she would seize the Federal property within her limits, and defend herself."[23]

Long-time fire-eater Edmund Ruffin was on hand that night and recorded in his diary that he hoped the rump's "demonstration of popular will . . . will have some effect in urging on the laggard movements of the legislature." Even so, Ruffin "entertained but little hope" that an Atlanta convention would be voted for by the Virginia lawmakers.[24]

The next day Starke wrote Governor Letcher a lengthy letter, the substance of which amounted to a discussion of political affairs. The Mississippian took great pains to clarify his state's position relative to the Union, and in carefully shaded terms asserted that if his state had been "influenced by a determination or even a desire to withdraw from this sisterhood of States, I am

[22] New York *Times*, February 22, 1860; Jackson *Semi-Weekly Mississippian*, February 1, 1860; State of Mississippi, *Communications From Peter Starke*, 3.
[23] New York *Times*, February 20, 1860; William K. Scarborough (ed.), *The Diary of Edmund Ruffin* (Baton Rouge, 1972), I, 403.
[24] Scarborough (ed.), *Diary of Edmund Ruffin*, I, 403.

very sure that she would have selected another agent to plead her cause before the state of Virginia."[25]

On February 21, Governor Letcher addressed his legislature and conveyed the encouraging opinion that the lawmakers would no doubt respond to Starke's assignment in a favorable manner. Meanwhile, a round of parties was in the offing and every politeness was extended to the visitor from Mississippi.

Peter Starke elected not to speak before the Virginia legislature, believing that the recent South Carolina envoy had set forth the arguments for a convention most convincingly. Moreover, a declaration of collective action seemed almost a certainty, especially since the host legislature approved a motion calling for the printing and circulation of 10,000 copies of his communications.[26]

Edmund Ruffin and Starke conferred on the evening of February 24. The latter was optimistic regarding the chances for the successful completion of his mission. Conversely, Ruffin expressed the belief that "no favorable response [would] be made" and that to look to the border states for leadership was fruitless.[27]

When no official word had been received by the end of the month, Starke grew disenchanted. Since the Virginia legislature's session was moving toward adjournment, the Mississippian penned a rather sharp note to Governor Letcher. Conveying the impression of possible embarrassment to himself and Governor Pettus, Starke virtually demanded a swift answer to the question of a southern conference, adding that he saw no reason why such a project should not be approved. Letcher, as noted earlier, had leaned toward participation in the Atlanta conference; but, because of increasing pressures from discordant political factions and the closeness of the National Democratic Convention, he now backed away from the issue altogether. In a message to the

[25] State of Mississippi, *Communications from Peter Starke*, 6–8. See also Natchez *Mississippi Free Trader*, March 12, 1860.
[26] Jackson *Semi-Weekly Mississippian*, February 28, 1860; State of Mississippi, *Communications From Peter Starke*, 11–20.
[27] Scarborough (ed.), *Diary of Edmund Ruffin*, I, 407.

Virginia legislature, Letcher sought pardon for "suggesting that a response was due to the States whose commissioners had been received." If a decision was to be forthcoming it was the law-makers' sole responsibility to determine the "character of that response."[28]

On March 8 the Virginia house and senate, by respective votes of 90 to 42 and 31 to 11, officially terminated the long-festering dilemma by adopting a series of six resolutions. The resolutions expressed special gratitude to the commissioners of both South Carolina and Mississippi and instructed Letcher to notify all other slaveholding states of the Old Dominion's reasoning in re-fusing to attend the Atlanta convention. The legislators felt that "efficient cooperation" between and among the cotton states could "be more safely obtained by such direct legislative action . . . as may be necessary and proper, than through the agency of an assembly which could exercise no legislative power except to debate and advise."[29] Hence, with his duties at an end, Peter Starke returned home with the empty fruits of his labor.

Reaction to Virginia's decision was varied. The New York *Times* hailed the legislature's action as a "piece of wisdom for which the whole nation should thank her." On the other hand, the Charleston *Mercury* charged that Virginia's refusal would have the "effect of inspiring the Black Republican party with confidence . . . and greatly tend to remove fear of a dissolution of the Union." Now it was "vain and cowardly to look to the Fron-tier States to lead the South to the recovery of her independence and security."[30]

By virtue of a negative stand Virginia dealt a heavy blow to the question of a unified southern program at this hour and was undoubtedly the determining factor in the eventual abandon-ment of the idea. Obviously affected by the Old Dominion ver-dict, the Tennessee legislature in March passed a similar series of resolutions expressing the view that it was inexpedient to send

[28] State of Mississippi, *Communications From Peter Starke*, 11–20.
[29] Virginia Resolutions on Federal Relations, March 10, 1860, in Governor's Correspondence, Vol. XLIX.
[30] New York *Times*, March 10, 1860; Charleston *Mercury*, March 10, 1860.

deputies to an Atlanta meeting.[31] Georgia followed suit, although it was admitted that some die-hard representatives from other states would probably assemble in Atlanta anyway. By way of caution the liberal Augusta *Daily Chronicle and Sentinel* on March 14 reminded its readers that the hot-bloods should "take warning from [Virginia's] lesson. Let them learn that however loud the press and the politicians may clamour . . . the people will not heed them."

Mississippians received the news of Virginia's judgment with mixed emotion. Governor John Pettus was depressed, and for good reason, as he had been actively engaged in seeking out personal commitments for the Atlanta meeting from other southern governors, especially Sam Houston of Texas. After the Virginia resolutions were passed, such men became more reluctant to take a stand on their own.[32]

Conference hopes had strong roots in the Magnolia State, but even the Jackson *Semi-Weekly Mississippian* observed that only South Carolina and Mississippi would be represented in Atlanta. Hoping that "no failure occur," the paper recommended that the convention be postponed until October or November, 1860. In this Governor Pettus concurred. In a letter to Governor William H. Gist of South Carolina, Pettus concluded that the time and place for an assemblage appeared inappropriate. Yet, since unified action was of utmost importance, the Mississippian offered to sponsor a temporary cancellation notice in order to avoid the stigma of failure.[33] Nothing came of the suggestion.

By the spring of 1860 the enthusiasm heralding joint southern action had dissipated everywhere, except in Mississippi, which had taken the liberty of selecting delegates to the proposed

[31] Tennessee Resolutions on Federal Relations, March 23, 1860, in Governor's Correspondence, Vol. XLIX. At a later date (January, 1861), Tennesseans did offer to carry through with a conference, but by then the time for such endeavors had long since evaporated. See Mary E. R. Campbell, *The Attitude of Tennesseans Toward the Union, 1847–1861* (New York, 1961), 161.

[32] Houston to Pettus, February 28, 1860, in Governor's Correspondence, Vol. XLIX.

[33] Jackson *Semi-Weekly Mississippian*, March 23, 1860; Pettus to Gist, April 7, 1860, in Governor's Executive Journal: Governors McRae, Pettus, Clark and Humphreys, 1856–1866, p. 207.

meeting. The remaining southern states continued to be either passive or, as in the case of South Carolina, held the opinion that separate state action was inevitable. National politics, of course, overshadowed other concerns by then.

During late May and early June all the previously elected Mississippi deputies, excluding ailing Henry Dickerson, responded to letters from Governor Pettus concerning their mission. Writing from Meadville on May 24, Hiram Cassedy took note of the fact that hardly anyone had agreed with the Atlanta plan and, fearing personal embarrassment, "respectfully declined" to accept the "farce of a journey to Atlanta." Deputies Clayton, Gholson, Harris, and Hill followed suit, and in a joint communiqué "deemed it unnecessary" to go to the Georgia capital. J. J. Boyd, exhibiting something less than optimism, indicated that his participation would be "sheer folly."[34]

Meanwhile, Governor Pettus sorrowfully notified Governor Gist that a southern meeting at this stage appeared most unlikely, but countered with a proposal for a similar type of gathering at Richmond, Virginia, which might have "better prospects of unanimity." The last flicker of hope for salvaging a conference came from ex-commissioner Peter Starke. In a letter to Pettus, he outlined the need for southern cooperation and affirmed that if Mississippi or South Carolina should "falter or take any step backwards, after the stand they have taken, then all is lost" and the nation should make ready "for the last great extremity."[35]

By the summer of 1860 the question of southern unity had been shoved aside and other considerations held center stage. Mississippians were concerned with the political and sectional developments that had transpired throughout the period when the Atlanta plan had been debated and analyzed. The slave states were as yet working at cross-purposes in attempting to deal with the vital issues of the day. Cooler minds still held sway and even the most hair-raising of counselors were forced to acknowledge

[34] Cassedy to Pettus, May 24, 1860, Harris et al. to Pettus, May 30, 1860, Boyd to Pettus, June 4, 1860, in Governor's Correspondence, Vol. XLIX.
[35] Pettus to Gist, May 12, 1860, in Governor's Executive Journal, 1856–66, p. 208; Starke to Pettus, July, 1860, in Governor's Correspondence, Vol. XLIX.

that 1860 presidential politics took precedent over any conference. Such feelings were probably best summed up by Alabama
Governor Andrew B. Moore. In a letter to Governor Gist, Moore
determined that it was "unnecessary to take any steps for the
purpose of appointing delegates to the proposed convention until
after the Charleston convention shall have met and acted."[36]
Charleston, scheduled to be the scene of the National Democratic party's presidential nominating congress, promised to be
the site of much political drama.

[36] Moore to Gist, April 2, 1860, in Andrew B. Moore Papers, Alabama Department of Archives and History, Montgomery, Alabama.

V

The Road to Disunion

PRIOR TO HIS ELECTION as governor of Mississippi, John Pettus had not been well known beyond the borders of his own state. But as a result of his campaign statements and sponsorship of the Atlanta convention project, his political stature increased, and as far away as South Carolina one began to associate his name with the cause of southern sectionalism.

The early months of office saw Pettus pursue the prospects of a southern conference. Such activity, however, was not the only tool deemed feasible for use in handling sectional issues. The legislature was called upon to begin examining the question of military needs. On December 15 a senate committee reported that the state arsenal contained a mere 344 rifles and muskets, 14 pistols, 118 sabers and swords, and 2 cannons. Additional investigation revealed that some state militia units had few, if any, arms at all. Such a gloomy weapons tabulation, the committee report concluded, demonstrated that the state was "in very poor condition for the defense of her Constitutional rights, if a contingency should occur making it necessary to resort to force.[1]

Obviously distressed by such information, Governor Pettus recommended that the situation be rectified as soon as possible. With unusual promptness the legislature appropriated $150,000 for the purchase of military supplies. Requests from local militia units for armaments reached the governor daily, and he did his

[1] Mississippi *Senate Journal* (1859), 164–65.

best to fill them, even if it meant doing business with northern manufacturers. Within a short while an order was placed for 4,000 muskets.[2]

So engrossed was the Mississippi legislature with sectional affairs and national politics during the opening weeks of 1860 that some criticism was directed its way. The Natchez *Weekly Courier*, a strong proponent of unionism, leveled the charge that it was bad enough to have Mississippi represented in Congress by "seven rampant fire-eating gentlemen" without having state legislators stir up "still more fiercely the fires of agitation, sectionalism and excitement." Other newspapers challenged the legislature's resolutions on federal relations and the plan for an Atlanta convention, believing that such actions would lead to a "fearful catastrophe." Marching off to Georgia against "an imaginary army of abolitionist invaders" would be tantamount to treason.[3]

Seemingly unaffected by adverse publicity, the lawmakers continued to pass judgment on the issues of the hour. A Pettus-backed resolution concerning the possible curtailment of commercial intercourse with northern states was approved on January 27. The same day state slave patrol laws were strengthened to a point consistent with the protection of "persons and property . . . against the insidious machinations of itinerate emmisaries [*sic*] of enemies of Southern citizens and their domestic institutions."[4]

Chief executive Pettus continued to prepare for any eventuality in sectional affairs by urging more internal improvements for the state. In January he was on hand to drive the ceremonial spike necessary to complete an expansion of the Mississippi

[2] Jackson *Semi-Weekly Mississippian*, December 27, 1859; Jack W. Gunn, "Mississippi in 1860 As Reflected in the Activities of the Governor's Office," *Journal of Mississippi History*, XXII (July, 1960), 186; Eli Whitney Arms Company to Pettus, January 1860, in Governor's Correspondence, Vol. XLIX; Pettus to R. W. James, March 9, 1860, in Governor's Executive Journal, 1856–66, p. 205.
[3] Natchez *Weekly Courier*, February 3, 1860; Vicksburg *Daily Whig*, January 10, 28, 1860; Vicksburg *Sun*, January 16, 1860.
[4] Mississippi *Senate Journal* (1859), 329–30.

Central Railroad. Other bridge and railroad projects also received his encouragement and support.[5]

Many of the events that transpired in Mississippi throughout late 1859 and early 1860 could not avoid being linked to the broader scope of national affairs. For instance, when the Thirty-sixth Congress assembled in Washington in December, 1859, bitter sectional rivalry flared into the open, reaching such proportions that it was even feared that a physical collision would occur. Unable to garner sufficient support to elect a speaker of the House, that body proceeded without rules, and debates over slavery and other sectional differences disrupted normal legislative routine. During one fiery exchange of words, Mississippi Congressman Lucius Q. C. Lamar charged Republicans with co-conspiracy in John Brown's raid and with the murder of "innocent men."[6] Amid the verbal conflict of embittered oratory, William Pennington, sent to Congress by the People's party of New Jersey,[7] was finally elected to the speakership, thus ending the tortuous business. Yet, the intense anger and excitement generated by such debate could only further the spread of sectional emotionalism throughout the nation. Hatred, suspicion, threats, and attempts at economic reprisals highlighted the spirit of the times. "A black list of New York merchants, called abolition houses, and a white list, called constitutional houses were published in the South, and Southern buyers were advised, even warned, to place their orders with the proper parties."[8]

Under such heated conditions John Pettus and the Mississippi legislature dealt with vital questions of the day. Much political activity in the state during the early months of 1860 was cen-

[5] E. G. Barney to Pettus, January 31, 1860, in Governor's Correspondence, Vol. XLIX; Mississippi Senate Journal (1859).

[6] James Ford Rhodes, History of the United States From the Compromise of 1850 to the McKinley–Bryan Campaign of 1896 (2d ed.; New York, 1920), II, 377; Allan Nevins, The Emergence of Lincoln (New York, 1950), II, 124; Edward Mayes, Lucius Q. C. Lamar: His Life, Times and Speeches (2nd ed.; Nashville, 1896),623.

[7] The People's party is not to be confused with the Populist or People's party of the late nineteenth century.

[8] Rhodes, History of the United States, II, 382–83.

tered around the demands the Mississippi delegation would make at the forthcoming national Democratic convention, scheduled to open in Charleston, South Carolina, on April 23. Although opinion was divided on this subject, there were some points that many individuals recognized as being valid. The "boldness and dexterity" of the antislavery movement was a foremost consideration, along with the knowledge that "success in the approaching presidential election was of the utmost importance to slavery, and that the election would likely be decisive."[9]

State Democrats generally found themselves in accord in seeking both a National Democratic presidential nominee who was sympathetic toward slavery and a strong platform that would assure congressional protection of that institution in the federal territories. Distasteful to many Mississippians was the possible selection of Illinois Senator Stephen A. Douglas to head the party's ticket. Douglas was distrusted and had been known in certain circles for some time as a "political reprobate" and "a turbulent demagogue" who possessed the "remarkable capacity to betray." On the national level the feelings of Mississippi Democrats were carried to the halls of Congress by Jefferson Davis, who made it clear in February of 1860 that his constituents would have none of Douglas.[10]

Mississippi Whigs, on the other hand, had no national forum from which to air their views, but felt it necessary to oppose, or at least temper, the radical tendencies of the national Democratic party. Not since the fall elections of 1859 had the Oppositionists been given such cause for alarm, and they left little undone in an effort to cry down the fire-eaters. John Pettus, symbol of all that was evil in local politics, did not escape the verbal barrage— being labeled "a most bigoted prejudiced Nincompoop!"[11] Un-

[9] Daniel W. Howe, *Political History of Secession to the Beginning of the American Civil War* (New York, 1914), 387; Gilbert H. Barnes, *The Anti-Slavery Impulse, 1830–1844* (New York, 1933), 195.
[10] Natchez *Weekly Courier*, July 6, 1859; Horace Greeley, *The American Conflict: A History of the Great Rebellion in the United States of America, 1860–1864* (Hartford, 1864), I, 306; Dunbar Rowland (ed.), *Jefferson Davis, Constitutionalist: His Letters, Papers and Speeches* (New York, 1923), IV, 167–84.
[11] Sydnor, *A Gentleman of the Old Natchez Region*, 292.

like the disorganized effort they had put on during the gubernatorial campaign of 1859, the Opposition party was ready and determined to do something about approaching political affairs,
and as far as possible, champion the position of moderation.

Shortly after the 1859 state elections, efforts to provide a continuing alternative source to the obvious revolutionary tendencies of the Democratic leadership shifted to the Central Committee of the Opposition party. At the head of that body was
William L. Sharkey, who in mid-December had called an Opposition convention to meet in Jackson in late March, 1860. The
stated purpose of the gathering was that of preventing the distor-
tion of true Mississippi views "by the art of politicians" who
"seriously endanger our national existence."[12]

But Democrats were not silent and did not intend to leave the
political field to the Oppositionists. Instead, they too met in
December of 1859 and reaffirmed their most recent platform of
the previous summer. Jefferson Davis was put forth as a candidate for the party's presidential nomination and, by way of
warning to the national Democratic leadership, served notice
that the state Democratic Central Committee was "authorized
to take such action as may be demanded by the exigencies" that
could arise during the Charleston convention.[13]

In the weeks immediately prior to the opening of the Democratic conclave, charges and counter-charges were hurled in
newspapers throughout the state. William Sharkey told his followers to "beat back the tide of fanaticism and disunion" by
public displays of moderation and reason. One group of Hinds
County citizens did just that and went on record as being opposed both to "the continuance of the present fierce and hostile agitation of the slavery question," and to "all disunion
conventions."[14]

In sharp contrast, many Democrats beat the drum of sectionalism, led on the state level by Governor Pettus. Comment-

ing on the coming political gathering, the Jackson *Semi-Weekly Mississippian* needed no persuasion to editorialize on March 21 that the state would have "a sound platform and a reliable candidate or none. She will not support Douglas on any platform. We go into the Convention upon the condition that it will nominate a Democrat."

On April 23, Democrats from across the nation assembled at Charleston—perhaps the worst atmosphere available for constructive thinking. The first few days witnessed little in the way of tangible accomplishment; the seating of rival New York delegations and the question of whether a platform or candidate should be the first item of business were the matters receiving most attention. Nevertheless, it was apparent from the very start of the proceedings that the party platform was to represent the most controversial issue of all.

Fundamentally, two opposing philosophies were at stake, both of which concerned slavery. On the one hand, northern delegates favored allowing either the courts or the residents of federal territories to handle the question of slavery in the public domain. Conversely, southern delegates, for whom Alabama's William Lowndes Yancey was the leading spokesman, supported the position of a strong federal code as a guarantee of protecting slavery in the territories. On April 30, after considerable debate and the formal rejection of southern demands, the delegates voted 165 to 138 to adopt portions of the Cincinnati platform of 1856. Southerners obviously objected to this course of action because it was believed that the institution of slavery would not be adequately safeguarded if left open to popular sovereignty. Thereupon, the Alabama delegation, led by Yancey, announced its withdrawal from the proceedings. The slavery issue, which had been the chief source of sectional hardship for years, had now reached the point of tearing the Democratic party asunder.[15]

The eleven-man Mississippi delegation, comprised of a pre-

[15] Clement Eaton, *A History of the Old South* (New York, 1949), 571; Austin L. Venable, "The Conflict Between the Douglas and Yancey Forces in the Charleston Convention," *Journal of Southern History*, VIII (May, 1942), 226.

ponderance of long-time activists in the fire-eater cause, followed the Alabama lead—but not before making their position crystal clear. Delegation chairman David C. Glenn delivered a harshly worded indictment of convention activities. Amid applause and a chorus of cheers Glenn disclosed that in view of the current "situation of things . . . it is right that we should part. Go your way and we will go ours. The South leaves you." Mississippi delegate Ethelbert Barksdale, outspoken owner of the Jackson *Semi-Weekly Mississippian*, also addressed the gathering and likewise gave an elegant refutation of the unpopular Cincinnati platform.[16]

Other southern delegations withdrew from the main convention, but attended a series of meetings in the same city until May 3. During the course of these deliberations arrangements were made for another conclave at Richmond on June 11. Meanwhile, the national Democratic convention had no alternative in view of the walk-out but to disband. Before doing so, another convention was called for Baltimore on June 18, and secessionist state delegations were instructed to send representatives to the new assembly.

On the heels of the ill-fated Charleston convention, Mississippi Governor Pettus felt a rise in sectional animosity was likely. State adjutant-general Francis W. Sykes was ordered "to visit Northern armories, arsenals and factories, and obtain several thousand stands of Mississippi rifles with bayonets attached." Further, Pettus corresponded with Tennessee merchant and political observer Joseph Barbrene regarding the merits of establishing contacts for direct trade with Europe so that the South might "break the shackles that bind her to the North." Although such a program was not new, it was an additional method of bringing pressure on northern abolitionists.[17]

Political events moved rapidly in Mississippi during the anx-

---

[16] Greeley, *The American Conflict*, I, 314; Owen Peterson, "Ethelbert Barksdale in the Democratic National Convention of 1860," *Journal of Mississippi History*, XIV (October, 1952), 274–75.

[17] Rowland, *Encyclopedia of Mississippi History*, II, 412; Barbrene to Pettus, April 14, 1860, in Governor's Correspondence, Vol. XLIX.

ious weeks following the disruption of the Charleston convention. Both Democratic and Opposition newspapers expressed conflicting opinions regarding the behavior of Mississippi's Charleston delegation. The Vicksburg *Sun* endorsed "fully and unequivocally" the vigor displayed, holding that the representatives were justified in their withdrawal from a "convention which refused to treat them as equals." Governor Pettus labeled the incident as the "first proud step that has as yet been taken by the South," applauding those involved with the affirmation "well done, thou good and faithful servant." The Natchez *Weekly Courier* took an Oppositionist line and called the recent debacle "disgusting to the nice feelings of every sincere patriot." It editorialized that the power struggle in evidence at Charleston would certainly play into the hands of moderates because the Democracy was not judged to be in tune with contemporary political reality. A neighboring Louisiana tabloid took issue with this reaction and categorized the walk-out as "natural and justifiable" because of the "arrogant pretensions set up by the Northern delegations."[18]

With upcoming conventions scheduled for Baltimore and Richmond, Mississippi Democrats found it necessary to determine which of the conventions to honor and with which slate of delegates. Pursuant to this objective a meeting was held May 13 in Jackson to debate the question, but it failed to resolve the problem after three days of deliberation. Judging from the available evidence it appeared that the majority of Democrats favored the recent Charleston walk-out and wanted the same delegation returned to Baltimore.[19]

While Mississippi Democrats were evaluating their own political posture, the Republican party held its national convention in Chicago, and nominated Abraham Lincoln for president. When the news reached Mississippi, Governor Pettus declared that the South would never become a "vassal or slave to the

---

[18] Natchez *Weekly Courier*, May 3, 8, 1860; Jackson *Semi-Weekly Mississippian*, May 30, 1860; New Orleans *Daily Delta*, May 2, 1860.
[19] Jackson *Semi-Weekly Mississippian*, May 23, 30, 1860.

60   JOHN JONES PETTUS

abolitionists." If by chance Lincoln was somehow elected, revolution, based upon the "principles of liberty and community
independence" would surely follow.[20]

But it was the unanswered question of what to do about the
planned Richmond convention that proved the most difficult
problem for Mississippi Democrats to resolve. An attempt by a
small group of Douglas followers to have the state's new delegation accredited only to the Baltimore national convention failed
to attract enough numbers to make more than token opposition.
Meeting in the chamber of the state house of representatives on
May 30, another Mississippi Democratic party convention played
to an overflow audience. Members of the earlier Charleston delegation were on hand and defended their every action in vigorous
terms. According to one report the "greatest harmony . . . and the
most cordial unanimity of feeling" characterized the gathering.
In short order it was decided that the former Charleston delegation should be reaccredited to Baltimore; but, if a tranquil atmosphere favorable to southern interests did not prevail, the
representatives were to proceed to a separate meeting at
Richmond.[21]

Simultaneously, Governor Pettus kept vigil over military matters by summoning militia generals and captains of volunteer
companies to a working conference in Jackson. Such energetic
action was widely publicized and performed the two-fold function of seeing to the state's defense while serving notice that the
Deep South political viewpoint must be upheld at all cost.

On June 11, 1860, delegations from several southern states
assembled at Richmond, but went into recess and traveled to
Baltimore for the national convention. In the latter city, on June
22, came a second secession of southerners with political and
sectional axes to grind. This development took few observers
by surprise. The seceders left Baltimore and promptly returned
to Richmond, adopting the name Constitutional Democratic

[20] *Ibid.*, May 29, 1860.
[21] Natchez *Mississippi Free Trader*, June 5, 1860; Jackson *Semi-Weekly
Mississippian*, June 2, 1860.

party, and nominating John C. Breckinridge for president.[22] The National Democrats put forth Stephen A. Douglas, while the moderate Constitutional Union party nominated John Bell of Tennessee for the presidency.

By the end of June all participants in the four-way race to the White House had been chosen. The overriding issue of the campaign was clearly that of slavery and its protection in the territories. The only group able to escape the controversial question by maintaining a somewhat nebulous middle ground was the Union party. But this fact worked to the Unionists' disadvantage, as did candidate Bell's lack of sympathy with secession. In contrast, northern Republicans and southern states' rights Democrats held ground at opposite ends of the political spectrum, while National Democrats proved incapable of attracting their normal following. And as the long-awaited election canvass began to gather momentum, the exactness of proliferated views made reason and toleration all but impossible. Too many men, in too many ways "subscribed to a code of conduct and a plan of action that was the antithesis of moderation and conciliation."[23]

Mississippi, like much of the Deep South, was swept by the sharpness of the issues and the bitterness they invoked. Seldom before in state history had a presidential campaign generated such intensity. Charges and counter-charges were hurled in debates, speeches, public rallies, and the press. Supporters of each presidential aspirant—with the notable exception of Lincoln— took to the stump on behalf of their respective favorites. Democrats of the fire-eater variety led the Breckinridge cause, while in typical and tragic fashion, old-style Whigs squabbled with a minority of National Democrats between the choice of Bell or Douglas.

Throughout the summer of 1860, Mississippi hot-spurs pressed the offensive and devoted themselves tirelessly to the cause of disorder in national affairs. A Lincoln victory would, one orator put it, make secession a necessity and a "patriotic" duty. North-

---

[22] Rainwater, *Mississippi: Storm Center of Secession*, 132–34.
[23] John H. Franklin, *The Militant South: 1800–1861* (Cambridge, 1956), ix.

erners were equated with witches and trouble-makers who would not be satisfied until they "deluge the land in blood to achieve their aims." In a speech at Columbus, Governor Pettus called for the abandonment of the Fourth of July as a national holiday should Lincoln be elected. If another day of celebration were needed, said Pettus, "by the eternals we will make a new one."[24]

The tide of emotion sweeping the state was so strong that many considered physical conflict with the North inevitable, whether the Republicans won the election or not. In a letter to Governor Pettus, William J. Rankin, a planter and one-time legislative aspirant who undoubtedly had caught a case of secession fever, believed that armed hostilities could not be far off and offered the services of the Fordsville Militia Volunteers to the "Confederate States for and during the war." It was that unit's desire "to meet the enemy as quick as possible and as far away from home as they can." But, while fire-eaters exhorted a martial spirit, such gospel did not go unchallenged. There were those who insisted that no election could be grounds for secession. The Vicksburg *Weekly Whig* took its usual stand and assailed Governor Pettus, in particular, for "wielding the battle axe" on behalf of candidates pledged to radical solutions.[25]

By early October, 1860, the presidential contest in Mississippi had clearly narrowed to a struggle between Breckinridge and Bell, although Douglas supporters were in evidence. One of the latter's followers was former governor Henry Foote who, during a speech at Holly Springs, depicted Douglas "fully as a friend of the South." Breckinridge men were labeled "conspirators against the Union, and traitors to the sacred cause of Constitutional liberty."[26]

[24] Richard T. Archer, *Speech of Richard T. Archer, August 10, 1860, at Port Gibson, Mississippi* (Port Gibson, 1860), 6; Natchez *Mississippi Free Trader*, June 13, 1860; Vicksburg *Weekly Whig*, November 1, 1860.
[25] Rankin to Pettus, June 29, 1860, in Governor's Correspondence, Vol. XLIX; Vicksburg *Weekly Whig*, September 14, 1860.
[26] Natchez *Weekly Courier*, October 15, 23, 1860. It should be mentioned that

Meanwhile, Constitutional Democrats ardently strove to fuse Mississippi into some semblance of solidarity, using as their theme the defense of southern institutions and civilization. The state resounded with "mass meetings, barbecues, public speaking, torchlight processions, flag presentations, fireworks, and patriotic slogans." Most prominent Democratic leaders turned out for Breckinridge and expounded his merits and philosophy at the hustings without pause. At a rally in Canton it was reported that Governor Pettus spoke so loudly that he made the "court house shake to its foundations."[27]

Former Whigs or Oppositionists now carried the Union party banner. As in the past, they found it difficult to mount an all-out drive against the firmly entrenched Democracy. Nonetheless, they made their presence known. Young Union Clubs were formed, whose members were urged to "buckle on [their] armor and go forth to do battle for the success of the Union candidates." As much opposed to the possibility of secession as they were to John Breckinridge, some Unionists viewed the election canvass as a "plot" by fire-eaters to bring about the destruction of constitutional government. Although their fight was an uphill one, Unionist spokesmen maintained a remarkable degree of optimism, and in late October estimated that John Bell would take Mississippi's electoral votes, then go on to preserve the American Republic by winning a national victory.[28]

Throughout the closing weeks of the contest, Democrats increased the cadence of political affairs. "Dismemberment of the Union" was their loudest and most frequent charge. Radicals spent so much time and energy extolling the cause of secession and damning Lincoln that their fundamental objective

---

a Douglas wing of the Democratic party did exist in Mississippi. This is in contrast to Lillian A. Pereyra, *James Lusk Alcorn: Persistent Whig* (Baton Rouge, 1968), 37.

[27] Rainwater, *Mississippi: Storm Center of Secession*, 135–36; Vicksburg *Weekly Whig*, September 14, 1860; New Orleans *Bee*, September 22, 1860.

[28] Vicksburg *Weekly Whig*, October 10, 1860; Vicksburg *Daily Whig*, October 19, 30, 31, 1860; Natchez *Daily Courier*, October 6, 1860; Natchez *Weekly Courier*, October 26, 1860.

of getting Breckinridge votes was often relegated to a low priority. Secession was not a true and direct issue in the campaign, and Lincoln's chances of winning any votes in Mississippi were slim or nonexistent. But hot-bloods used such themes with great will and preyed upon constituent fears to such an extent that they obscured the political realities of the day.

Governor Pettus' language was particularly disturbing and packed with prejudice of the highest order. Mississippi, he insisted, would never become a "Black Republican province" as long as he was governor. Republicans were as untrustworthy as Comanche Indians. The secessionist press so bombarded their readers with similar philosophy that one contemporary opined that the "damnable policy" of disunion was largely the work of activist Democratic newspapers. In any event, the Vicksburg *Weekly Whig* probably caught the essence of this form of electioneering when it proclaimed: "The disunionist wants turmoil. He desires agitation; anything to stir up strife. He is the petrel of the political waters, and delights in, and screams over, the tempest-tossed waves."[29]

As the day of political decision neared, the Jackson *Semi-Weekly Mississippian* went so far as to predict that ninty-nine out of every one hundred men supporting Breckinridge would favor secession, if Lincoln managed to win the presidency. Governor Pettus, in a Macon speech, gave the Republicans a thorough going-over and announced that the same telegraph lines that brought word of a Lincoln victory would, the next instant, carry back an executive order for the convening of a special session of the state legislature. Members of that body upon hearing the worst possible news, said Pettus, might as well "set out for the Capitol . . . the next minute." By election eve the political lines in Mississippi were so fiercely drawn and equally distorted that even "Bell men" were equated with "Black" Republican-

[29] Fernandina (Florida) *East Floridian*, October 31, 1860; Henry Stuart Foote, *War of the Rebellion: Or Scylla and Charybdis. Consisting of Consequences of the Late Civil War in the United States* (New York, 1866), 284; Vicksburg *Weekly Whig*, October 23, 1860.

ism.[30] Compromise and understanding were all but impossible under such circumstances.

To a South full of fury and hyperemotionalism generated by many months of campaign excitement came the news of a Lincoln win. The Republicans had won a *sectional* triumph. Yet, it remained to be seen if the forecast of the fire-eaters could be galvanized into reality.

Reaction to the presidential election among leading Mississippi radicals differed only in respect to which form the disunion movement should take, be it unilateral or in joint concert with other southern states. Mississippi voters gave John Breckinridge a handsome 15,000 vote majority over John Bell, while Douglas ran a far distant third. Even so, a vote for Breckinridge could not be construed as a vote for secession nor could the election be interpreted as a referendum on the issue. If anything, the balloting had "demonstrated [that] a not inconsiderable minority of Unionists" still existed. Whether right or wrong, however, Mississippi fire-eaters viewed the campaign results as a vindication of their ultra views and a mandate to proceed with their plans. By late 1860 a good number of Mississippians felt trapped between "two enfilading fires" and even candidate Bell came reluctantly to the sad conclusion that the state's radical tide was not likely to be stemmed.[31]

During the anxious post-election days the influence of South Carolina's more rapid course of action undoubtedly weighed

[30] Jackson *Semi-Weekly Mississippian*, October 31, 1860: Vicksburg *Weekly Whig*, November 1, 1860; Natchez *Mississippi Free Trader*, November 3, 1860; John B. Thrasher, *Slavery A Divine Institution: A Speech Made Before the Breckinridge and Lane Club, November 5th, 1860* (Port Gibson, Miss., 1861), 22; John Camden to Pettus, November 5, 1860, in Governor's Correspondence, Vol. XLIX.

[31] Ollinger Crenshaw, *The Slave States in the Presidential Election of 1860* (Baltimore, 1945), 267. (Results of the voting were: Breckinridge, 39,962; Bell, 24,693; Douglas, 4,365. See Rainwater, *Mississippi: Storm Center of Secession*, 200. According to the records of the secretary of state, the statistics are as follows: Breckinridge, 40,464; Bell, 25,335; Douglas, 3,636.) Percy L. Rainwater, "An Analysis of the Secession Controversy in Mississippi, 1854–1861," *Mississippi Valley Historical Review*, XXIV (June, 1937), 35; Joseph H. Parks, *John Bell of Tennessee* (Baton Rouge, 1950), 390.

heavily upon the minds of Mississippi leaders. Governor William Gist of South Carolina kept John Pettus fully apprised of events transpiring in the Palmetto State. On November 6 Gist wrote that he had "never witnessed such an enthusiastic demonstration" on behalf of secession. Two days later it was proudly proclaimed that the South Carolina legislature was in historic session that would undoubtedly witness the disintegration of the Union. "We have opened the wall," Gist wrote; "South Carolina leads the way. Will not Mississippi stand by her side?"[32] Indeed, the flood gates of a movement unprecedented in the annals of the American Republic were being opened. The field of resentment, fear, and suspicion had been sown too long not now to be reaped.

Throughout Mississippi the political situation took on an air of semi-intoxication. Many individuals believed that Lincoln's election had "settled the question that safety could no longer be found in the union." "The Union is dead," proclaimed Albert Gallatin Brown, "and nothing now remains to be done but to bury the rotten carcass."[33] The spirit of the times saw federal office-holders resign, a multitude of requests for weapons and military supplies pour into Mississippi's executive mansion, and militia units muster for the first time in the state's history. The handwriting was on the wall—Mississippi would leave the Union.

With converts moving into the fire-eater camp in ever increasing numbers, Pettus' role as governor took on added dimension. Typical of the growing shift to radicalism was the testimony of J. B. Hancock of Marion County, who said that his former Unionist sentiment had now given way to the magic of the moment and urged the governor to summon the legislature into session "at an early day" so as to deal appropriately with the matter at hand. "Hurry" was the watchword of the most extreme disunion worshippers. "Delay is dangerous," wrote the editor of

[32] Gist to Pettus, November 6, 8, 1860, in Governor's Correspondence, Vol. XLIX.
[33] Montgomery, *Reminiscences of a Mississippian*, 36; Vicksburg *Weekly Whig*, November 28, 1860.

a Jackson newspaper. "Now is the time to strike. Let not a moment be lost." While Buchanan was still president "the Federal Government is in friendly hands." Dismemberment of the Union must come swiftly "before the enemy can make good his promise to overwhelm us."[34]

While some individuals demanded speed others wanted time for debate and reflection. Benjamin L. C. Wailes put such attitudes into perspective when he wrote in his diary that some persons "feared that Gov. Pettus [would] by some hasty and intemperate action seek to precipitate the State into secession."[35] But the temperature of the times permitted little room for free and cool deliberation.

John Pettus kept pace with the rapid movement of events and translated his long-standing principles into reality by issuing a directive for the legislature to meet in extraordinary session on the twenty-sixth day of November. On that occasion the "propriety and necessity of providing surer and better safeguards for the lives and liberties" of Mississippi citizens would be taken up. Pettus also felt obliged to supplement political activity with an order of 9,000 rifles and muskets, 200,000 cartridges, and ample quantities of cannon powder and shot from the federal arsenal in Baton Rouge, Louisiana. Indeed, it looked as if a New Orleans *Daily Picayune* prediction that Pettus was "for disunion . . . at all hazards" might well come true.[36]

The governor's message summoning the legislature into session was well received in Mississippi and in neighboring Louisiana as well, being "fully up to the most heated degree of immediate and unconditional secession." Yet, there was a sense of horror among some persons who viewed all this political hurly-burly as anticipatory of something far more evil. One-time Whig planter Josiah Winchester publicly challenged the entire dis-

[34] Hancock to Pettus, November 14, 1860, Governor's Correspondence, Vol. XLIX; Jackson *Semi-Weekly Mississippian*, November 14, 1860.
[35] Entry for November 7, 1860, in Benjamin L. C. Wailes Diary, Duke University.
[36] Jackson *Semi-Weekly Mississippian*, November 16, 1860; Jefferson Davis Bragg, *Louisiana In the Confederacy* (Baton Rouge, 1941), 51; New Orleans *Daily Picayune*, November 3, 1860.

union philosophy, believing that it "would crush us with a load of taxes, reduce the value of our property, impoverish our people, and involve us in bankruptcy and war." In short, Winchester saw as much logic in the secessionist doctrine as "committing suicide for fear we shall die a natural death."[37]

Meanwhile, as Governor Pettus waxed bold in public, the responsibility of high office dictated a more thoughtful position in private. In order to sample and subsequently weigh the counsel of others in regard to the policy he should follow in dealing with the legislature during its coming special session, Pettus arranged for Mississippi's congressional delegation to meet with him at the executive mansion. With the exception of John McRae all parties were in attendance on the morning of November 22, at which time a thorough review of recent political events took place.

The two-day caucus stressed the theme of unity, but debate did ensue over three important questions, the first of which concerned whether or not the legislature should be asked to call a secession convention. Everyone agreed on the necessity of a convention, but a heated argument transpired on the issue of separate state action. Jefferson Davis, L. Q. C. Lamar, and Albert Gallatin Brown favored the withdrawal of Mississippi from the Union only after other states had taken the lead. Senator Davis felt that disunion could not be "peaceably accomplished" and it would be extremely dangerous to risk a unilateral decision. Although asked by Pettus prior to the meeting to serve as a spokesman for immediate, unqualified secession, Davis refused to alter his position.[38] The third question concerned South Caro-

---

[37] New Orleans *Daily Picayune*, November 29, 1860; Natchez *Daily Courier*, November 24, 1860.

[38] Jefferson Davis, *A Short History of the Confederate States of America* (New York, 1890), 40; Jefferson Davis, *The Rise and Fall of the Confederate Government* (2nd ed.; New York, 1958), I, 57; Burton J. Hendrick, *Statesmen of the Lost Cause: Jefferson Davis and His Cabinet* (New York, 1939), 53; Hudson Strode, *Jefferson Davis: American Patriot, 1808–1861* (New York, 1955), I, 363; Robert W. Winston, *High Stakes and Hair Trigger: The Life of Jefferson Davis* (New York, 1930), 163–64; Rowland (ed.), *Jefferson Davis Constitutionalist*, VIII, 202.

lina. Davis, Brown, and Lamar voted to advise Governor Gist to delay any ordinance of secession and to await concert of action, at least until Lincoln's inauguration. Representatives Reuben Davis, Otho R. Singleton, and William Barksdale supported the more radical alternatives to the second and third items of business. The deciding vote in both cases was cast by Governor Pettus, who favored a hard-line. The three dissenters reluctantly acquiesced, giving the conference a false impression of unanimity. The emotions of constituents around the state made it doubtful that approaching developments could have been slowed in the slightest, even if the policy votes had gone the opposite way. Now, as Reuben Davis noted, there "would be no pause or tarrying."[39]

On Monday, November 26, 1860, amid the hubbub of extraordinary times, the Mississippi legislature convened in Jackson. Nearly three-fourths of the members of that body owned slaves and held property valued, on the average, at between $15,000 and $20,000. While the vast bulk of the solons were planters, farmers, and lawyers, few could be considered extremely wealthy. Twenty-nine of the lawmakers (approximately 15 percent) owned no slaves at all and only six held more than one hundred bondsmen. Slavery, Governor Pettus noted in his address to the legislature, had been placed on trial by the North and judged sinful. Therefore, upon the decisions reached at this juncture "hangs the destiny . . . of all generations which come after us, for an indefinite term of centuries." The lives and property of Mississippians could no longer be entrusted to the federal government, Pettus declared.[40]

Referring to the recent presidential election, the governor remarked that the South could find no safety in a Union run by

[39] Willie D. Halsell, "The Friendship of L. Q. C. Lamar and Jefferson Davis," *Journal of Mississippi History*, VI (July, 1944), 135; James B. Ranck, *Albert Gallatin Brown: Radical Southern Nationalist* (New York, 1937), 284–85; Davis, *Recollections of Mississippi*, 392. The meeting underwent reexamination several years later. See Jackson *Clarion*, June 5, 12, 1878; Jackson *Times*, July 6, 1878.
[40] Ralph A. Wooster, *The People In Power: Courthouse and Statehouse in the Lower South, 1850–1860* (Knoxville, 1969), 40–41, 141–43; Mississippi *Senate Journal*, Called Session (November, 1860), 5.

men guilty of "violence and bad faith," and to maintain such an association merely added "weight to the arm that strikes." Mississippians should, in one united voice, inform the "Black Republicans" that they were peacefully withdrawing from the compact of states. In case the North should resist the dismemberment of the Union, Pettus felt it wise to now call for still more military appropriations. Conditions also seemed to warrant laws that would stay the bringing of suits against the state and prohibit the transport of slaves into Mississippi from border states.

Getting down to the real business of the legislature, Pettus urged that a convention be called at an early date to decide Mississippi's fate in the Union. The governor asked that commissioners be dispatched simultaneously to every corner of the cotton kingdom for the purpose of urging that similar steps be taken in every slave state. Such a plan would almost force all southerners to join hands and "go down into Egypt while Herod rules in Judea."[41]

In a final burst of frenzied outrage, Pettus again warned the assembly of the necessity for prompt disposition of the matters he had discussed. Do not "be caught by the fatal bait of temporary ease and quiet," he cautioned, adding that some individuals could mistakenly think the enemies of the state were mere products of imagination. Nothing should be left to chance, said Pettus; "if we falter now, we and our sons must pay the penalty in future years, of bloody, if not fruitless efforts to retrieve the fallen fortunes of the State." Failure to respond positively would forever curse the South "with Black Republican politics and free Negro morals" and the region would become "a cesspool of vice, crime and infamy." "Can we hesitate," he inquired, "when one bold resolve, bravely executed makes powerless the aggressor, one united effort makes safe our homes?" Let the federal government "prepare to meet the spirit of '76," he thundered.[42]

Upon the conclusion of the governor's tirade ten thousand

---

[41] Mississippi *Senate Journal*, Called Session (November, 1860), 11–12.
[42] *Ibid.*

copies of his speech were ordered printed for public distribution and the solons lost no time in pursuing both the spirit and the letter of his remarks. Resolutions and statutes were approved in a fast and furious manner, with little or no debate. The governor was even authorized to prepare a coat of arms for the state. Indeed, the lawmakers too had surrendered to the wave of fanaticism and were reported to be almost "unanimous for secession."[43]

On November 28 the legislature approved a measure providing for the selection of delegates, equal to the number of representatives in both the state house and senate, to a convention which would meet at Jackson on December 20. The reason for the special assembly was vindication of the "sovereignty of the State and the protection of its institutions." On November 29, the senate sanctioned a motion calling for the dispatch of envoys to the other slave states. These agents were encouraged to express the hope that all slaveholders would follow the programs adopted by Mississippi. Pettus appointed the commissioners as follows: Henry Dickerson, to Delaware; A. H. Handy, to Maryland; Charles E. Hooker, to South Carolina; Joseph W. Matthews, to Alabama; David R. Russell, to Missouri; Edward M. Yerger, to Florida; T. J. Wharton, to Tennessee; Horace H. Miller, to Texas; Wirt Adams, to Louisiana; Jacob Thompson, to North Carolina; Fulton Anderson and Walker Brooke, to Virginia; George R. Fall, to Arkansas; Winfield S. Featherston, to Kentucky; William L. Harris and Thomas W. White, to Georgia. Former Whigs and moderate Democrats were among the messengers, thus indicating an effort on behalf of the governor to promote an exhibition of state unity while hoping to convince others to rectify "the present threatening relations of the Northern and Southern sections of the United States" in the same way.[44] While the academic concept of conspiracy to effect revo-

---

[43] New Orleans *Daily Delta*, November 27, 1860; Rainwater, *Mississippi: Storm Center of Secession*, 171.
[44] State of Mississippi, *Laws of the State of Mississippi*, Called Session (November, 1860), 32; Mississippi *Senate Journal*, Called Session (November, 1860), 23, 25; Pettus to Joseph E. Brown, December 5, 1860, in Governor's Correspondence, Vol. XLIX.

lution can be debated, activities of this calibre do not tend to dispute the point.

In December, 1860, the fires of southern secession had been kindled. John Pettus stood nearest the disunion flame in Mississippi seemingly typifying the dominant political mind in those troubled times. A statement which had appeared in the pages of the Woodville *Republican* over twenty years before now gave promise of fulfillment: "The question will not be settled by negotiation, but by the sword,—by balls and the *Bayonet—We can do without the North.*"[45]

[45] Clement Eaton, *The Growth of Southern Civilization, 1790–1860* (New York, 1961), 324; Woodville *Republican*, August 22, 1835.

VI

The Day of the Hawk:
Secession, 1861

THE COURSE OF POLITICAL AFFAIRS in Mississippi had moved at
an ever quickening pace during the final months of 1860. Lincoln's election to the presidency had prompted Governor John
Pettus to summon a special session of the legislature in order to
obtain approval for calling a convention to decide, once and for
all, Mississippi's relationship to the Union. Under such circumstances it was almost impossible for any politician in a Deep
South state to take any other "ground of resistance below secession." Contributing more to the sweep of events, however, was
the fact that large numbers of southerners held the view that it
was "both abhorrent and dangerous to continue to live under the
same government with the people of the North."[1]

Although enjoying wide support by this time, such a drastic
measure as secession still had a number of hurdles to overcome,
not the least of which involved Whig and Unionist forces. Many
of these individuals were at first stunned by the governor's call
for a disunion convention, but felt compelled to let matters drift
along. After all, such rhetoric had been heard before and nothing
ever came of it. Some experienced politicians still doubted that
such an ordinance could ever be adopted.

On the other side of the fence stood the more activist minded

---

[1] G. Harrison to Pettus, November 19, 1860, in Governor's Correspondence,
Vol. XLIX; Frank L. Owsley, "The Fundamental Cause of the Civil War:
Egocentric Sectionalism," *Journal of Southern History*, VII (August, 1941), 6.

Whigs who pondered the language and deeds of both the state's fire-eater power structure and the lame duck Buchanan administration. Benjamin L. C. Wailes, outspoken critic of the entire secessionist movement, evidenced his dissatisfaction by calling the president "a poor imbecile" and a "blundering, incompetent executive." Governor Pettus was not held in much higher esteem, being labeled by Wailes a "miserable demagogue," who, like Buchanan, should do public penance "in sackcloth and ashes." The Vicksburg *Weekly Whig* agreed with these evaluations, noting that the "bitter fruits of secession or revolution would be strife, discord, bloodshed, war, if not anarchy."[2] Yet, these antisecession Whigs were realistic enough to know that the thrust of their efforts had to go toward modifying the intensity of the disunion spirit, rather than trying to stop it altogether.

On the heels of the governor's legislative call for a secession convention, Opposition elements proposed a giant rally for Vicksburg on November 29. Although backed by leading Whigs and circulated in every corner of the state, the summons met a pitiful response. Only four counties (Adams, Hinds, Rankin, and Warren) sent representatives; unquestionably, time and distance played a role in the poor turnout. Nevertheless, the assemblage did go on record as passing resolutions heavily tainted with Unionist sentiment and urging moderation in sectional affairs.[3]

The increased disunion sentiment in Mississippi was partially due to the fact that economic prosperity was at a high level; hence, the citizenry could more easily afford to act, or overreact, to sectional pressures. Moreover, similar political activities developed concurrently in neighboring states, the results of which contributed additional mental fuel to the desires of Mississippi radicals. Louisiana Governor Thomas O. Moore, for example, had also called his state's general assembly into special session, while Alabama Governor Andrew B. Moore sent observers to

---

[2] Entries for December 20, 23, 26, 1860, in Benjamin L. C. Wailes Diary, Duke University; Vicksburg *Weekly Whig*, November 8, 1860.

[3] Vicksburg *Weekly Whig*, November 20, 1860; Jackson *Semi-Weekly Mississippian*, December 5, 1860.

Mississippi and Louisiana for the purpose of keeping him appraised of political developments.[4]

Meanwhile, public and private messages regarding secession and states' rights flooded Governor Pettus' office daily. Even public utilities championed the new cause. L. J. Fleming, president of the Mobile and Ohio Railroad, offered to "transport, free of charge, . . . any arms or other munitions of warfare, which Mississippi may desire to distribute among the citizens for the protection and defense of the State."[5]

Perhaps more reflective of the pulse of the people were the churches. Various denominations adopted the same color and spirit of the secession movement as did their communicants. The Baptist Church of Bethesda, Mississippi, was typical. A series of resolutions adopted by the congregation in December, 1860, proclaimed unqualified support for Governor Pettus' policies. Above all the call for a secession convention was heralded as "a warning voice to the people—that we may put our house in order —for our Enemies are marshalling their forces for our distruction [sic]." Sermons preached throughout the state came boldly to grips with politics. "Resistance to tyranny is obedience to God," was a favorite pulpit theme. Not above invoking the spirit of the Almighty for his own purposes, Pettus set aside the day of December 31 for public "humiliation and prayer."[6]

Meanwhile, the commissioners who had been sent to the other slave states for the purpose of rallying support for disunion began to report back. The first to do so was V. D. Groner, who was added to the earlier list of Mississippi emissaries. From the key state of Virginia he wrote that the political situation was still undecided. It was his estimation that only when the states of the Deep South left the Union would Virginia follow suit. "We are

[4] Herbert Weaver, *Mississippi Farmers, 1850–1860* (Nashville, 1945), 125; G. P. Whittington, "Thomas O. Moore: Governor of Louisiana, 1860–1864," *Louisiana Historical Quarterly*, XIII (January, 1930), 7; Edmund W. Pettus to Andrew Moore, December 2, 1860, in Andrew B. Moore Papers.

[5] Fleming to Pettus, December 1, 1860, in Governor's Correspondence, Vol. XLIX.

[6] Jackson *Semi-Weekly Mississippian*, December 12, 1860; Rowland, *Encyclopedia of Mississippi History*, I, 76–77.

dependent upon your activity," he told Governor Pettus, "so go
on in your work with the assurance that every true heart in the
Old Dominion is beating for your success." Pettus lost little time
in replying that Mississippians certainly did intend "to commit
their lives and fortunes to the hazards of war rather than to sub-
mit to a government by the Black Republican minnaec [sic]."
If secession materialized, then it would be the result of "a calm
and resolved people at convention." The governor further assured Groner that he had "no doubt" that the state legislature
would authorize him "to take such steps as are necessary for the
defense of our rights."[7] Even so, Virginia was not to be moved
until the force of federal arms threatened its people.

By December, 1860, Mississippi's withdrawal from the Union
seemed little more than a matter of due course. However, advocates of unified southern action on such a serious matter stepped
forward to urge that the lower South, and especially Mississippi,
not proceed in unilateral fashion. Fear that the end result might
boomerang, with one or two states left holding the political bag,
prompted such thinking. Cooperationists, as these individuals
were known, counted moderate Democrats and certain Whigs
in their numbers. The latter, realizing the fruitlessness of opposing secession head on, had thus elected to channel their energies
and by this means slow the movement.[8]

Cooperationist aims rested on the twin pillars of moderation
and, if need be, concert of action among all slave states in the
cause of forming a separate national government. In short, while
neither completely denying nor totally accepting the theory of
secession, the Cooperationists urged that the struggle for rights
and protection of southern interests take place *within* the Union.
Only after failing to achieve desired objectives could separation
be sanctioned.

John Pettus, acknowledged symbol of the Mississippi secession movement, was a convenient target for much Cooperation-

[7] V. D. Groner to Pettus, December 6, 1860, Pettus to Groner, December 8,
1860, in Governor's Correspondence, Vol. XLIX.

[8] Rainwater, *Mississippi: Storm Center of Secession*, 181; Clarence P. Denman,
The Secession Movement in Alabama (Montgomery, 1933), 93.

ist anti-disunion abuse. A playlet set in the state lunatic asylum portrayed the governor as a fire-eater of the first magnitude, who quoted biblical scripture and gave every indication of being a psychopathic madman. Appearing in several newspapers, the political satire unfolded thus:

> *Junius*: Mr. Superintendent, permit me to introduce you to governor Pettus (aside). He is the representative of a large party who should become acquainted with you. You will find him a very pleasant gentleman, and on many subjects he will talk sensibly. If however, you ever begin to doubt his insanity, whisper the word, 'Abolition,' and you will see his knees tremble, the color leave his cheeks, his eye-balls start, his whole countenance become distorted with fear. He will halloo to the politicians to run 'down into Egypt' with the young child, the Little South, and tell you of his silly plan of DISUNITING, in order to REUNITE 'the South.'
>
> Should you still doubt, allude to the fact of his being frightened and you will find that whilst shivering with fear, he regards his party as the courageous party and himself as an heroic leader; and that he sincerely believes his RUNNING party to be the only one capable of intimidating the Abolitionists; and that all Southern men, who do not fear and tremble as he does, who do not think nine millions of free white people are a LITTLE CHILD to be protected by running with it down into Egypt; or that these States should be DISUNITED in order to be 'RE-UNITED,' are cowards, traitors, or fools.
>
> *Superintendent*: You say the Governor is the representative of a large party. You mean a party of voters?
>
> *Junius*: Yes. This is epidemic. It is raging among three classes of the people. The old who are in, or approaching their dotage; young adult males, who are ignorant and green, or self-conceited; and the political or irreligious persons. It is beginning to spread among the modest and sensible, and seems instantly to dwarf or craze the most powerful intellect.
>
> *Superintendent*: Then, oh my God! our country is lost.[9]

In the anxious weeks between the call for a secession convention and the election of delegates to that conclave, a number of Mississippians expressed concern over the long-range results of

---

[9] Vicksburg *Weekly Whig*, December 20, 1860.

disunion. Uppermost was the future of economic activity, for in the event the Magnolia State left the Union and Alabama and Louisiana did not do likewise, access to a seaport could hamper business relations. Governor Pettus, aware of the issue, dispatched envoy Wirt Adams to Baton Rouge and instructed him to stress the absolute necessity of maintaining close commercial ties among the contiguous states of the Deep South. The desired assurances relating to the use of ports were swiftly pledged along with the commitment to "act together in this contest."[10]

Such pronouncements did not satisfy the opposition. And when normal commercial enterprise slowed in New Orleans on account of the uncertainty of political affairs, further alarm ensued. Unable to sell their produce, planters and merchants remained fearful, while the fire-eaters argued that the South would "thrive on Free Trade." Apparently the prospects of declining commerce worried others in high places. Governor Andrew Moore of Alabama, for example, sent Judge Edmund Winston Pettus (brother of the Mississippi governor) to Jackson and New Orleans for the purpose of evaluating the probable aftermath of secession. Judge Pettus reported that he had no doubt that Mississippi would withdraw from the Union and that his brother intended "to use his official influence to aid in separating . . . from the present federal government." In regard to the consequences of secession, the Alabama commissioner saw "great excitement among the merchants and other trading people," and concluded that it would produce "no good results."[11]

This issue forced John Pettus to pause and ponder the gravity of the movement already in motion. When he further learned that President Buchanan had ordered the completion of con-

[10] Adams to Pettus, December 11, 1860, in Mississippi *Senate Journal*, Called Session (January, 1861), Appendix, 88–91. See also Jackson *Semi-Weekly Mississippian*, December 19, 1860; Natchez *Mississippi Free Trader*, December 20, 1860.

[11] Milledge L. Bonham, "Financial and Economic Disturbance in New Orleans On the Eve of Secession," *Louisiana Historical Quarterly*, XIII (January, 1930), 33; Sydnor, *A Gentleman of the Old Natchez Region*, 292; Natchez *Mississippi Free Trader*, December 3, 1860; E. W. Pettus to Moore, December 2, 1860, in Andrew B. Moore Papers.

struction of a federal fort on Ship Island, the threat to Mississippi commerce appeared more menacing. Since this stronghold was located in the Gulf of Mexico, a short distance from Biloxi, government forces would be in a position to interfere with the state's sea trade and to land troops on Mississippi soil. Expressing his apprehension in regard to all this, Pettus sought the counsel of Jefferson Davis. The governor inquired if he should endeavor to postpone action on disunion "until other states can get ready." Davis replied, "We should not halt, least of all hesitate; the moral power of steady progress must not be impaired."[12]

Despite any last minute reservations, Mississippians went to the polls on December 20, 1860—ironically the same day that South Carolina withdrew from the Union—and elected delegates to a state convention, scheduled for January 7 of the following year. Although the balloting produced an obvious victory for the secessionist forces, close inspection of the returns yielded some surprising discoveries. Vying for the 100 convention seats had been a total of 210 candidates. Whigs and Unionists, depending upon the county involved, had sponsored either their own nominee or had been forced by a preponderance of disunion feeling to back Cooperationists. In the latter case the primary aim was to slow the fire-eater drive from inside the convention. Many of the hard-core anti-secessionist aspirants, however, had put forth only the meagerest of initiatives and had made little or no effort to sway the voter toward any alternative course of action.[13] At this stage it was reasonable to suggest that Unionists believed the question of disunion was virtually decided anyway.

Further analysis of the voting returns sheds more light on the late 1860 Mississippi political scene. First, there was a marked drop of about 40 percent in voter turnout in this election, as compared with the recent presidential contest. Second, based

[12] Kenneth M. Stampp, *And the War Came: The North and the Secession Crisis, 1860–1861* (Baton Rouge, 1950), 256; Pettus to Davis, December 27, 1860, Davis to Pettus, January 4, 1861, cited in Robert M. McElroy, *Jefferson Davis: The Unreal and the Real* (New York, 1937) I, 242–43.

[13] Ralph A. Wooster, *The Secession Conventions of the South* (Princeton, 1962), 29; Vicksburg *Daily Whig*, December 19, 1860.

80   JOHN JONES PETTUS

upon the stands taken by the respective candidates, an over-whelming majority of the voters indicated a preference for withdrawing the state from the Union. Nevertheless, immediate or unilateral action on this question was not the view apparently held by at least one-third of those casting ballots. When this number is combined with the approximately 20 percent who could be labeled "Coalitionists" (those in the middle on the issue), the net effect tends to indicate that about one-half of all the voters either were opposed to secession or wanted to wait until other states had left the Union before having Mississippi do so.[14]

While the election of convention delegates was not a popular referendum on secession itself, it did, indirectly, amount to the same thing. What was probably most unfortunate was that so many individuals stayed away from the polls. Had they voiced an opinion it is interesting to speculate as to what it might have been. However, in the long run, a fairly large number of Mississippians went along with the secession doctrine and voted to have their feelings represented in the forthcoming convention. Thomas B. Webber of Byhalia might have expressed the people's attitude best when he wrote: "Because the north is disloyal to the constitutional rights of our section of the country . . . my honor compelles [sic] me to think . . . that we can have no security for our rights and no guarantees of our freedom under his [Lincoln's] administration. . . . Secession or revolution is the only remedy."[15]

While many individuals were noticeably gratified by the outcome of the December elections, others were bitter. Soon afterward accusations were made that the Democrats had failed to allow sufficient time for discussing the issues, let alone their consequences. It was charged that haste had made for confusion and voters had felt so intimidated that they did not appear at

[14] Natchez *Weekly Courier*, December 27, 1860; Rainwater, *Mississippi: Storm Center of Secession*, 198–200; State of Mississippi, *Journal of the State Convention and Ordinances and Resolutions* (1861), Appendix.
[15] Entries for January 3 and 7, 1861, in Thomas B. Webber Diary, Duke University Library, Durham, N.C.

the polls. In cases where these allegations did not apply, Unionists accused the fire-eaters of buying votes, trickery, and false promises.[16]

Following the election, a number of the commissioners who had been dispatched to the other slave states reported to Governor Pettus. Of the seventeen men involved in such missions, those sent to the border states deserve special consideration, for it appeared necessary to the southern cause that the frontier states join with those of the lower South to enhance the success of any disunion movement. In Arkansas, for instance, the secession question was reported to be a new one. Even so, commissioner George Fall found much evidence of "a determination on the part of Arkansas to cooperate with the Southern states on the formation of a Southern Confederacy."[17]

On a parallel mission Jacob Thompson journeyed to Raleigh, North Carolina, and conferred with both Governor John W. Ellis and members of the state legislature. Thompson noted a certain warmth for the maintenance of the Union, but assured Pettus that "as soon as all hope of a satisfactory adjustment of the slavery issue is abandoned, the voice of North Carolina will be well nigh unanimous for a Southern Confederacy." According to Thompson the "spirit of the patriots of . . . 1775 is entering the hearts of the people everywhere." In Kentucky, Winfield S. Featherston discharged his duties by conversing with Governor Beriah Magoffin, who affirmed that his state was as emphatically pro-slavery as any in the Deep South. Elated, Featherston urged Governor Pettus to hurry on with the secession of Mississippi because Kentucky was obviously "moving in the right direction."[18]

All such appraisals from the border states were favorable, save

[16] Vicksburg *Daily Whig*, December 25, 1860; Natchez *Weekly Courier*, December 27, 1860.
[17] Edward C. Smith, *The Borderland In the Civil War* (New York, 1927), 25; George Fall to Pettus, December 25, 1860, in Governor's Correspondence, Vol. L.
[18] Jacob Thompson to Pettus, December 26, 1860, in Governor's Correspondence, Vol. L. For further detail on Thompson's visit see Joseph C. Sitterson, *The Secession Movement In North Carolina* (Chapel Hill, 1939), 187; Winfield Featherston to Pettus, December 19, 1860, in Mississippi *Senate Journal*, Called Session (January, 1861), Appendix, 8.

one. Alexander H. Handy, envoy to Maryland, found a considerable coolness upon his arrival along with much disposition
toward moderation. In a letter to Handy, Maryland Governor
Thomas H. Hicks, a man of unionist sympathies, noted that he
would exercise caution on the secession issue. Hicks reasoned
that the border states must first counsel together before rendering a verdict, since they were likely to suffer more than any
other area in the event of disunion and war.[19]

On a somewhat more optimistic note, Horace Miller, commissioner to Texas, learned of the results of the recent election
of delegates to the Mississippi convention and sent word of
personal encouragement. The entire question had now been
settled, thought Miller, and would undoubtedly serve to influence the course of Texas history. But much to the commissioner's chagrin, the final issue of secession had not yet been
settled. Hawkish elements, although in command of the situation, had not seen the struggle through to the last battleground
—the convention itself, where it was estimated that Cooperationists would make every effort against separate state action.[20]

Meanwhile, the excitement of political conditions was gen-
erating much in the way of military activity. Even from the
border states, where disunionism was not moving fast enough
to suit many, came offers to enlist in the armed forces of Mississippi. Missourian O. B. Young, for example, announced that
he viewed "with much gratification and pride the high and just
grounds" that Governor Pettus had taken and offered the services
of a unit known as the Western League of United Southrons. As
for native Mississippians, they were not immune to the mush-
rooming martial spirit. W. G. Paxton, writing from Vicksburg,
told Pettus that while a large majority in his city was now in favor
of secession he personally disliked the "unpleasant necessity of
waiting upon the slow movements of conditions." Similarly, a
Brandon Artillery Company resolution affirmed that it was now

[19] Thomas Hicks to A. H. Handy, December 19, 1860, in Governor's Correspondence, Vol. L.
[20] Horace Miller to Pettus, December 27, 1860, in Governor's Correspondence,
Vol. L; Vicksburg *Weekly Whig*, December 21–29, 1860.

the "duty of every good citizen of the state to be prepared at a moments [sic] warning" to meet the dastardly Yankees.[21]

Preparing for the worst, Governor Pettus overlooked no opportunity to acquire military hardware. In mid-December he wrote Jefferson Davis in Washington that delegates to the secession convention would be elected "by a larger majority than we gave to Breckinridge." Therefore, Davis was instructed to contact New York or St. Louis munitions companies and have them send 15,000 pounds of gunpowder and between 30,000 and 40,000 pounds of lead. The supplies would be paid for by state treasury warrants, as tax dollars were not yet in hand. These military resources would hopefully supplement those obtained by Adjutant General Sykes from the federal arsenal at Baton Rouge. A short while later Pettus again urged Davis to lend a hand in obtaining weapons because he, the governor, found it difficult to "convert auditors warrants into rifles." Because volunteer companies were "forming in every County of the State," Pettus could not "furnish arms as fast as they call for them." Davis was also instructed to return to Mississippi, and "if Lincoln makes fight as I doubt not he will I think you had better be getting ready to meet Gen. [Winfield] Scott at the head of 200,000 wide awakes."[22]

Jefferson Davis' return to Mississippi coincided with the opening of the 1861 convention and was accompanied by much fanfare. Admirers and self-appointed escorts filled the train on which he was riding, and by the time it reached Jackson the railroad station was crowded with well-wishers. Governor Pettus was on hand to present the senator with a commission as major general, head of the armed forces of Mississippi. Soon afterward the governor and Davis conferred on the consequences of disunion. The former, while not believing that secession necessarily called for bloodshed, did insist that 75,000 firearms should be

[21] O. B. Young to Pettus, December 26, 1860, W. G. Paxton to Pettus, December 11, 1860, Resolutions of the Brandon Artillery Company to Pettus, December 27, 1860, in Governor's Correspondence, Vol. L.
[22] Pettus to Davis, December 16, 31, 1860, in Jefferson Davis Papers, Duke University Library, Durham, N.C.

ordered. Davis, conversely, held an opposing view, but was chided for overrating the hazards.[23]

The Mississippi convention of 1861 convened in Jackson on January 7. Everything seemed conducive to the fire-eater spirit. Even the city took on a festive, if not carnival atmosphere. The stage was set for the long-awaited drama. The day of the hawk had arrived, and with rare insight a contemporary put things into proper perspective when he wrote: "The doctrine of States Rights had been too long preached . . . , not to be practiced . . . it was too great a favorite to be kept suspended and held in abeyance forever."[24]

At noon Samuel J. Gholson gaveled the one-hundred-man assembly to order. Most social, economic, and political elements were represented, thus indicating an average cross-section of Mississippians. Planters and lawyers were in the majority, but a few yeoman farmers took seats. The mean age of the delegates has been put at forty-two years. While slavery appears to have been the dominant vested interest, it should be pointed out that no delegate possessed over 300 Negroes. In fact, 15 percent of the assemblage did not own a single bondsman, while 65 percent held less than thirty. In this case at least, large slaveholders were not in a position to exercise much in the way of political clout. When indebtedness and outstanding financial obligations were taken into account, the small slaveowner and the yeoman farmer were fully as prosperous as the big planters.[25]

Since a majority of the convention delegates were connected in some way with the institution of slavery, it may be well to examine the issue further. The ownership of slaves in Mississippi represented a vehicle for ascending the social structure. Even more, the institution typified a state of mind—more imaginary than real—which the Vicksburg *Sun* accurately described in the

[23] Strode, *Jefferson Davis*, I, 397; Varina Howell Davis, *Jefferson Davis: Ex-President of the Confederate States of America* (New York, 1890), II, 508.
[24] C. C. S. Farrar, *The War: Its Causes and Consequences* (Memphis, 1864), 234.
[25] Wooster, *Secession Conventions of the South*, 30–31, 34; Rainwater, *Mississippi: Storm Center of Secession*, 204; Weaver, *Mississippi Farmers*, 125.

spring of 1860: "A large plantation and negroes are the ULTIMA THULE of every Southern gentleman's ambitions. The mind is thus trained from infancy to think of and prepare for the attainment of this end."[26] Such was the standard of antebellum society, and the delegates at Jackson could hardly have failed to be influenced by it. Challenges, current or future, real or otherwise, to the cornerstone of southern civilization left those men only the narrowest of alternatives.

In the opening moments of the convention Reverend Charles K. Marshall, a slaveholder from Vicksburg, gave the invocation and pronounced it a "day of sore trial to Patriots and Christians." If any doubt remained as to the sympathies of the vast majority of delegates, they were swiftly erased when William S. Barry, a passionate disunionist, was elected president of the assembly. However, James Lusk Alcorn, a Whig, ran a good second in the contest and forced the balloting to go three rounds before a decision was reached. Even so, sectional animosity was in ample supply, and convention member Thomas H. Woods noted that the "advocates of immediate and independent action were complete masters of the situation, and . . . it was manifest to the most superficial observer that the die had been cast."[27]

On the same day, January 7, L. Q. C. Lamar introduced a resolution calling for the appointment of a committee of fifteen, whose task it would be to prepare an ordinance to withdraw the state from the Union. Lamar's motion passed overwhelmingly and the following day a committee was selected. However, the opposition had something to say first. Warren County Whig J. Shall Yerger requested a vote on another resolution that would have made the convention's work one of seeking "further Constitutional guarantees within the present Union" rather than

26 Vicksburg *Sun*, April 9, 1860.
27 Mississippi *Journal of the State Convention* (1861), 3, 7; J. L. Power (ed.), "Proceedings and Debates of the Mississippi State Convention of 1861," in J. F. H. Claiborne Papers, University of North Carolina Library; Thomas H. Woods, "A Sketch of the Mississippi Secession Convention of 1861—Its Membership and Work," in Franklin L. Riley (ed.), *Publications of the Mississippi Historical Society* (Oxford, Miss., 1902), VI, 93.

leaving it. Although Yerger's proposal was soundly defeated, 78 to 21, it did not stop another die-hard Whig, James Lusk Alcorn, from suggesting that disunion not take effect until the other states of the lower South had followed a similar path. Still another alternative was put forward calling for the submission of any secession ordinance to a popular referendum.[28] Both of these proposals went down to defeat by wide margins.

Whigs and Unionists sitting in the convention apparently expected that their alternatives would have carried more weight than they did. For many of the latter were prominent political figures in the state and hoped to capitalize on that asset and steer a course away from immediate disunion. When Alcorn wrote to his wife a short while later, he took note of this fact and made mention of the "great confidence" he expected the convention to accord him and his ideals.[29] But it was not to be.

With minimum delay an Ordinance of Secession was prepared, brought before the assemblage on January 9, and adopted by a vote of 84 to 15.[30] In spite of any differences a harmonious atmosphere prevailed, and as one delegate recalled: "The debates were brief; there was no set orations; and there was absolute freedom from all acrimony."[31] Generally, those not favoring the ordinance came from counties with either high or low percentages of slaves.

In what constituted an exoneration of the convention act, Alexander Mosby Clayton spoke at length on the reasons for the state's withdrawal from the Union. The protection of slavery, both at home and in the federal territories, headed the list. Not far behind was abolitionist pressure and the failure of northerners to treat southerners as equals in the Union. The ultimate

[28] Mississippi *Journal of the State Convention* (1861), 12–16. Alcorn's actions were partially responsible for making him a lasting political enemy of Governor Pettus. See Pereyra, *James Lusk Alcorn*, 48–49.
[29] James Alcorn to Amelia Alcorn, January 15, 1861, in James Lusk Alcorn Papers, University of North Carolina Library, Chapel Hill, N.C.
[30] Mississippi *Journal of the State Convention* (1861), 16. The president did not vote.
[31] Woods, "Sketch of the Mississippi Secession Convention," 98.

justification was deemed to be a matter of principle, the same as that of the American Revolution. With freedom on the wane, no alternative other than seeking independence was now advisable.[32]

The Ordinance of Secession consisted of four sections. Now that the state was "sovereign and independent," all obligations binding Mississippi to the federal Union were declared repealed. The oath that state officeholders were required to take to the constitution of the United States was abolished, but provisions were included for the continuance of such laws as were not incompatible with the instrument of disunion. A stipulation that Mississippi stood ready to join with other states in creating a new type of national government was also attached. The official signing ceremony took place on Tuesday morning, January 15. At that time, in an obvious display of unanimity, all but two members of the convention initialed the document.[33]

During and immediately preceding the convention, Mississippi was visited by commissioners from other states—namely, Armistead Burt of South Carolina and Edmund W. Pettus of Alabama. These envoys had been dispatched for the same reasons that had earlier sent the Mississippi commissioners elsewhere. Burt, in particular, was asked to speak before the assembly on January 11. Since both states were now out of the Union his remarks were very well received and "frequently and loudly applauded."[34]

As for Edmund Pettus, his mission was twofold—to lend moral support for hastening Mississippi's withdrawal from the Union and to provide assurances that port facilities at Mobile would be at the disposal of the Magnolia State. In a report to Alabama Governor A. B. Moore, Edmund Pettus noted that "immediate dissolution" was obviously the order of the day and

[32] Mississippi *Journal of the State Convention* (1861), 86–88.
[33] *Ibid.*, 27–28, 119–22. The two members who refused to sign the ordinance were John W. Wood of Attala County and Dr. J. J. Thornton of Rankin County.
[34] Power (ed.), "Proceedings and Debates of the Mississippi State Convention of 1861."

that "no bitter personalities marred the harmony" of the convention proceedings.[35]

Reaction to these historic events differed widely throughout the state. When news of the withdrawal reached Oxford, lights burned late into the night while citizens hastened about firing guns, ringing bells, and shouting "cheers for our gallant State!" Recently resigned Congressman Reuben Davis traveled from Corinth to Aberdeen by rail and "was scarcely out of the sound of cannon all the way." At the University of Mississippi, hot-blooded students were unable to hold back their enthusiasm and marched through the streets to the music of fife and drum. A Presbyterian minister in Lee County noted that members of his flock "fired cannon all day . . . in honour of the event." A Kosciusko resident, calling himself a "secessionist—stock lock and barrel," revealed that the martial spirit was so strong that a local militia company was "almost ready" to leave for South Carolina in pursuit of glory on the field of honor.[36]

While many constituents applauded the secession convention's deed, even Cooperationists and Whigs—for reasons of practicality—finding it expedient to join the mainstream of politics, there were still detractors in evidence. In a variety of ways hard-core opponents of disunion manifested a reluctance to swallow the bitter pill of defeat. J. F. H. Claiborne, for one, was a man of unimpeachable loyalty to the Union. So disgusted with political events did he become that he returned to his Laurel Wood plantation on the Gulf Coast, and in effect pouted him-

[35] Mississippi *Journal of the State Convention* (1861), 13; E. W. Pettus to Moore, January 21, 1861 in R. N. Scott et al., *War of the Rebellion: A Compilation of the Official Records of the Union and Confederate Armies* (Washington, D.C., 1880–1901), Ser. IV, Vol. I, 76–77. For additional information on the public career of Edmund Pettus see Mark Boatner, *The Civil War Dictionary* (New York, 1959), 649; Denman, *Secession Movement In Alabama*, 92, 111, 114, 134; U.S. War Department, *List of Staff Officers of the Confederate States Army, 1861–1865* (Washington, D.C., 1891), 128.

[36] Oxford *Intelligencer*, January 10, 1861; Davis, *Recollections of Mississippi*, 402; Clifford Dowdey, *The Land They Fought For: The Story of the South as the Confederacy, 1832–1865* (New York, 1955), 82; Entry for January 12, 1861, in Diary of Samuel A. Agnew, University of North Carolina Library, Chapel Hill, N.C.; William H. McClanahan to Joseph Stapp, January 14, 1861, in Joseph D. Stapp Papers, Duke University Library, Durham, N.C.

THE DAY OF THE HAWK

self into exile, away from the realities of the day. Similarly, the chancellor of the University of Mississippi, Frederick A. P. Barnard, deplored the fact that students flew state flags from dormitory roofs and that the entire population of the surrounding community seemed "to have suddenly gone wild." Very much against secession and equally "powerless to oppose it," he soon left the state.[37]

From outside Mississippi both positive and negative response to the withdrawal question was forthcoming. Neighboring Louisianians kept an eye on the convention activities and pushed forward with their own plans for disunion. The Louisville, Kentucky, *Daily Courier* of January 10, 1861, viewed Mississippi's action as a simple matter of due course. Conversely, the New York *Tribune* of the same date held that no state ever had any independence or sovereignty and flatly stated that it would "really like to know upon what grounds she [Mississippi] attempts to justify her actions."

Negative sentiment was not confined to the North. Discontented elements at home continued to urge submission of the Ordinance of Secession to a popular election, even planning to put forth in the fall a gubernatorial candidate who agreed with that position.[38] This particular charge was an absorbing one, if only from an academic standpoint. Had the ordinance been given to the public to vote on, the result might have proved interesting. Little doubt should exist as to the outcome of such a development, but at least it would have given posterity a better picture of the way constituents felt. To be sure, there were some individuals who believed that such a vote would have been adverse.

[37] Franklin L. Riley, "Life of Col. J. F. H. Claiborne," in Franklin L. Riley (ed.), *Publications of the Mississippi Historical Society* (Oxford, Miss., 1903), VIII, 234–35; Herbert H. Lang, "J. F. H. Claiborne At 'Laurel Wood' Plantation, 1850–1870," *Journal of Mississippi History*, XVIII (January, 1956), 1–17; Frederick A. P. Barnard, "Autobiographical Sketch of Dr. F. A. P. Barnard," in Franklin L. Riley (ed.), *Publications of the Mississippi Historical Society* (Oxford, Miss., 1912), XII, 116; John Fulton, *Memoirs of Frederick A. P. Barnard* (New York, 1901) 272.
[38] Rainwater *Mississippi: Storm Center of Secession*, 214.

By February, 1861, the fires of resistance to disunion had all but gone out in Mississippi. Secession was an accomplished fact; whatever chances of reversing the popular tide there may have been earlier had vanished. Outright opposition to changing events was replaced by a more subtle verbal guerrilla warfare. One by one, however, the advocates of compromise and reason were crossing to the side of the dominant philosophy. Many, far from taking a gloomy view, became eager to atone for not having supported the secession movement sooner. Giles H. Hillyer, editor of the Natchez *Daily Courier*, unknowingly wrote the epitaph of the anti-disunion spirit when he remarked that the last spark of hope had just disappeared from the "smouldering fire upon the altar of Liberty."[39] Last minute efforts to avoid the inevitable had been countered at every turn. And the few clear-eyed Mississippians who remained viewed the future with a sense of impending doom.

Although the state convention's proceedings held center stage for several weeks, the office of the governor was the scene of much activity. Contrary to what one historian has written, John Pettus was not content "to let things slide." Far from it. Instead, he had laid his plans carefully and deliberately. Not only did he announce his intention to call the legislature into special session after the convention withdrew the state from the Union, but he also took the crafty step of writing United States Secretary of War John B. Floyd requesting that Mississippi be sent its quota of federal arms for a year in advance. Further, the governor maintained a watchful eye on political events in the border states and did all he could toward driving the latter into the secessionist camp.[40]

Captivated by the flood tide of disunion spirit, the Mississippi legislature met in January, according to the governor's call. Pettus addressed the gathering and announced that "perplexing

[39] Natchez *Daily Courier*, February 13, 1861.
[40] Bettersworth, *Confederate Mississippi*, 14; Pettus to Jefferson Davis, December 31, 1860, in Jefferson Davis Papers, Duke University Library; Pettus to Floyd, December 31, 1860, in *Official Records*, Ser. III, Vol. I, 22; Handy to Pettus, January 10, 1861, in Governor's Correspondence, Vol. LI.

and novel circumstances" were at hand and that dire "questions growing out of the present relations of Mississippi with the surrounding States, must be met and solved." As chief executive, he had already been active in seeing to the state's military posture. Some state troops were engaged by his order in the siege of a federal fort, Pickens, in Florida, while others had been sent to Vicksburg to fortify that city so as to prevent hostile forces from descending the Mississippi River.[41]

Looking to the future, Pettus suggested that the legislators enact more stringent laws against inciting slaves to insurrection, provide for more military supplies, and see to the general needs of the people. A "stormy sea" awaited. But "if justice, prudence and moderation" could not be utilized to maximum advantage, said Pettus, then Mississippi must "lay her lance in rest and cry God defend the Right."[42] The solons, however, elected to remain inactive, at least until the state convention had finished its deliberations.

By early 1861 Mississippi was out of the Union. Dissent had evaporated. Military activities, if only minor, were underway and the people basked in the sunshine of a new order of things.

[41] Mississippi *Senate Journal*, Called Session (January, 1861), 5–8.
[42] *Ibid.*, 8–9.

VII

The End of Innocence:
The Realities of 1861

THE EARLY MONTHS OF 1861 comprised a period of high excitement, uncertainty, and extreme pressure. Rumors of all kinds circulated far and wide, including a particularly distressing bit of news concerning slave insurrections. A resident of Illinois, for example, informed Governor Pettus that a secret organization known as the "Mississippi Society" had been created. Its members planned to go South, obtain employment as overseers, and perpetrate another John Brown uprising.[1] In view of the near pandemonium of the times it was not surprising that few individuals saw things in proper perspective. Therefore, much that transpired in early 1861 was often both confusing and indecisive.

Greatly adding to the vagueness of the Mississippi political climate of January and February was the fact that both the secession convention and the legislature were in session at the same time. The latter body did little and simply left most of the work of governmental realignment to the convention. Especially in relation to military matters, the new Republic of Mississippi hardly got its defense preparations off the ground. Such conditions were, in part, fostered by the uncertainty of the hour —which was bloated by infatuation and momentary self-indulgence on the part of politicians and constituents alike.

Members of the convention and the legislature, neither anxious

[1] Anonymous to Pettus, February 22, 1861, C. B. New to Pettus, January 14, 1861, in Governor's Correspondence, Vol. LI.

92

to rock the political boat any more than necessary, felt that to provide for rash measures of a military character might not be advisable at this stage. The convention even went so far as to turn down an offer to "sell the state the finest machinery for manufacturing small arms in America." The reason for the refusal was that many convention members believed that the Ordinance of Secession was merely "a demonstration inviting concession." Thus, weapons were not needed in great supply because the "disrupted Union [would be] fully restored within the next twelve months."[2]

Since Lincoln had not yet been inaugurated, it was anyone's guess as to what position he would take concerning disunion. In view of this, the idea that secession was a mere device to pry concessions from the North apparently was not an isolated phenomenon. Many a politician felt that withdrawal of the slave states from the Union would bring about a settlement. Northern businessmen were sure to bring pressure to bear on the Republicans and, for economic reasons, see to it that the Union was brought back together.

Governor Pettus held such talk in the lowest regard. To his way of thinking, secession was the only means of finding a permanent solution to southern grievances. Therefore, he proceeded to carry on a campaign of military preparedness. Throughout January, Pettus ordered the establishment of a state armory, sent troops to help capture federal installations in Florida, and dispatched seven militia companies to Mobile. Governor Andrew Moore was notified to call on Mississippi if additional soldiers were needed for service in Alabama.[3]

For fear that the governor's martial spirit might get entirely out of hand and perhaps involve the state in a needless war, the convention appointed a council of three men to advise Pettus on military matters until such time as Mississippi should enter

[2] Davis, *Recollections of Mississippi*, 403–404.
[3] Pettus to A. B. Moore, January 20, 1861, Pettus to Charles H. Albert, January 26, 1862, in Governor's Executive Journal, 1856–1866, pp. 210–11. See also Don Carlos Seitz, *Braxton Bragg* (Columbia, S.C., 1924), 51; Pettus to Moore, January 12, 1861, in Andrew B. Moore Papers.

a southern confederacy. In a further effort to restrain the state's chief executive, a five-member Military Board was created, the consent of whose members was necessary on any armed services matter. The meager sum of $1,000 was all the convention saw fit to appropriate for military expenses.[4]

As absurd as these decisions would seem at a later date, the immediate likelihood of conflagration did appear to be far removed from the minds of many Mississippians. A survey of the governor's correspondence reveals that numerous individuals were far more concerned with the prospect of having postal operations disrupted than with armed conflict with the North. Those who were eager for the taste of battle were thought of as unstable and it was predicted that "they will want to come back worse than they did go."[5]

As for Pettus, he chose not to stand idly by while either the legislature or the state convention inhibited his interpretation of executive duty. Since March of the preceding year he had been canvassing neighboring states in search of weapons. With secession now a reality, any device of war that he could acquire seemed worthy of the effort needed, even if such endeavors proved offensive to state solons. Pettus was not the only one who viewed war as a distinct possibility, and to Jefferson Davis a noticeable lack of armaments represented "clear proof" that hostilities could not be sustained for long, if things came to that.[6]

Inasmuch as Mississippi's chief executive was for adopting a belligerent posture toward anything that smacked of the federal

[4] Rowland, *Encyclopedia of Mississippi History*, II, 413; Mississippi *Journal of the State Convention* (1861), 18, 126–32. Jefferson Davis was named major-general, while James L. Alcorn, Charles Clark, Earl Van Dorn, and C. H. Mott were selected brigadier generals. Whether advisable or not similar actions had been taken in other states. See Odom, "Political Career of Thomas O. Moore," 996.

[5] A. Rozie to Pettus, January 25, 1861, J. S. Biazley to Pettus, March 10, 1861, J. Lorory to Pettus, March 11, 1861, in Governor's Correspondence, Vol. LI; William H. McClanahan to Joseph Stapp, January 14, 1861, in Joseph D. Stapp Papers.

[6] Pettus to John Zacharie, March 9, 1860, in Governor's Executive Journal, 1856–1866, p. 205; Davis, *Rise and Fall of the Confederate Government*, I, 228, 471–72.

government, his actions could hardly have been unexpected. On January 11, he advocated the capture of the United States gunboat *Silver Wave*, which had been sighted on the Mississippi River. The purpose of this action was to employ that vessel's guns in defense of Ship Island, which he planned to occupy in the near future. In short order Pettus also dispatched eight more companies of state troops to Pensacola to assist Alabama and Florida volunteers in securing federal forts in the vicinity. Within a few weeks, however, some of the Mississippians returned home for lack of funds, confusion over who should direct their movements, and for displeasing the host states by demanding excessive use of force against Union strongholds.[7]

On January 12 the governor, realizing full well the strategic importance of the Mississippi River, forwarded troops to Vicksburg and simultaneously raised seven more companies for uninvited service in Florida. By the middle of the month William L. Sykes, adjutant-general, was able to tell Pettus that sixty-five militia companies had been organized thus far, contracts for weapons were in the proper hands, and many of the "old arms and accouterments (a pile of rubbish) in the arsenal were overhauled and examined, cleaned, and stored away for an emergency."[8] To meet the threat of just such an exigency, the governor thought it time to inform the Military Board of his recent handiwork.

Pettus' conduct of military affairs during the early months of 1861 has been viewed by certain historians as being one of "lighthearted indulgence." The charge has also been leveled that he made almost no effort to secure arms for the volunteers.

[7] Pettus to H. H. Miller, January 11, 1861, in Governor's Executive Journal, 1856–1866, p. 209; Baxter McFarland, "A Forgotten Expedition to Pensacola in January, 1861," in Franklin L. Riley (ed.), *Publications of the Mississippi Historical Society* (Oxford, Miss., 1906), IX, 18–21; Thomas D. Duncan, *Recollections of Thomas D. Duncan, A Confederate Soldier* (Nashville, 1922), 10–11; A. B. Moore to William M. Brooks, January 18, 1861, in *Official Records*, Ser. I, Vol. I, 446; William W. Davis, *The Civil War and Reconstruction In Florida* (2nd. ed.; Gainesville, Fla., 1964), 85.
[8] Charles E. Hooker, "Mississippi," in Clement A. Evans (ed.), *Confederate Military History* (Atlanta, 1899), VII, 17–18; Sykes to Pettus, January 18, 1861, in *Official Records*, Ser. IV, Vol. I, 61–67.

The thrust of this argument seems to stem from the observation left by a contemporary, Horace S. Fulkerson. On one occasion Fulkerson and Pettus did examine some weapons and "shot away much ammunition trying to hit an imaginary Yankee at long range." Afterward, those on hand "retired to the Governor's office at the State house where he entertained [them] with one of his best bear stories." It is true that Fulkerson was unsuccessful in getting the governor to place an order for these weapons, but that was chiefly because the company was located in Belgium.[9] As has been noted, Pettus was quite active in the effort to arm Mississippians. Moreover, it was not always the governor who was responsible for failing to acquire military hardware.

As always, events pressed forward in rapid fashion, regardless of the indecisive manner in which the issues of the day were handled. On January 30 it was learned that several ragtag expeditions of devotees were poised for an attempt to commandeer Ship Island from the federals. Although pleased in principle, the governor indicated a reluctance to officially sanction the action, because he lacked appropriations with which to furnish and defend the place once it was acquired. Ultimately, the federals evacuated without a contest, but Pettus was still faced with the necessity of supplying weapons to a growing number of state troops. Response to war fever had been so great that existing supplies of military gear were soon exhausted. However, the pressure was momentarily lifted when contracts for war materials were placed in Europe and a supply of rifles, muskets, and cannons was received from a recently occupied federal arsenal at Baton Rouge.[10]

---

[9] Bettersworth, *Confederate Mississippi*, 17; Horace S. Fulkerson, *A Civilian's Recollection of the War Between the States*, ed. Percy L. Rainwater (2nd. ed.; Baton Rouge, 1939), 47.

[10] Frederick E. Prime to J. G. Totten, January 30, 1861, Governor Thomas O. Moore to Louisiana Legislature, January 22, 1861, in *Official Records*, Ser. I, Vol. I, 329, 495; Pettus to Thomas O. Moore, January 20, 1861, in Governor's Executive Journal, 1856–1866, p. 210; Milledge L. Bonham, "Louisiana's Seizure of the Federal Arsenal at Baton Rouge, January, 1861," *Proceedings of the Historical Society of East and West Baton Rouge*, VIII (1917–18), 49; J. J. Smylie to Pettus, August 8, 1861, in Governor's Correspondence, Vol. LIII.

Overall, the people of the South were in high spirits during the early months of 1861 and thoroughly convinced of the rightness of their cause. Mississippians proved no exception to the rule and reports of militia musterings, the volunteering of old cannons, offers to convert secular colleges into military institutions, and military enlistments of persons from all walks of life were commonplace. Women, not to be outdone, formed sewing and nursing societies. Something resembling a crusading fervor was in the air. Churches of every denomination responded favorably to the disunion movement, often comparing the likelihood of armed hostilities with a holy war. Copies of the *New Testament* were distributed among the militia by zealous missionaries, who offered to accompany soldiers to the field.[11] Mississippians were indeed eager to follow the drum, and would get the chance sooner than they expected.

Not all was wine and roses, however, and in some areas news traveled slowly. Although the state convention had sent a highly qualified group of men to Montgomery, Alabama, to help frame a new national government, uncertainty as to the future political status of Mississippi was apparent. A Kosciusko resident was troubled by the possibility of war, but was more concerned over the "great confusion . . . in political affairs," complaining that the ordinary man was not being kept posted on transactions of the secession government. He added, "I have not heard much of what they [delegates to Montgomery] done."[12]

In other quarters, certain individuals insisted that planter and

[11] C. H. Banks to Pettus, January 1, 1861, W. W. Wood to Pettus, January 8, 1861, F. A. P. Barnard to Pettus, April 28, 1861, in Governor's Correspondence, Vol. LI; Mrs. B. Beaumont, *Twelve Years of My Life: An Autobiography* (Philadelphia, 1887), 175; W. H. Weathersby, "A History of Mississippi College," in Dunbar Rowland (ed.), *Publications of the Mississippi Historical Society* (Oxford, Miss., 1925), V, 199; Z. T. Leavell and T. J. Bailey, *A Complete History of Mississippi Baptists From the Earliest Times* (Jackson, 1904), I, 153, 188; Francis A. Cabaniss and James A. Cabaniss, "Religion In Mississippi Since 1860," *Journal of Mississippi History*, IX (October, 1947), 199; J. B. Cain, *Methodism In the Mississippi Conference, 1846–1870* (Jackson, 1939), 297; James W. Silver, *Confederate Morale and Church Propaganda* (Tuscaloosa, Ala., 1957), 17, 43, 56, 77–78.

[12] William H. McClanahan to Joseph Stapp, February 25, 1861, in Joseph D. Stapp Papers.

yeoman alike were not in accord with either secession or the prospect of war. Some malcontents proclaimed that they would never fight for the cause under any circumstances. In fact, rumor had it that Whigs and Cooperationists were planning to circulate a ticket in the fall elections of 1861, with the end in mind of repealing the Ordinance of Secession.[13] Other voices of dissent simply bewailed the dangers to trade and commerce that secession was sure to bring with it. For the most part, however, out-and-out diverse political sentiment was at a low ebb.

Changes were so rapid during early 1861 that many persons were unable to cope with them. A colonel in the 31st Mississippi Militia, for example, resigned his commission, confiding: "I don't know anything about it all." Still others, conversely, discovered that secession and events surrounding it might be a useful avenue for resolving their personal problems. "I am now out of imployment [sic]," J. M. McPhail wrote to Governor Pettus, "and wish to give my servises [sic] to my State." Another activist was so carried away by the sweep of events that he advocated that Mississippi exercise all possible haste in building an empire. This could have no better beginning than by taking over the New Mexico territory.[14] But things closer to home needed attending to.

February and March, 1861, found John Pettus embroiled in a variety of issues. On top of the troubled state of military affairs—which often witnessed more argument within the Military Board over detailed descriptions pertaining to uniform specifications than over weapon quality—Jefferson Davis had resigned as major general of the Army of Mississippi in order to assume the presidency of the Confederacy. Thereupon, the governor appointed Bolivar County planter Charles Clark to replace Davis. Clark was known for his "indomitable will" and "intellectual capacity of the highest order."[15]

13 Fulkerson, A Civilian's Recollections, 9.
14 John McIntosh to Pettus, January 18, 1861, J. M. McPhail to Pettus, January 16, 1861, in Governor's Correspondence, Vol. LI; A. M. Jackson to Reuben Davis, February 1, 1861, in Jefferson Davis Papers, Duke University Library.
15 Davis to Pettus, February 12, 1861, in Rowland (ed.), Jefferson Davis, Con-

In some circles the response to Clark's appointment was less than warm. Scarcely had he assumed the duties of his post, when, in an inflammatory speech at Natchez, he defended Governor Pettus' war preparations before a hostile crowd. Two local militia units were "pitched into" and the residents of that community were urged to look to the chief executive for military leadership, instead of local officials. To be effective, programs must be directed by only one man, said Clark. The outspoken general did not become a local favorite when he told his listeners that Natchez militia forces resembled "women with broom handles."[16]

Elsewhere, the economic structure of the state furnished clear and depressing evidence of approaching disaster. A growing number of persons, being too preoccupied with the political scene to plant crops, were soon on the verge of starvation and bankruptcy. The governor was informed of the condition and took immediate action. Since the legislature had confronted this problem only briefly by providing the paltry sum of $1,500 for the relief of but one county, other avenues had to be sought out. Pettus turned to the state convention for remedy and in a letter to William Barry outlined the especially depressed conditions of central Mississippi. The convention responded in a wholly inadequate manner by allowing the affected counties to issue limited quantities of bonds against the state treasury.[17]

The military situation, however, was by far the paramount issue in Mississippi throughout most of 1861. With the advent of secession, Governor Pettus had been directed to muster four regiments of twelve-month volunteers. But the response was underestimated and enlistments proved to be "very rapid." Before long the excited governor, desirous of being ready for any mili-

stitutionalist, V, 46; McElroy, Jefferson Davis, I, 261; Montgomery, Reminiscences of a Mississippian, 39.

16 Natchez Daily Courier, March 6, 1861.

17 A. M. Williamson et al. to Pettus, February 16, 1861, Anonymous to Pettus, March 22, 1861, Pettus to Barry, March 28, 1861, in Governor's Correspondence, Vol. LI; Mississippi Laws of the State of Mississippi, Called Session (January, 1861), 43–44; Mississippi Journal of the State Convention (1861), 31, 81–82.

tary eventuality, had exceeded his authority, accepted the services of eighty companies, and sent them to rendezvous points at Corinth, Enterprise, Grenada, and Iuka. As the number of volunteer units continued to expand, it became apparent that there was little for them to do. Although the Confederate attorney general, Judah P. Benjamin, was authorized to call upon Mississippi for seven regiments for the newly forming Confederate Army, a restlessness among the remaining companies was evident.[18]

Typical of the statewide military excitement was the "Noxubee Cavalry Squadron." On the occasion of a rally in the town square young ladies were on hand. A $100 silk banner, complete with gold tassels, floated in the air while a Baptist minister prayed for the blessings of the Lord.[19] With the martial spirit at an unprecedented level the people could not get into the military fast enough. The governor obliged.

Pettus soon came to realize that he had, at least for the time being, allowed too many into the ranks. Although managing to dispatch 700 troops to Forts Morgan and Pickens in Alabama and Florida respectively, provide two additional regiments to the Confederate Army, and prevail upon the Military Board to forward twenty-three companies to Pensacola for training, the riddle of what to do with the surplus was far from being solved. Faced with an ever accelerating number of enlistments, Pettus attempted to curtail the flow by friendly persuasion. Many individuals resented this action, and one irate constituent confronted him by asking: "What the Devil do you care for events prospected?"[20]

---

[18] Benjamin to Pettus, February 1, 1861, in Governor's Correspondence, Vol. LI.

[19] J. G. Deupree, "The Noxubee Squadron of the First Mississippi Cavalry, C. S. A., 1861–1865," in Dunbar Rowland (ed.), Publications of the Mississippi Historical Society (Oxford, Miss., 1918), II, 16–18.

[20] Beulah M. D'Olive Price (ed.), "Excerpts From the Diary of Walter Alexander Overton, 1860–1863," Journal of Mississippi History, XVII (July, 1955), 197; Pettus to L. P. Walker, March 28, 1861, in Official Records, Ser. I, Vol. LII, Part II, 31; Minutes of the Military Board of the State of Mississippi, Ser. L, Vol. LXXXVI, March 26, 1861; D. W. Kern to Pettus, March 31, 1861, in Governor's Correspondence, Vol. LI.

With a variety of important questions at hand, Governor Pettus often discovered that answers were not easily come by. Not only was his normal authority incumbered by the Military Board, but members of that organization, on occasion, did not even attend called meetings. War preparations were further hampered by a failure to obtain sufficient arms, ammunition, and clothing for the volunteers. A majority of the federal weapons recently received from the Baton Rouge arsenal were sent to the Confederate government, believing that it had a prior hold on them. It was indeed a rare occurrence when any unit could report itself well armed.[21]

Matters were made worse when neither the legislature nor the state convention enacted appropriate military legislation to meet the needs of the times. In late 1860, when disunion appeared imminent even to the casual observer, the power for organizing and disciplining the state militia was still legislative private domain. The governor, although allowed to call up the militia, could not hold the troops for more than one year nor draw any money on their behalf. No changes in the stature of executive military authority, aside from those already mentioned, transpired during early 1861, and it was only with the greatest of reluctance that the lawmakers consented to allow the governor to convene the legislature at some place other than Jackson, should it ever be necessary to do so. Similarly, the state convention not only left Governor Pettus militarily penniless, but also refused to shoulder any responsibility for maintaining customs houses, hospitals, fortifications, and lighthouses within the borders of Mississippi. These burdens were assigned to the Confederate government.[22]

[21] Pettus to W. L. Barry, March 28, 1861, in Governor's Correspondence, Vol. LI. Clothing was extremely hard to obtain and Mississippi's infant textile industry proved incapable of meeting the challenge. See John H. Moore, "Mississippi's Ante-Bellum Textile Industry," *Journal of Mississippi History*, XVI (April, 1954), 81–98.
[22] Mississippi, *Laws of the State of Mississippi*, Called Session (November, 1860), 21–23, (January, 1861), 17; Mississippi *Journal of the State Convention* (1861), 85–86, 92, 94–95, 126–32. The sum of $1,000,000 in the form of war certificates, it should be noted, was allocated, but the governor was not permitted

Aside from military issues the state convention also succeeded in contributing to the governor's troubles by voting to adopt the newly framed Confederate Constitution without submitting it to a popular referendum. Whereas a majority of individuals did not seem to mind the fact that the Ordinance of Secession had not been voted on, a number of dissenters took issue with this policy, believing that the convention had overstepped its bounds.[23]

Apparently, convention members were divided on the issue as much as private citizens. Debate inside the meeting hall was occasionally hot. Alexander Clayton, for example, favored letting the people have a voice in the matter, affirming that convention powers were plenary, and thereby no such authority existed. Speaking for the majority, David Glenn insisted that the convention had "the power and right to act and that duty, expediency and the crisis demanded we should act." The Glenn position carried the day by a margin of 78 to 7.[24] Although some constituents opposed the decision and predicted that the people would not stand for it, Mississippi entered the Confederacy on March 29, 1861, like it or not.

Amid the frustration and chaos of these unsettled times, Governor Pettus was often forced to deal with problems in a unilateral fashion in the absence of clear-cut authority. In an effort to get Confederate courts functioning within his state and to open a customs house on the Mississippi River, he had to rely upon the new national government for support. But if state politicians often refused to confront pressing matters, dealings with Montgomery officials proved equally frustrating. Messages between Jackson and the Confederate capitol were occasionally lost, took

---

to offer them for public sale until mid-March, 1861. See Natchez *Daily Courier*, March 14, 1861.

[23] Vicksburg *Daily Whig*, March 20, 1861; Natchez *Daily Courier*, March 27, 1861.

[24] "Speech of A. M. Clayton Before the Secession Convention," "Memoranda by D. C. Glenn on Secession Convention," in J. F. H. Claiborne Papers, University of North Carolina Library; Mississippi *Journal of the State Convention* (1861), 33–36.

too long to arrive, or involved decisions for which guidelines had not yet been formulated.[25]

Along military lines, John Pettus continued his uninhibited movements. Contacting his chief of ordnance, he revealed his grand strategy for defeating the federals, should they endeavor to invade. Ostensibly, the governor planned to equip the Army of Mississippi with shotguns. The director of ordnance, Samuel G. French, was skeptical, but did as he was instructed and placed orders for this type of firearm. When the guns arrived it was noted that the "god of war never beheld such a collection of antique weapons. . . . There were guns without a vent, to be fired with a live coal, guns without ramrods, barrels without stocks, stocks without barrels, guns without cocks, cocks without pans." Moreover, Pettus gave every foolhardy indication of actually inviting the "pestiferous Yankees" into the state for the purpose of ambushing them.[26]

March and April, 1861, found the popular subscription of state volunteer companies continuing to maintain itself at a fever pitch. In Panola, a "high war enthusiasm" prevailed, complete with militia meetings and parades. And as if this type situation were not enough, offers to tender military duty also came in from as far away as Wisconsin, with one individual complaining that he was "tired of that . . . anti-slavery foundation of the north."[27]

By far the chief difficulty in all this military readiness was the

[25] Jefferson Davis to Confederate Congress, April 29, 1861, in James D. Richardson (ed.), *A Compilation of the Messages and Papers of the Confederacy* (Nashville, 1905), I, 78; Montgomery, *Reminiscences of a Mississippian*, 39; Pettus to Leroy P. Walker, March 17, 18, 1861, in Telegrams Received by the CSA Secretary of War, 1861–1865, National Archives, Washington, D.C.

[26] Samuel G. French, *Two Wars: An Autobiography of General Samuel G. French* (Nashville, 1901), 137–39. Although the governor's idea did seem foolish, it nevertheless was well accepted both within Mississippi and in neighboring Alabama as well. See M. W. Wilbourn to Pettus, June 13, 1861, in Governor's Correspondence, Vol. LII; Canton *American Citizen*, July 6, 20, 1861.

[27] Entry for April 22, 1861, in Everard G. Baker Diary, University of North Carolina Library, Chapel Hill, N.C., George H. Paul to Pettus, March 12, 1861, in Governor's Correspondence, Vol. LI.

inactivity of the volunteer companies. It was not long before criticism found its way to the governor's doorstep. One writer grumbled that his unit, the "Natchez Fencibles," had been "bamboozled" into believing that they were going to war. The *Mississippi Free Trader* observed that the people were "indignant, *not* because they are compelled to fight, but because they are not allowed a *chance* to fight." Related complaints regarding a lack of firearms, which some organizations even offered to purchase for themselves, reached the governor's desk daily. An Abbeville, Mississippi, resident probably got to the heart of the matter when he wrote: "if we do have to fight we want to do some execution."[28]

Pettus, with no power to veto a decision of the Military Board to accept all volunteers, was reminded by state brigadier general and long-time friend Reuben Davis that growing volunteer discontent could well influence the fall elections, if allowed to continue. Since Pettus planned on standing for reelection, political prudence demanded that something be done. With military assignments at a premium, many units soon proved unmanageable. Captain Francis L. Full wrote from Vicksburg that his men were in "open mutiny" and requested instructions on how to control them, adding, they "dought [*sic*] your authority as to compell [*sic*] them to obey your orders."[29]

In an attempt to stabilize the situation, Governor Pettus turned to the Confederate War Department for relief. "Companies fuller than expected," he wrote in one dispatch. In a typical response to what few troop requisitions did arrive in Jackson, the governor on one occasion sent two hundred more men than asked for. "I hope the Pres. will receive them," he noted. On April 13 Pettus informed Confederate Secretary of War Leroy P. Walker that he had at least thirty companies ready for service

[28] John Fowler to Pettus, April 9, 1861, Owen to Pettus, April 28, 1861, in Governor's Correspondence, Vol. LI; Natchez *Mississippi Free Trader*, April 19, 1861.

[29] Davis to Pettus, April 8, 1861, Full to Pettus, April 2, 1861, in Governor's Correspondence, Vol. LI.

and that they were impatient for orders. When no word was forthcoming the governor wired Walker again, with a plan to force his hand. Playing upon the issue that Mississippians had heard that southern property was being confiscated at Cincinnati, Ohio, Pettus indicated that some hot-bloods were ready to attack northward on their own. "It is difficult to restrain river people," he wrote. "I wait instructions for retaliation."[30] None came.

What news there was in those trying spring days only added to the gloomy military forecast. Even when three companies of artillery were called up for Confederate service, the Mississippi governor had to send them along without horses or harnesses. Secretary Walker could be of immediate assistance only insofar as to promise that the troops would receive marching orders sometime in the future.[31]

Left to his own devices, John Pettus attempted to dissipate the dissatisfaction by visiting several units and personally distributing rifles and reviewing them on parade. But this was not enough, and by May the volunteer problem had reached nearly crisis proportions—with ninety-three companies in state service. Compounding the obvious were other loudly articulated complaints relating to the enrollment of certain companies ahead of others, the acquisition of weapons, pay allotments, buttons for uniforms, lack of clothing, and desertion.[32]

Disappointment among the volunteer units was not without consequences, and within a short period newspapers were open-

[30] Pettus to Leroy P. Walker, March 31, 1861, in Telegrams Received by the CSA Secretary of War, National Archives; Pettus to Walker, April 13, 17, 1861, in *Official Records*, Ser. I ,Vol. LII, Part II, 46, Vol. LIII, 672.
[31] Pettus to Leroy P. Walker, April 8, 1861, in Telegrams Received by the CSA Secretary of War, National Archives; Walker to Pettus, April 25, 1861, in Telegrams Sent by the CSA Secretary of War, 1861–1865, National Archives, Washington, D.C.
[32] Percy L. Rainwater (ed.), "W. A. Montgomery's Record of the Raymond Fencibles," *Journal of Mississippi History*, VI (April, 1944), 113; James W. Silver, *A Life For the Confederacy: As Recorded In the Pocket Diaries of Private Robert A. Moore* (Jackson, Tenn., 1959), 26; Natchez *Daily Courier*, May 1, 1861.

ly chiding the Pettus administration's handling of military affairs. The Vicksburg *Weekly Whig* went so far as to call for an end to the "imbecility" at Jackson and put forth the name of Samuel Benton of Marshall County as a likely candidate for governor in the fall elections. Described as a "self-made man, an upright and enlightened christian gentleman," Benton was an outspoken critic of events thus far.[33]

With the political repercussions more than obvious, Pettus marshalled all resources at his disposal in an attempt to quiet this kind of talk. By threat and persuasion he finally prevailed upon the Military Board to grant a temporary halt to the enlistment of any more new companies. On May 14 it was announced that the door to further volunteering was closed, at least for the time being. As might have been expected, the moratorium drew a volley of protest from disappointed individuals throughout the state. Many expressed bitter resentment toward the new ruling, feeling they would not be permitted to participate in the great drama growing near.

Leaving no stone unturned, the energetic governor continued his search for a way to rid himself of his excess troops. Another appeal for relief went to friend and cousin Jefferson Davis, with the notation that enlistees were "anxiously waiting orders." To General Gideon J. Pillow went a request to summon the military "as fast as possible." For all this labor, the result was paltry— just two regiments, "armed with heavy Double-Barreled Shotguns," were called for by the War Department.[34]

As if Pettus' dilemma were not overwhelming enough already, another military problem arose in early June when Charles Clark tendered his resignation as major general of the Army of Mississippi in order to assume a similar post in the Confederate Army. Clark's action proved to be the catalyst for still more

---

[33] Natchez *Daily Courier*, May 2, 1861; Vicksburg *Weekly Whig*, May 4, 1861.
[34] Pettus to Davis, May 18, 1861, in *Official Records*, Ser. IV, Vol. I, 334; Pettus to Pillow, May 18, 1861, in John J. Pettus Papers; Mississippi Department of Archives and History, Jackson; Leroy P. Walker to Pettus, May 18, 1861, in Telegrams Sent by the CSA Secretary of War.

controversy of political as well as military significance. For the next person in line to fill the vacated post was James Lusk Alcorn, a Whig who had opposed unilateral secession in the first place. In Pettus' eyes, this was tantamount to absolute subversion and had the effect of making Alcorn *"persona non grata."*[35]

Meanwhile, Reuben Davis, a long-time associate of the governor, indicated his desire for Clark's former position. Pettus, affirming that he would "never promote Alcorn," appointed Davis, and in so doing contributed to the animosity of dissidents of long standing. Davis' accession to the important post added to the aggressiveness in the governor's military program, both men being dedicated to carrying out bold plans.[36] The Davis–Alcorn incident, however, was but a small gust of wind in the middle of the storm that continued to swirl about the state of military affairs.

During June, pressure upon the governor to repeal his moratorium on volunteering mounted. Militia organizations still mustered with fanfare and cermony. On one such occasion in Bolivar County, local men publicly pledged that their flag would never fall into the hands of the enemy. But temporarily, at least, such individuals were dressed up with no place to go. But charges of insufficient pay and a failure to be mustered into service were only some of the grievances brought before Pettus. Also of prime concern were the other problems that excessive volunteering had fostered. Numbers of soldiers had apparently become so submerged in political and military affairs that they had neglected to plant crops; by the summer of 1861 many were in danger of having their property confiscated for non-payment of liens and taxes. This pitiful situation caused a Copiah County resident to remark: "I am plum out of anything to eat but bread

---

[35] Clark to Pettus, June 10, 1861, in Governor's Correspondence, Vol. LII; Charles J. Swift, "James Lusk Alcorn," in James Lusk Alcorn Papers, Mississippi Department of Archives and History, Jackson, Miss.
[36] Davis to Pettus, June 10, 1861, in Governor's Correspondence, Vol. LII; Davis, *Recollections of Mississippi*, 405–406; Pereyra, *James Lusk Alcorn*, 48–49; May S. Ringold, "James Lusk Alcorn," *Journal of Mississippi History*, XXV (January, 1963), 4.

i have not got a sent of money to nor cant get money nor provision."[37]

Disgusted by the turn of events, Governor Pettus released a proclamation which was designed both to soothe the temperament of constituents and explain the reasons for the deplorable state of affairs in which Mississippi now found herself. "Arms manufactured specially for war," Pettus told the people, "cannot be secured in sufficient numbers to arm all who are willing and anxious to take part in the present conflict." At least 25,000 troops would be needed in the near future, on which occasion it was highly "probable that Mississippi will be called upon to put forth her full military strength." To aid in resolving present issues the legislature was once again to be called into special session.[38]

Pettus' call for the legislature came not a moment too soon. For the Military Board, bowing to public pressure, suddenly threw open the flood gates to allow the unimpeded acceptance of more volunteers. By the time the lawmakers were in session the number of companies on muster rolls had reached an all-time high of 125.[39]

When the solons gathered in Jackson, Pettus went before them to vent his wrath at what he felt to be ineptness on their part and to lash out at his personal critics by trying to place the burden of blame for what had gone wrong on the legislature. Noting that some of his actions thus far had been arbitrary, the outspoken governor indicated that he felt justified in taking certain military steps because the citizens had manifested a desire that he do so by responding to the sectional crisis "in a manner unknown in modern times."[40]

By way of specifics the governor went on to urge that a stay law be enacted to prevent the collection of debts from those

[37] Florence W. Sillers, *History of Bolivar County, Mississippi* (Jackson, 1948), 145; Issac L. Smith to Pettus, April 4, 1861, in Governor's Correspondence, Vol. LII.
[38] Pettus Proclamation of June 23, 1861, in Frank Moore (ed.), *The Rebellion Record: A Diary of American Events* (New York, 1862–71), II, 195–96.
[39] Minutes of the Military Board, Ser. L, Vol. LXXV, July 20, 1861.
[40] Mississippi *House Journal*, Called Session (July, 1861), 6.

serving the state, and that new taxes be provided. In respect to military affairs he emphatically denounced the Military Board for interfering with his activities, called for a law to permit absentee voting by soldiers in the field, and announced the completion of an executive agreement with the governors of Alabama and Louisiana for the joint procurement of steamers to patrol the coastal areas of the Gulf of Mexico. Pettus closed his address on a patriotic note with religious overtones: "May the God of Justice give success to our arms and safety to our sons."[41]

Apparently many members of the legislature took the governor's words lightly. For in view of recent good fortunes on the battlefield, particularly at the First Battle of Manassas, several lawmakers were of the opinion that the war was rapidly drawing to a close. In line with such reasoning a bill was introduced calling for the abolition of the Military Board and a drastic reduction of the state's armed forces. Needless to say, Governor Pettus and chief advisor Reuben Davis were unalterably opposed to such action. The latter, acting under the governor's directive, attempted to browbeat the legislators into defeating these proposals by warning that the state was about to be invaded. The scheme failed, and in so doing brought Davis to a moment of unguarded passion, at which time he threatened to "hang" anyone who dared vote to dismantle the military machinery. He was determined that the solons "should not trifle with the safety of the people."[42]

In seeming retaliation for this type of heavy-handedness, the legislature showed a near total lack of concern for the difficulties already apparent by failing to enact a single piece of worthwhile legislation. Two laws, one dealing with harsher penalties

[41] Ibid., 6–7, 9; Pettus to Thomas O. Moore, June 28, 1861, Pettus to A. B. Moore, July 18, 1861, in Governor's Executive Journal, 1856–1866, 217–18; Andrew B. Moore to Colonel Walker, July 15, 1861, in Andrew B. Moore Papers. In addition Pettus had been busy obtaining pledges for free transportation of troops and supplies from railroads and in advocating the confiscation of northern owned property within Mississippi. See C. F. Vance to Pettus, March 2, 1861, H. J. Ranney to Pettus, April 20, 1861, in Governor's Correspondence, Vol. LI; James W. Garner, Reconstruction In Mississippi (New York, 1901), 27.
[42] Davis, Recollections of Mississippi, 411.

for "tampering with slaves" and another to prevent cohabitation and fornication between whites and Negroes, were deemed of greater importance.[43] Disgusted, Pettus had to continue his own quest for solutions to contemporary problems.

By the summer of 1861 the Mississippi governor's political future seemed bleak indeed. Efforts to create a sense of unity among opposing political factions by appointing several Whigs and Cooperationists to various offices boomeranged and drew a volley of criticism from the rank and file of his own party. When he selected I. M. Patridge, former editor of the anti-secessionist Vicksburg *Weekly Whig*, to head a division of the state militia, Democrats denounced him. Always a stickler for detail, Pettus was criticized by former U.S. Congressman William Barksdale, who had briefly held the post of state quartermaster-general. Barksdale resigned because he could not meet Pettus' requirement of "showing accurately and correctly where every tin cup, spoon, canteen, [and] knapsack has gone."[44] Barksdale felt that if the governor demanded accountability from others, the same should be required of the governor.

Since early that year residents of the Gulf Coast had been reminding Governor Pettus of both the importance and exposed position of the entire region. With the bulk of forces concentrated in the northern or central parts of the state, it was natural that the people in the southernmost counties would be concerned. Among the many points of contention during the summer was concern for Ship Island, which had never been properly secured and fortified by the state forces stationed there. When, for lack of supplies, little was done, the people exhibited "a general feeling of insecurity" while rumors circulated that "Dictator Lincoln" would blockade the entire coast and "pounce upon" shipping at will.[45]

---

[43] Mississippi, *Laws of the State of Mississippi*, Called Session (July, 1861), 31–35, 67–68, 70–71.

[44] Natchez *Daily Courier*, February 21, 1861; Patridge to Pettus, May 10, 1861, in Governor's Correspondence, Vol. LII; Barksdale to Pettus, July 26, 1861, in John J. Pettus Papers.

[45] J. C. Monet to Pettus, January 2, 1861, D. S. Pattison to Pettus, January 13,

Pettus did not believe that the Gulf Coast situation was quite so critical, but took no chances and wired President Davis that arms should be forwarded to the area. Pettus should have listened harder and investigated further. Confederate General T. E. Twiggs soon afterward found his efforts to enlist troops from that region thwarted and met with a "positive refusal" because of the prevailing opinion there that invasion was imminent.[46]

Elsewhere, reports of dissatisfaction among the volunteer units continued to persist. Several companies simply disbanded, while others left the state altogether in order to get into battle. A militia colonel, caught up in the unsettled times, wrote the governor for advice. Are my men to be "allowed to go and come just when they pleased," he asked.[47]

Backed into a corner, Pettus on the one hand quietly suggested that some of the units discontinue activities, while on the other he telegraphed the Confederate government, begging for an encouraging word in regard to the enlistment situation. However hard he tried, the complicated puzzle was no closer to solution, and the distribution of rifles that would fire only once in every ten attempts was not about to pacify the angry volunteers.[48]

The unsatisfactory military situation and corresponding discontent could not but become a factor in politics. In late April, newspapers had begun openly advocating a change in the governor's office. Among those mentioned as alternatives to Pettus

1861, R. Seal to Pettus, April 6, 1861, J. B. Mullane to Pettus May 4, 1861, A. E. Lewis to Pettus, June 30, 1861, W. R. Clark to Pettus, July 4, 1861, in Governor's Correspondence, Vol. LII.
[46] Pettus to Davis, August 3, 1861, in *Official Records*, Ser. E, Vol. LII, Part II, 124; T. E. Twiggs to Pettus, September 19, 21, 1861, in Governor's Correspondence, Vol. LXIII.
[47] T. A. Graves to Pettus, June 24, 1861, in Governor's Correspondence, Vol. LXIII.
[48] Pettus and J. A. Powell to L. P. Walker, May 10, 1861, in *Official Records*, Ser. I, Vol. LII, part II, 92; Pettus to Jefferson Davis, May 3, 1861, *ibid.*, Ser. IV, Vol. I, 277; Pettus to Robert D. Hacken, May 10, 1861, in Governor's Executive Journal, 1856–1866; Davis, *Recollections of Mississippi*, 416.

were such public figures as James Alcorn, Fulton Anderson, William Lake, and J. Shall Yerger. A short while later, the governor's public image received another sharp setback when a published report quite unfavorable to him circulated throughout the state. William Howard Russell, an employee of *The Times* of London, had visited Mississippi and found the executive mansion filled with a "republican simplicity" that included broken windows, "ragged" carpets, and a ceiling "discoloured by mildew." As for Pettus, the Englishman depicted his office as easily accessible as a "publichouse," with a "grim, silent man, tobacco-ruminant, abrupt-speeched" as its prime occupant. The governor, Russell noted, believed that the "society in which he exists, wherein there are monthly foul murders perpetrated . . . is the most . . . civilized in the world." Commenting on international affairs, Pettus was quoted as saying:

> "Well, sir" he said, dropping a portentous plug of tobacco just outside the spittoon with the air of a man who wished to show he could have hit the centre if he liked, "England is no doubt a great country, and has got fleets and the like of that, and may have a good deal to do in Eu-rope; but the sovereign state of Mississippi can do a great deal better without England than England can do wthout her."[49]

Russell's unflattering comments did not go unchallenged. The Jackson *Weekly Mississippian* rallied to the executive's defense on August 14, 1861, by asking if it were not better to be accessible to the people than to be shut off in the "salon of the tyrant, furnished by the sweat of the over-taxed operative."

Meanwhile, for better or worse, John Pettus was renominated as the Democratic candidate for governor by convention caucus in late July. Although the move encountered certain opposition and a few convention delegates demonstrated "a good deal of

---

[49] William Howard Russell, *My Diary North and South* (New York, 1863), 113; William Howard Russell, *Pictures of Southern Life, Social, Political and Military* (New York, 1861), 116.

dissatisfaction," it was generally conceded that Pettus was the best choice available.[50]

Despite his renomination, Pettus' political prospects for the immediate future remained dim, at least in the press. The Oxford *Mercury* and the Yazoo City *Banner* came out for Jacob Thompson, a former member of the Buchanan cabinet. The Vicksburg *Weekly Whig*, on the other hand, reflected a desire for either one-time Whig Samuel Benton or moderate Democrat Madison McAfee. The Canton *American Citizen*, although supporting the incumbent, did so in feeble fashion and warned that a number of Mississippians were growing tired of a "few unscrupulous, wire-working, pot-house and street-corner politicians, who meet in caucus [and] nominate their own particular favorites—perhaps as supple tools to carry out some rascally scheme."[51]

Several of the governor's friends soon brought to his attention a long list of names of persons pledged to support the candidacy of Madison McAfee, the state quartermaster-general and long-time opponent of the governor on the Military Board. While a common charge leveled against Pettus was that he had been "too slow to act," the most universal complaint always seemed to return to the volunteer system. A number of militia companies that had recently visited Jackson believed that they were badly treated by the governor, who should have "encamped" them in the capitol building or the executive mansion and otherwise made their stay in that city into a "sort of grand pageantry and jubilee." Even those state troops who had been sent elsewhere on duty were not always content. One Mississippi soldier found Mobile to his disliking because the people gave him "a real cold reception" and quartered him "in a large cotton shed near the wharf." When the same individual was transferred to Florida, he remained dissatisfied because "other Mississippi

<hr>

[50] Davis, *Recollections of Mississippi*, 414. See also Jackson *Weekly Mississippian*, July 27, 1861.
[51] Canton *American Citizen*, August 10, 1861.

troops who enlisted long after" were off somewhere else "fighting the battle of the Country" and winning "imperishable honor
. . . and unfading Laurels." But the fundamental obstacle to
Pettus' reelection was the idle volunteer companies. Still, the
Confederate government refused to take surplus volunteers off
his hands.[52]

As time dragged on, Pettus' slowly growing storehouse of
frustration soon manifested itself. In a public letter the bitter
chief executive appealed to the voters to investigate the charges
leveled at him. They would find, he maintained, that the accusations were little more than personal attacks and the individuals
who made them were the same ones who had opposed secession.
Pettus maintained that he had "labored diligently, faithfully, and
zealously for the safety, prosperity and happiness of the State."
This rebuttal only worked to the governor's disadvantage, however, even displeasing the Jackson *Weekly Mississippian*, whose
editor took special pains to remind Pettus to keep his remarks
confined to real issues.[53]

During August and September, Governor Pettus' political
fortune hung on the verge of despair. Volunteers deserted, and
requests for winter uniforms, blankets, underwear, and weapons
went unfilled. Old-line dissenters continued to cry down the
governor, while one-time supporters denounced his military
strategy.[54]

Consequently, Pettus began to discuss the propriety of withdrawing from the contest, but Reuben Davis advised against
such action, even though the political storm "darkened rapidly,

[52] E. B. Gardner to Pettus, August 3, 1861, John Marshall to Pettus, August 30,
1861, Robert S. Hudson to Pettus, August 30, 1861, in Governor's Correspondence, Vol. LII; Entries for March 30, April 2, July 20, 1861, in Thomas B. Webber Diary, Duke University Library.
[53] Paulding *Eastern Clarion*, August 23, 1861; Jackson *Weekly Mississippian*,
September 25, 1861.
[54] James Alcorn to Pettus, August 26, 1861, W. K. Douglass to Pettus, August
26, 1861, Jeff Wilson to Pettus, September 4, 1861, R. C. E. Esteo to Pettus,
September 6, 1861, W. S. Randall to Pettus, September 10, 1861, in Governor's
Correspondence, Vol. LIII; Paulding *Eastern Clarion*, September 6, 1861.

and seemed to portend disaster." In an effort to take the heat off his chief, Reuben Davis offered to announce as a candidate for the Confederate congress and stump the state on a platform calling for the governor's vindication. And there were some constituents who yet sent along personal endorsements praising the governor and expressing the belief that he should remain in the race.[55]

Pettus must have taken heart for he was soon in the thick of things once more. Madison McAfee, the major rival, was temporarily disposed of, the governor sending him to Richmond, Virginia, under the pretext "of procuring an adjustment of accounts due from the Confederate Government." McAfee, perhaps sensing the discomfort of his position, withdrew from the canvass and a month later came to the governor's defense by stating that he also was "equally responsible" for the military failures of the Pettus administration. McAfee's retirement was not without significance and was heralded as a deed that would place him in the executive mansion in 1863. With the quartermaster-general out of the way, the prediction that the incumbent would "leisurely walk over the course" was hardly surprising. Not above being patronized, Pettus further sought to bolster his chances by exchanging state printing contracts for political support from the Vicksburg *Sun*.[56]

In the meantime, the federals were busy along the Gulf Coast. The U.S.S. *Massachusetts* forced Confederate troops off Ship Island on the evening of September 16, and two days later succeeded in cutting the submarine telegraph cable between Shieldsboro and Pass Christian. Old fears among local residents reached new heights. But this time the governor was on top of things and literally begged President Davis for swift assis-

[55] Davis, *Recollections of Mississippi*, 413–14; John Kyle to Pettus, August 14, 1861, in Governor's Correspondence, Vol. LIII.
[56] Pettus to McAfee, August 8, 1861, T. S. Martin to Pettus, October 7, 1861, in Governor's Correspondence, Vol. LIV; Jackson *Weekly Mississippian*, September 18, 1861; Paulding *Eastern Clarion*, August 9, 1861; Canton *American Citizen*, September 21, 1861.

tance.[57] A few companies did reach the coast, but not until early October.

More gratifying to Pettus, however, was the fact that in September orders for the large-scale mobilization of soldiers for the Confederate Army began to arrive in Jackson. Such information was withheld from the public until September 28, 1861, at which time Governor Pettus issued the long-awaited call for 10,000 men to assemble at Grenada and Vicksburg, with an additional twenty companies to be enrolled at New Orleans.[58] The impact of the muster order was both obvious and calculated to affect the election campaign. As if by magic, the political air cleared, and not a moment too soon.

The outcome of the October elections was never in doubt after the release of the muster orders. Incumbent Pettus carried every county but four (Amite, Hancock, Harrison, and Lauderdale), defeating nearest rival Jacob Thompson by a margin of almost ten to one. The counties that Pettus lost were, in the main, located on the Gulf Coast. A complete tabulation of the balloting showed: John Pettus, 31,169; Jacob Thompson, 3,556; Madison McAfee, 234; and a scattering of "favorite son" candidates, 662. Pettus' total might have gone even higher had arrangements been made for absentee voting. There must have been more than one soldier who could not understand how it was that the lawmakers of Mississippi could be "so patriotic as to disfranchise its soldiers."[59] Although Governor Pettus' policies and his handling of military and political affairs appeared to have been exonerated, the fact remains that opposition of one kind or another was not eliminated. The persistent myth that the Whig and Oppo-

[57] Report of Commander Melancton Smith, September 20, 1861, in Moore (ed.), *The Rebellion Record*, III, 125; Pettus to Davis, September 20, 1861, in Telegrams Received by the CSA Secretary of War.

[58] Davis, *Recollections of Mississippi*, 415; Jefferson Davis to Leonidas Polk, September 15, 1861, in *Official Records*, Ser. I, Vol. IV, 188; Proclamation of September 28, 1861, in Governor's Executive Journal, 1857–1870, 302; Natchez *Daily Courier*, October 4, 1861.

[59] Mississippi *House Journal* (November, 1861), 38–39; Entry for November 6, 1861, in Thomas B. Webber Diary.

sition factions had agreeably entered the mainstream of Mississippi politics during 1861 would prove to be erroneous.

By late 1861, however, the time had come for Mississippians to end their bout with the bustle, drama, and idealism of secession and transfer their energies to the reality of war. Some, of course, had recognized this for a long time. In January, 1861, one observer had predicted: "Our happy homes many will be clothed in sorrow. The sound of the drum must take the place of the hammer and spinning wheel. Troubles are coming many and unavoidable."[60]

With the full measure of civil conflict about to overtake them, the fortunes of politicians and soldiers alike would soon wax and wane in proportion to the results of war. Pettus, in particular, would drift in and out of public esteem when the true test of crisis came. But, for the moment at least, the horrors of war were to be thought of in terms of the abstract, the romantic, and the poetic.

> Southrons, hear your Country call you!
> Up! lest worse than death befall you!
> To arms! To arms! To arms! in Dixie!
> Lo! All the beacon-fires are lighted,
> Let all hearts be now united![61]

[60] Entries for January 10, 11, 1861, in Thomas B. Webber Diary.
[61] Albert Pike, "Dixie," in Albert Bushnell Hart (ed.), *Welding of the Nation, 1845–1900* (New York, 1901), 277.

VIII
The Struggle
for Unity and Direction

THE CLOSING MONTHS OF 1861 were troubled ones for Mississippi's chief executive. Not only had he overcome an important personal crisis, reelection, but he was painfully aware that had a more aggressive challenger entered the campaign against him, the outcome could well have been reversed, or at least the margin of safety might have been reduced.

Although heavily preoccupied with events relating to his own political future, Governor Pettus did not neglect the duties of office. He even took time out from the campaign to recommend presidential clemency for three youthful soldiers who were "sentenced to be shot at Pensacola" for desertion. "They are too young," he told the War Department.[1]

Concerning military matters, the governor's policy—whether for selfish reasons or not—was one of cooperation with the Richmond government. No sooner had Albert Sidney Johnston been ordered to take charge of Confederate operations in the western part of Mississippi, for instance, than Pettus volunteered to turn over forty militia companies for Confederate service. There was a pitfall in transferring those units, however; Richmond authorities refused to accept any organization unless it was fully armed. In this connection, gunpowder was of extreme value, for without it all the major types of weapons that the state was be-

[1] Pettus to Leroy P. Walker, August 29, 1861, in Telegrams Received by the CSA Secretary of War.

ginning to manufacture were useless. Unable to secure such a product, the governor sarcastically inquired if Johnston might be able to supply "from 1 to 100,000 pounds" of the precious commodity. Johnston objected to this War Department policy, but was powerless to alter it. So when it came to counting noses, in late 1861 Mississippi was able to furnish only one fully supplied regiment for immediate service. Pettus had to be content to operate in piecemeal fashion—sending forward armed men "by companies, squads and indivduals" instead of regular units.[2]

Elsewhere, Pettus did his utmost to promote the state's best interests in a variety of ways, some of which bore positive and negative results. As many troops as could be spared were hurried to the Gulf Coast in order to quiet the nervous residents of that place, but both they and their weapons were slow in arriving. And in the latter instance the Confederate War Department intercepted a shipment of rifles which Pettus had ordered, and sold them without his consent to Governor Moore of Louisiana. This made Pettus hopping mad, especially since the Union blockade now prevented another shipment of firearms from reaching Mississippi via Havana, Cuba.[3]

Mississippi troops, on duty in the state as well as beyond, exhibited mixed feelings in respect to camp life during the early stages of the Civil War. One soldier stationed near Biloxi found his plight a good one, thanks to a "splendid camp and good water, splendid breeze all the time," and an abundance of excellent food. Writing from Virginia, another Mississippian in the ranks noted that he had plenty of food and clothes. But in Kentucky things were different. Troops serving there encountered problems with disease and much confusion over how long they were obligated for duty.[4] Matters were complicated even further by

[2] Pettus to Johnston, September 28, 1861, in *Official Records*, Ser. I, Vol. IV, 432; Charles P. Roland, *Albert Sidney Johnston: Soldier of Three Republics* (Austin, 1964), 274–76; Pettus to Jefferson Davis, November 23, 1861, in Telegrams Received by the CSA Secretary of War.

[3] Pettus to Judah P. Benjamin, December 3, 7, 1861 and January 6, 1862, in Telegrams Received by the CSA Secretary of War.

[4] F. Jay Taylor (ed.), *Reluctant Rebel: The Secret Diary of Robert Patrick,*

disputes concerning who should issue orders to state forces.

Meanwhile, the busy governor was instrumental in helping the state's railroads to "issue notes in considerable amounts," which were to serve as substitutes for cash payments for the use of their facilities. The original spirit of wartime cooperation had worn thin by the fall of 1861, and those railroad men who had previously offered to haul military supplies for free in reevaluating their stand had come up with the figure of either 50 percent of the normal charges or only one free shipment per week.[5]

During the same period arrangements were made for salt to be imported to Mississippi from Mobile by means of an agreement among Pettus, Alabama Governor Moore, and the railway companies. The need to secure an adequate supply of salt, while not critical yet, was made more urgent by the Union blockade. Aware of the issue, Pettus ordered state geologist Eugene Hilgard to canvass Mississippi in search of any such deposits that could be utilized in the event they were needed.[6]

In military circles, the overzealous governor continued to transfer as many state troops to Confederate command as possible. Two such regiments were handed over, the governor knowing full well that two-thirds of them had the measles. Likewise, the cumbersome Military Board was always the topic of some complaint.[7]

Throughout the waning months of 1861, personal critics of Pettus were still in evidence. Men of the cloth, who had once

1861–1865 (Baton Rouge, 1959), 32; J. C. McIntyre to Anonymous, November 23, 1861, in Miscellaneous Confederate Army Letters, 1863–1865, Duke University Library, Durham, N.C.; Davis, *Recollections of Mississippi*, 422–26.

[5] John C. Schwab, *The Confederate States of America, 1861–1865: A Financial and Industrial History of the South During the Civil War* (New York, 1901), 155; James Goodman to Pettus, May 21, 1861, in Governor's Correspondence, Vol. LII.

[6] A. B. Moore to Pettus, November 14, 1861, in Andrew B. Moore Papers; G. W. Brame to Pettus, November 28, 1861, in Governor's Correspondence, Vol. LIV.

[7] John W. O'Ferrald to Jefferson Davis, October 16, 1861, in *Official Records*, Ser. I, Vol. IV, 454; Pettus to Jefferson Davis, October 29, 1861, *ibid.*, Ser. IV, Vol. I, 712.

smiled with favor on secession, now took special precautions "against letting down and prostituting the pulpit, to a level with a low and corrupt hustings." A resident of Sharon, Mississippi, noted this change of heart and was suspect of "several preachers whose sympathies are for the north," one of whom had "not prayed a good Confederate prayer this year."[8]

There was little that John Pettus could do about such talk. But when he did possess the means, those who voiced dissent found themselves bearing the brunt of a vindictive vengeance. A case in point was that of E. C. Boynton, professor of chemistry at the University of Mississippi, who was fired for having been too vocal in his pro-Union attitudes. Generally, however, this kind of action was not necessary in large doses and the bulk of Mississippians were probably, as a Tippah County resident put it, "in a high state of discipline" and ready to follow the governor's lead.[9]

On the lighter side, Pettus was able to find time for brief relaxation in the form of hunting and fishing expeditions. A widower for several years, the governor even managed to take time out from his active schedule for courtship. On October 1, John Pettus wed a Tuscaloosa, Alabama, widow, Mrs. Sarah H. Potts, described as a "happy choice."[10] But the times left little room for domestic affairs or private pursuits.

Problems similar to those present in the recent gubernatorial campaign continued to fester long after the balloting. The price of foodstuffs rose steadily. Bacon, normally cheap, was high. Cloth and buttons for uniforms were in short supply, and many farmers were unable to procure very little beyond the bare necessities of life. The governor was even held responsible for the dwindling salt resources. Counterfeit ten-dollar bills circulated

[8] Entry for June 13, 1861, in Journal of Reverend James A. Lyon, in Mississippi Department of Archives and History, Jackson; A. B. Bledsoe to Parents, November 24, 1861, in William C. Cobb Papers, Duke University Library.

[9] Paulding *Eastern Clarion*, September 22, 1861; Francis A. Wolff to Pettus, October 6, 1861, in Governor's Correspondence, Vol. LIV.

[10] John L. Ball to Pettus, October 11, 1861, in Governor's Correspondence, Vol. LIV.

freely, and Confederate dollars had a market value of only eighty cents in late 1861.[11]

If the failure to muster troops for active duty had caused Governor Pettus great alarm prior to the fall elections, something of the reverse was true afterward, especially when the realities of war became unmistakable. The hoarding of much needed weapons was a common phenomenon, with many residents preferring to hold their firearms for defense of county or town rather than donate them to the state war-chest. The closing days of October found the situation more critical. A DeSoto County resident gloomily noted that many men in that vicinity were not as anxious to volunteer for military duty as they once had been. An irate citizen of Marion County complained to the governor that a certain Zacharia Tornvegay, described as a "mischievous, meddlesome rascally man" who told "mischief making lies," was freely announcing his intention of not joining the army. Still other Mississippians elected to join secret "Peace Societies" when the trials of war came upon them or, as in the case of one William R. Croxton, even to desert the armed services.[12] The pre-war enthusiasm had succumbed to the hardships of soldier life.

Amid the tribulations of the same period Governor Pettus learned of the death of one of his sons, John. The boy, determined to meet the enemy as soon as possible, had joined a unit that was sent to Virginia. Near Leesburg, at the battle of Ball's Bluff, he paid the ultimate price. According to his company commander, young John "fought bravely and killed his share of yankees before he fell."[13] Less than a month later, and much against the wishes of the father, the governor's other son, William Winston, left college and joined the army.

[11] Robert C. Wood, *Confederate Handbook: A Compilation of Important Data and Other Interesting and Valuable Matters Relating to the War Between the States, 1861–1865* (New Orleans, 1900), 76.

[12] Joseph T. Hollowell to Pettus, October 22, 1861, R. W. Vince to Pettus, October 26, 1861, O. E. Stewart to Pettus, October 5, 1861, in Governor's Correspondence, Vol. LIII; Georgia Lee Tatum, *Disloyalty In the Confederacy* (Chapel Hill, 1934), 88.

[13] J. C. Campbell to Pettus, October 25, 1861, in Governor's Corespondence, Vol. LIII. See also Jackson *Weekly Mississippian*, November 13, 1861. For

Although the governor had personally tasted the bitter sorrow of war, he found the strength to address the opening of the regular session of the legislature on November 4, 1861. As anticipated, his discourse centered upon military themes. At least 35,000 men, it was pointed out, had responded to the recent summons for 10,000 troops, thus demonstrating "a unanimity unparalleled in the history of republican governments." Pettus felt that the only shortcoming appeared to be that he had not been given the authority to better prepare these forces to meet the enemy.[14] Nevertheless, 4,000 double-barreled shotguns and rifles were in the hands of volunteers. But this was not enough, and the governor chided the legislators for not doing more toward financing the war effort. Specifically, he had been unable to obtain gold or silver through the sale of treasury bonds authorized earlier.[15] This had forced him to use bonds as promissory notes for the purchase of military supplies. The state, Pettus insisted, must develop "some well-digested financial scheme" to meet the emergency. As a partial remedy, he suggested that the lawmakers allow the Confederate government to become the only source of paper currency, instead of having the state resort to printing its own inflated money. As if to underscore his personal interest in a policy of conserving funds for the war effort, Pettus let it be known that the capitol building was not to be repainted because the price seemed excessive.

In final words of disgust the Mississippi chief executive urged, as he had done during the previous summer, that the legislature abolish the abominable Military Board and that a "less expensive and less complicated system" be devised. He warned that the state might soon be plundered by northerners and that he was equally certain the "magnitude and duration of the war" were

---

impact of the battle consult E. P. Alexander, *Military Memoirs of A Confederate: A Critical Narrative* (Bloomington, Ind., 1962), 57–58.

[14] Mississippi *House Journal* (November, 1861), 10–15.

[15] The bonds spoken of were initially subscribed to in large quantities. Due, however, to rapid inflation they were no longer considered a good risk. See Woodville *Republican*, July 13, 1861; W. A. C. Loupety to Pettus, June 17, 1861, in Governor's Correspondence, Vol. LII.

not "fully appreciated" by many of the lawmakers. "We must triumph or perish," he insisted.[16]

While the solons pondered the straightforward message, political and military minded Mississippians made it clear that the truth had been spoken. The Jackson *Weekly Mississippian* called the address "able and sound" and stood beside the governor in the belief that the "war must go until peace can be made upon our own terms." Elsewhere, free Negroes were known to have given as high as one hundred bushels of corn to the war effort, while patriotic whites concluded that the Yankees must be defeated at any cost so that "if our friends fall we have the consolation in knowing that they fell in a noble cause."[17]

Slowly the legislature began to respond to the problems outlined by the governor. By late November it had taken steps to permit borrowing on state treasury notes for weapons purchases and to allow Pettus to call up state militia units for duty, but only for the ridiculously short period of sixty days. Such other pressing demands as the acquisition of tents, economic help for poverty-stricken families of state troops, the rising cost of salt, provisions for hospitals, and a host of other difficulties were scarcely attended to.[18] Unfortunately, Governor Pettus alone could find no lasting solutions to these issues; without legislative assistance, he was often rendered helpless.

The legislators gathered at Jackson remained sluggish, apparently failing to grasp the urgency of the circumstances at hand. It was not until December 16 that the lawmakers got around to providing some minor method of relief for destitute families whose men were in uniform. And while an act permitting the governor to set up hospitals was also passed, the accompanying stipend amounted to a paltry $25,000. No gen-

[16] Mississippi *House Journal* (November, 1861), 16.
[17] Jackson *Weekly Mississippian*, November 13, 1861; H. Reynolds to Pettus, November 6, 1861, E. W. Freely to Pettus, November 5, 1861, in Governor's Correspondence, Vol. LIV.
[18] Mississippi, *Laws of the State of Mississippi* (November, 1861–January, 1862), 45, 48–49; Pettus to Madison McAfee, November 27, 1861, Reuben Davis to Pettus, November 28, 1861, G. W. Brume to Pettus, November 28, 1861, in Governor's Correspondence, Vol. LIV.

eral appropriation for the military was sanctioned—only individual companies were designated to receive funds.[19]

Up to this point legislative reaction to the growing list of troubles was casual, at best. But with the unfolding of other events, the lawmakers were spurred into motion. Specifically, it was the fear of slave unrest and the thought that bondsmen would, if given the opportunity, join federal troops and slay white people that must have aroused the legislature. In rapid fashion they reinforced slave laws so that no black could "reside at any distance greater than one mile from the residence of the master." Such sentiment spilled over into military affairs; all original twelve-month volunteers were now ordered to remain in the service for an indefinite period. Similarly, $250,000 was appropriated for the procurement of gunboats to defend the Gulf Coast, volunteer and militia units were unified into a single command structure, and the objectionable Military Board was abolished.[20]

Another thorny question that had persevered for some time was that of cotton. In the face of wartime requirements for subsistence commodities and the growing reality of Lincoln's blockade, Governor Pettus advocated the elimination of most cotton production. Displaying a profound ability to grasp both the meaning of war and the demands of it, he suggested that the raising of staple cotton be replaced by wheat or corn production. To enforce this plan, Pettus recommended to the state legislature that the tax structure be adjusted so as to discourage persons who insisted on continuing to cultivate the product in large quantity. He reasoned that the war would drive the price of cotton up. In turn, this would stimulate the demand for other fabrics. "The people of the world must wear clothes, and if they cannot get cotton, they will make them of hemp, flax and wool." More important, Pettus said, if the federal blockade of southern

[19] Mississippi, *Laws of the State of Mississippi* (November, 1861–January, 1862), 53–58, 67–73.
[20] C. G. Dahlgren to Pettus, December 5, 1861, in Governor's Correspondence, Vol. LIV; Mississippi, *Laws of the State of Mississippi* (November, 1861–January, 1862), 82, 132–33, 142–43, 176, 220–21.

ports "should last five years, there would not be as great a demand for our cotton" at the end of the conflict as there was at present. Cotton, if continued to be used in world markets, would likely be imported from some nation other than the Confederate States of America. Despite the validity of the governor's argument, the legislature failed to act on his plan and thereby unofficially condoned the unlimited raising of cotton. One prime reason was the fact that many large and influential planters had adopted the practice of issuing their own money, and used their crops as security for it.[21] In any event, cotton was still king and Pettus was clearly against the mainstream of thought on the matter.

In the meantime, the ever-present specter of warfare prompted the Mississippi governor to take additional steps to insure the defense of the state and the well-being of its troops. He pressed convicts at the state penitentiary in Jackson into service weaving cloth for uniforms, and he strengthened the defense of the vital city of Vicksburg. As the Gulf Coast was still somewhat exposed, Pettus asked President Davis not to order the Third Regiment of Mississippi Volunteers out of the state, and assign them to the coast instead.[22] This request was granted, but too late. In early January, 1862, the enemy landed on Mississippi's shore in force. Twenty additional companies were immediately called up for active duty, but the emergency soon passed, as the bluecoats retired from the area.

By 1862, the riddle of insuring a continuous flow of military supplies proved far from being resolved. A late December report from state Brigadier General James Alcorn warned that Confederate authorities would be forced to either release or disband Mississippi troops from service, for want of provisions. The factors responsible for this deplorable situation were many.

[21] Pettus to the Legislature, December 4, 1861, in Governor's Executive Journal, 1857–1870, 330–31; Natchez *Daily Courier*, December 18, 1861.
[22] Pettus to Davis, December 12, January 2, 1861, Davis to Pettus, December 13, 1861, John J. McRae to Jefferson Davis, December 14, 1861, in *Official Records*, Ser. I, Vol. VI, 780–81.

Prices of powder and shot rose rapidly, while speculators refused to accept state treasury notes as payment for such supplies. Previous action by the Military Board, calling for cash-on-the-line, was believed to be at the bottom of this dilemma, as well as unadjusted financial claims between the Richmond government and the state. Governor Pettus was forced into the position of asking twelve-month volunteers to serve for less time in order to save on expenses.[23]

In an effort to correct or at least ease the strain of such deficiencies, Pettus endeavored to secure much needed capital by attempting to sell state bonds to financial houses in Virginia. Likewise, he instructed local police boards to seize all available firearms. Additional gunboats were ordered, and by late February, 1862, the governor had managed to prevail upon Confederate authorities to accept into service all Mississippians, whether armed or not, "as fast as they are sworn."[24]

But the secession spirit was beginning to wane. From Hancock County came the news that between three and four hundred men, characterized as "deserters," had banded together and sworn not to serve in the army. Some of their number had even gone over to the federals, while a few turned a profit by "pillaging and plundering private property." Similar incidents of banditry as well as pro-Union sentiment surfaced in other sections of the state. From Vicksburg it was reported that many persons were taking an oath of allegiance to Lincoln's government, while in Baldwin people were accused of being overjoyed when "hearing of our soldiers being sick and dying." Trouble in the ranks of certain military units operating around Oxford was also brought to the governor's attention. Thomas W. Caskey

[23] Alcorn to Pettus, December 20, 1861, C. G. Dahlgren to Pettus, January 2, 1862, Edward Fontaine to Pettus, January 11, 1862, in Governor's Correspondence, Vol. LVI; Pettus to A. S. Johnston, December 2, 1861, January 7, 31, 1863 in Official Records, Ser. I, Vol. VII, 732–33, 823–24, 851.
[24] Thomas Brach to Pettus, January 22, 1861, Edward Jack to Pettus, March 17, 1862, Judah P. Benjamin to Pettus, February 21, 1862, in Governor's Correspondence, Vols. LVI, LXIII; Pettus to Withers, February 15, 1862, in Governor's Executive Journal, 1857–1870, 351.

reported the constant struggle of his men "for petty power," attributing such conditions to "poor human nature."[25]

These disturbing reports were often disputed throughout the state. The Jackson *Daily Mississippian* minimized the adverse military situation by concluding that it was often caused by "sensational dispatches from nervous Generals." A writer from Enterprise assured Governor Pettus that eastern Mississippi was "a perfect blaze of patriotism." Even General Pierre G. T. Beauregard sounded a note of optimism when he told the governor that there was "life in the Old Land yet."[26] The general consensus seemed to be that things were not all that bad, Mississippians holding to the idea that the state possessed sufficient manpower to defend itself from any adversary.

True, all was not quite as dark as it appeared on the surface. Countless examples of cooperation, patriotism, and unflagging devotion dot the contemporary evidence of the period. For instance, a former British subject gave one-fourth of everything he possessed to aid the southern cause. In religious circles, Catholic nuns did considerable charity work, setting up hospitals and caring for wounded soldiers. Women in Vicksburg manufactured hats, took the place of men as schoolteachers, and cooked for the war effort. The bell in a Baptist Church at Jackson was taken down, melted, and made into a cannon, then given to state authorities.[27]

Not satisfied with letting matters take their own course, Governor Pettus came to favor some sort of Confederate conscrip-

[25] Howard W. Wilkinson to Pettus, January 1, 1862, W. J. Reeves to Pettus, January 5, 1862, C. G. Dahlgren to Pettus, January 12, 1862, D. L. Smythe to Pettus, March 4, 1862, Caskey to Pettus, March 15, 1862, in Governor's Correspondence, Vol. LVI.

[26] Jackson *Daily Mississippian*, January 27, 1861; John W. O'Ferrall to Pettus, February 19, 1862, Beauregard to Pettus, March 8, 1862, in Governor's Correspondence, Vol. LVI.

[27] James Stewart to Pettus, March 10, 1862, C. Johnson et al. to Pettus, March 3, 1862, in Governor's Correspondence, Vol. LVI; Mother M. Bernard, *The Story of the Sisters of Mercy in Mississippi, 1860–1930* (New York, 1931), 12–19; Francis B. Simkins and James W. Patton, *The Women of the Confederacy* (New York, 1936), 117.

tion measure as a viable solution to the growing complexity of military affairs in early 1862. His attitude was undoubtedly influenced by the fact that Confederate personnel were recruiting men for twelve months of duty, with the promise of letting them out in time for spring planting. To many, this prospect was more appealing than that of joining state forces, which were now required to remain in the ranks until all hostilities ceased. The general public, judging from available correspondence, was cognizant of both the internal and external reasons for a military draft. So confident was the governor of constituent acceptance of a conscription policy, that he informed General Beauregard that the people were "much excited and ready to sacrifice anything necessary for success." Pettus anticipated no difficulties in raising men by such means. Convinced that a Confederate conscription policy would be enacted, he even planned to extend it to foreign citizens living within the state.[28]

Several of the overriding problems of early 1862 concerned inflation, the procurement of food, and salt—problems that affected civilian and military sectors alike. "Our people," wrote an Enterprise resident, "are much distressed for salt." Pettus' response to such a call was both rapid and positive, although not always successful. Contracts were let for 50,000 sacks of salt and commissioners were dispatched to New Orleans for that purpose. Much to the regret of many, salt could be obtained only on a "strictly cash" basis. Rapid depreciation of the Confederate dollar certainly played a role at this stage; each such dollar was worth only sixty cents in buying power by February, 1862.[29]

[28] J. Phelan to Pettus, February 10, 1862, Resolutions of Columbus, Mississippi, Town Meeting, February 10, 1862; John Battiff to Pettus, February 12, 1862, George Coppell to Pettus, February 26, 1862, in Governor's Correspondence, Vol. LVI; Pettus to Beauregard, February 24, 1862, in *Official Records*, Ser. I, Vol. LII, Part II, 276.

[29] Moody O'Ferrall to Pettus, January 1, 1862, J. N. Baker to Pettus, January 17, 1862, John Magee and Everret George to Pettus, February 7, 1862, in Governor's Correspondence, Vol. LVI; Wood, *Confederate Handbook*, 76. For official Confederate evaluation of the impact of the blockade on salt imports, see George Goldthwaite to Duff C. Green, March 20, 1862, in *Official Records*, Ser. IV, Vol. I, 1010.

Periodic thrusts by the federals into the state not only further weakened the governor's ability to procure supplies, but also caused a lack of confidence among Mississippians. One constituent compared the southern struggle with the Revolutionary War, equated Union troops with those of Britain in terms of ability, and sadly deplored the "unprepared [military] state in which we have been allowed to remain." Others had so "utterly lost their confidence in the generalship of Gen. A. S. Johnston" that they advocated that President Davis act as his own general and go into the field to lead the troops.[30]

Perhaps the most telling piece of news regarding supply procurement came in the form of a report issued by ordnance officer Edward Fontaine. The report made it clear that prices of war materials were rising sharply and that businessmen were refusing to take paper money in exchange for goods. "Some action must be taken by the State," wrote Fontaine, to counter the "cowardly, yankee spirited note-shaving" segment of society; otherwise "the money grasping knaves at home will deliver our state to Lincoln." Indeed, it was evident that at least a few persons were more concerned with selling cotton than they were with the war effort.[31]

Always abreast of military affairs, Governor Pettus continued to fortify Vicksburg, notifying the War Department that "any amount of labor [was] ready" to help with building projects. Elsewhere, Pettus met with the new governor of Alabama, J. Gill Shorter, for the purpose of discussing a program of regional defense, cooperative security, and economic stabilization. However, the conference produced only gloom, revealing the fact that the joint Alabama–Mississippi project of procuring gunboats had been halted by arguments over who should receive contracts and to what specifications the vessels should be built. To compound things still further, a gun factory at Aberdeen, Mississip-

[30] Entries for February 7, 10, 1862, in William A. Drennan Diary, Mississippi Department of Archives and History; A. B. Bacon to Jefferson Davs, February 25, 1862, in Jefferson Davis Papers, Duke University Library.
[31] Fontaine to Pettus, January 11, 1862, in Governor's Correspondence, Vol. LVI; Entry for January 22, 1862, in William A. Drennan Diary.

pi, which was used to supply the needs of both states, accidentally burned to the ground.[32]

The arrival of spring brought military reality home to Mississippians as never before. Until that time, federal troops had
posed no serious threat to the state. But during the early months
of 1862 Union Generals Don Carlos Buell and Ulysses S. Grant
arrived at Pittsburg Landing, Tennessee—just a few miles from
the northeastern border of Mississippi. From the city of Corinth,
Mississippi, a Confederate army under Beauregard was ordered
out to check any Union advance. At a place known as Shiloh the
two opposing armies met on April 6 with such intensity as to
place the ensuing battle in the pages of history as one of the
deadliest of the entire war. Badly outnumbered, the Confederates were forced from the field and retreated to Corinth for
reorganization and reinforcement.

Not content to remain idle, Yankee General Henry Halleck
soon followed the southerners to Corinth on April 28. No sooner
had Halleck arrived at Corinth and began to plan for a siege,
when Beauregard withdrew to Tupelo, Mississippi. The loss of
Corinth cost the Confederates much needed railroad facilities
and opened the state to further federal progress. Beauregard
partially blamed his military reverses on a "lack of proper food,"
which had caused sickness and disease to infest his army while
it was at Corinth. Fortunately for the rest of Mississippi, Halleck
did not elect to proceed deeper into the state for fear that the
summer heat might reduce the effectiveness of his troops.[33]

Elsewhere, federal forces continued to enjoy considerable
success on the military front throughout the same period. Between April and June, New Orleans was occupied, Memphis fell
into enemy hands, and northern Admiral David G. Farragut
dramatically illustrated the inability of Vicksburg to completely

[32] Pettus to Judah P. Benjamin, March 18, 1862, in Telegrams Received by the
CSA Secretary of War; C. G. Dahlgren to Pettus, March 8, 1862, E. C. Eggleston
to Pettus, April 7, 1862, in Governor's Correspondence, Vol. LVI.
[33] E. B. Long and Barbara Long, *The Civil War Day by Day: An Almanac
1861–1865* (New York, 1971), 221; H. H. Cunningham, *Doctors In Gray: The
Confederate Medical Service* (Baton Rouge, 1958), 177; Archer Jones, *Confederate Strategy From Shiloh to Vicksburg* (Baton Rouge, 1961), 57.

restrict Yankee movement on that portion of the Mississippi River by sailing past the batteries stationed there. As Union activity in and around Mississippi increased, so did disenchantment and disloyalty. Even while the pros and cons of a southern draft were still being debated, it was noted that the "spirit of volunteering" was already a dead letter. In Kosciusko babies were named in honor of the northern president, and open declarations expressing a willingness to "fight for Lincoln and his murderous self" were heard. A resident of Canton, while assuring Governor Pettus that many would resist the federals "in guerrilla warfare as long as they live," reluctantly admitted that a mounting pro-Union sentiment was in the wind. So alarmed over disloyal neighbors were Sunflower and Hinds countians that the drastic step of declaring martial law was proposed, along with using slaves as soldiers to smash such attitudes.[34]

Under the circumstances, the Pettus administration was often a convenient focal point for criticism. A Noxubee County newspaper editor, who was quite put out by displays of false allegiance, complained that it was the fault of the governor—who was guilty of "much talk, but no definite action." But it was the Natchez *Daily Courier* that issued the most pungent indictment, charging unqualified condemnation of politicians who would sit "in a comfortable chair and put up forts, plan campaigns, discipline armies," and win paper victories by the dozen.[35]

Still other less dramatic, but significant, expressions of disloyalty or personal self-indulgence were in evidence—even from the state's law-makers. The legislature, having failed to heed the governor's warning earlier in the year regarding cotton production, had thereby left the door open for unlimited cultivation of the product. When Pettus was notified that large stores of cotton were being accumulated in towns, in flagrant disregard to his pleadings to the contrary, he sprang to action. Since these stores

---

[34] V. M. White to Pettus, March 21, 1862, "A True Southern Girl" to Pettus, April 17, 1862, Franklin Smith to Pettus, April 25, 1862, James B. Walton et al. to Pettus, April, 1862, H. S. Dabney to Pettus April 28, 1862, in Governor's Correspondence, Vol. LVI.

[35] Macon *Beacon* April 16, 1862; Natchez *Daily Courier*, June 4, 1862.

ran the risk of falling into enemy hands, he took it upon himself to call upon the loyal citizenry to "silence those who love money more than their liberties." Pettus said that every bale of cotton taken from Mississippi would be a disgrace to the state, and if he failed to do everything in his power to prevent such action, he would personally "feel disgraced." Many Mississippians, however, did cooperate in this endeavor, if for no other reason than necessity. A typical example was one Sydney S. Champion, who reminded his wife to be sure "and make a good crop of corn" because "the object of our enemies is to starve us."[36]

While many individuals did forego staple cotton production, others did not elect to follow suit. Notable among the latter was Miles H. McGehee of Bolivar County. Opposed to secession before the war, McGehee attempted to make the best of a bad situation by selling cotton to northern merchants in occupied Memphis. When challenged by angry neighbors, McGehee hid several hundred bales "out in the cane." Such conditions left Governor Pettus no choice other than to issue an executive proclamation deeming it "unwise" to permit the unrestricted cultivation of cotton and requiring that growers "plant not more than one acre to the hand . . . and the remainder of their arable land in grain." Such a policy was, at least in some quarters, welcomed and accounted for as being long overdue. However, resistance to this plan soon became more a matter of necessity than disloyalty. For in order to obtain funds the legislature had established a "cotton money" policy, which meant that "any owner of cotton could draw five cents a pound from the State, if he would apply to the Governor and promise to deliver to the Governor the cotton whenever he should call for it."[37] Hence, should cotton production be curtailed, vital income would be

---

[36] S. Durham to Pettus, April 15, 1862, David Fulton to Pettus, April 25, 1862, Pettus to W. L. Poindexter, May 2, 1862, in Governor's Correspondence, Vol. LVI; Champion to Matilda Champion, May 24, 1862, in Sydney S. Champion Papers, Duke University Library, Durham, N.C.

[37] Montgomery, *Reminiscences of a Mississippian*, 77–78; Natchez *Weekly Courier*, May 28, 1862; Canton *American Citizen*, June 6, 1862; Thomas B. Carroll, *Historical Sketches of Oktibbeha County* (Gulfport, Miss., 1931), 107.

lost and, in turn, would have the effect of compounding economic hardships already present.

The military situation in the spring and early summer of 1862 continued to worsen on the home front. When in mid-May, for example, the federals carried out a brief raid on the outskirts of the city of Jackson, the emotional aftermath was almost predictable. Nevertheless, it was in the western part of the state that cause for alarm reached high levels. During May, 1862, the federal commanders began showing signs of interest in Vicksburg. Long recognized as being of extreme value, the city now took on top priority status.

Union ships were sent up the river from New Orleans toward Vicksburg in early May. Along the way one of the vessels passed the city of Natchez and was welcomed not by gunfire, but by a crowd of "men, women and children who cheared [sic] loudly for Jefferson Davis and the Confederate flag." The same vessel, the U.S.S. *Oneida*, made its way to Vicksburg and on May 18, 1862, the commander requested the surrender of the city. His efforts were answered by a volley of cannon fire.[38]

In June and July, Yankee troops stationed themselves across the river from Vicksburg on the Louisiana side. Although no actual direct major assault on the city transpired, rumors circulated far and wide that the northerners intended to construct a canal which would divert the course of the Mississippi River, thus leaving Vicksburg "high and dry." Efforts toward this end were shortly abandoned in favor of a month and a half siege, during which time an estimated 25,000–30,000 various types of shells were sent into the city from Union guns. The resulting casualties were surprisingly small, "there being but twenty-one soldiers killed and wounded, and one female and a negro killed."[39]

For his part, Governor Pettus was not idle through all this. At the first sign of trouble he issued a verbal commitment that

[38] Entries for May 12, 18, 1862, in U.S.S. *Oneida* Diary, University of North Carolina Library, Chapel Hill, N.C.
[39] Alexander S. Abrams, *A Full and Detailed History of the Siege of Vicksburg* (Atlanta, 1863), 7.

both he and the rest of the people of the state intended to resist aggression to the last man. The Vicksburg *Daily Whig* of May 15, however, was quick to point out that the residents of that river community were not interested in consigning their city to flames before surrendering, as the governor would surely advocate. As if to reassure the citizens of his good intentions, Pettus called out 2,000 more troops and personally dashed to the scene in the company of General Earl Van Dorn, the new Confederate commander of the city. For his part, Van Dorn lost no time in preparing the defenses there, even going so far as to seize a shipment of arms destined for the state of Louisiana. Pettus, on the other hand, returned to Jackson. Writing Van Dorn that he heard "the heavy guns from your beleaguered city," the governor expressed the encouraging belief that he had no doubts as to the result the Confederate general would achieve.[40]

Although in late July the federals discarded any large-scale effort to take Vicksburg, the subsequent siege did generate moments of controversy, especially afterward. William P. Johnston, special adjutant to President Davis, was sent to the area in order to demonstrate Richmond's official concern for the welfare of Vicksburg. His report noted that no real crisis existed and that defense preparations were most adequate. Another investigator reached the same conclusion, noting that the city was so well protected that state militia would be capable of defending it in the future without much difficulty. Hence, Confederate forces already there could be released for other duties. To this Pettus violently objected. Sensitive to the needs of his own state, the governor called attention to the fact that Mississippi had already been discriminated against in terms of its share of central government support, and he was not about to detail state troops for simple guard duty. Richmond authorities should know the importance of Vicksburg and see to it that constant vigilance was maintained.[41]

[40] Thomas Adams to Van Dorn, June 23, 1862, Pettus to Van Dorn, July 25, 1862, in Earl Van Dorn Letters and Telegrams, Library of Congress, Washington, D.C.
[41] Johnston to Pettus, July 29, 1862, in Governor's Correspondence, Vol. LVII;

The governor was apparently not the only one to view the role of the Richmond government with suspicion and distrust. The Hinds County *Gazette* seemed to indicate that President Davis was somehow responsible for allowing the federals anywhere close to Vicksburg in the first place. Calling Davis "a blockhead" who followed the lead of "parlor generals from morning to night," the paper on August 6, 1862, demanded that steps be taken to see to it that this sort of thing did not happen again. But at least one observer saw events at Vicksburg in a different light. A Confederate soldier at Vicksburg, Sydney Champion, emerged from the affair with a bitter resentment toward "the planters around [who] do not deserve to be protected." For these individuals had done nothing during the siege to aid the plight of the ordinary soldier, who had given up life's "ease and pleasure—to fight and protect those, who now extort the last pound of flesh, for the common necessaries of subsistence." Prices charged for goods during the siege, by merchants and planters alike, were too high. If it was not for his own family, the same soldier indicated that he "would be glad to see [Vicksburg] plundered and burnt to the ground." "A day of retaliation is coming," he warned; "we will not forget them."[42]

In a wider sense, the federal activities around Vicksburg and elsewhere served to stimulate panic and fear throughout Mississippi. All this made Governor Pettus' job increasingly difficult, as did a host of new or revitalized problems which confronted him during the same spring and summer months of 1862.

With the rise of military confrontation, a number of Mississippians took another look at their part in the war effort. Many individuals failed to report for military duty, in defiance of the Confederate Conscription Act of April, 1862. Similarly, sheriffs often bowed to local pressure and disobeyed the governor's order to collect all available guns within their jurisdiction. Vio-

Pettus to Jefferson Davis, July 27, 1862, in *Official Records*, Ser. I, Vol. LII, Part II, 332; Sterling Price to Earl Van Dorn July 21, 1862, Sterling Price to Pettus, August 4, 1862, in *Official Records*, Ser. I, Vol. XVII, Part II, 664–65.
[42] Sydney Champion to Matilda Champion, September 26, 1862, in Sydney S. Champion Papers.

lations of liquor laws were not enforced, military supplies remained short, and high prices prevailed.

Special fears relating to the possibility of slave rebellions also had to be contended with. In fact some constituents were more apprehensive about being killed by runaway Negroes than they were about confronting the federals. This condition forced Pettus to beg General Beauregard to detail several companies of men into Mississippi "to create a sense of security among the people and keep down any disorders among the slaves." Pettus supplemented these Confederate forces with 3,000 men from state troops, being careful to assure them that their call-up would not obligate them for Confederate conscription.[43]

Governor Pettus interpreted his prime function as that of looking to the safety of his own state, first. In so doing, however, it often brought him into disagreement with Confederate officials, especially when it came to the issue of military conscription. Confederate conscripting officers undertook their responsibilities in Mississippi shortly after the draft law went into effect. At first, response to their activity was mild, but before long, when the Richmond officials began to accomplish their task with special zeal, a number of questions came to the governor's attention. Since regulations concerning draft exemptions were not altogether specific, Pettus had to personally request that President Davis excuse tanners and gunsmiths from service for the good of the cause. As the weeks wore on, conscription officers began laying hold of a large number of planters and overseers. The inherent dangers were obvious. Pettus again contacted the Confederate president for advice, lamenting that there were "not white persons sufficient to keep the slaves in subordination." If something was not done, wrote Pettus, crop production would diminish by 55 percent, "if nothing worse happens from leaving so many Negroes with no managers." Only

---

[43] Pettus to Beauregard, May 1, 1862, in *Official Records*, Ser. I, Vol. LII, Part II, 309; Natchez *Weekly Courier*, May 6, 1862. The threat of Negro insurrection was apparently very real. In Natchez alone some eighty blacks had been either hanged or jailed since the opening of the war. See A. K. Farrar to Pettus, July 17, 1862, in Governor's Correspondence, Vol. LVII.

Davis could resolve this situation which the governor found himself "very greatly embarrassed" at being unable to control.[44] President Davis knew of the problems Pettus faced, but could only tell the governor that Congress had not yet made allowances for this emergency. The law would later be corrected in October, 1862, to provide for draft exemptions for plantation managers.

The spirit of sacrifice in Mississippi was indeed on the wane. Overseers, planters, millers, blacksmiths, gunsmiths, and even hatters, found common bond in seeking to avoid Confederate conscription. So thorough were the impressment officers in performing their duty that lightly populated Issaquena County was literally "drained of its white male population." The intense hunt for manpower in Clark and Newton counties was bewailed in the pages of the Jackson *Weekly Mississippian*. All Governor Pettus could do was sympathize with such grievances and inform would-be exemptioners that "state authorities . . . [were] entirely ignored" in the matter.[45]

Resistance to the draft was often coupled with outright desertion from the army. More often than not, at this stage of the war, the ranks of the military were diminished by the desire of soldiers to protect home and family, rather than cowardice or blatant disloyalty. Nevertheless, Mississippi soon earned a reputation as "deserter-country," and such knowledge was reinforced by the fact that the southernmost counties of the state were swarming "with deserters from almost every organization."[46]

Desertion and draft-dodging only led to a further tightening of military regulations. General Beauregard outlined the official Confederate position on the subject of abandoning one's military duty when he told Pettus that "all soldiers not regularly provided

[44] Davis to Pettus, May 1, 1862, in *Official Records*, Ser. IV, Vol. I, 1110; Pettus to Davis, May 14, 1862, in Jefferson Davis Papers, Duke University Library.

[45] C. L. Buck to Pettus, June 7, 1862, Ethelbert Barksdale to Pettus, June 25, 1862, Comment on letter from A. B. Longstreet to Pettus, June 7, 1862, in Governor's Correspondence, Vol. LVII.

[46] Ella Lonn, *Desertion During the Civil War* (New York, 1928), 229; Assistant Adjutant General Harrison to John C. Pemberton, June 6, 1862, in *Official Records*, Ser. I, Vol. II, Part II, 493.

with sick leaves or furloughs must be arrested and treated as deserters." The governor elected not to enforce this request, since Mississippi herself could use all the men she could get— whether Confederate deserters or not. It is quite possible that a state draft would have been more agreeable to the average citizen.[47]

Forced to seek a middle ground, Governor Pettus initiated a "minute-man" program—approximately two companies from each state regiment would be detailed to patrol the countryside, guard against slave unrest, and engage Yankee troops whenever possible. The minute-men were to operate as free agents and hopefully be able to move at a moment's notice to wherever they might be needed. Although this strategy was designed to pacify the public clamour for protection against possible slave revolt and circumvent the Confederate draft at the same time by allowing men to remain near their homes, it drew skepticism. Specifically, detractors charged that any unattached company, whether acting under state jurisdiction or not, was sure to be forced into the service of Richmond.[48]

Efforts by the Mississippi governor to procure Confederate military aid for his region often proved exasperating. In fact, President Davis freely admitted that his personal ability "to provide for the military wants" of the Magnolia State was "sadly frustrated." Pettus, left to rely on energetic measures of his own, on one occasion literally hijacked a shipment of rifles bound for government troops, but such measures could only partially alleviate the situation. It was no wonder that 1862 military life was far from attractive to the average Mississippian. Weapons were scarce and so were proper provisions. Hospital facilities were not the best either, and the prospective soldier knew it. One doctor reported that Early Grove medical care ranked far inferior to what was available elsewhere. Describing Columbus, Mississippi, as "one vast hospital," a Presbyterian minister de-

[47] Beauregard to Pettus, June 10, 1862, in Governor's Correspondence, Vol. LXIII; Albert B. Moore, *Conscription and Conflict In the Confederacy* (New York, 1924), 360.
[48] Jackson *Daily Mississippian*, June 9, 1862.

plored a situation in which "many miserable wretches died" for
want of proper attention. Prisoners, "especially the wounded
ones, suffered egregiously."[49]

Salt remained yet another critical problem with which civilian and military sectors alike had to contend. State sources,
particularly at Aberdeen and Columbus, could yield only limited
quantities of salt, so the governor dispatched commissioners
to Alabama, Louisiana, and Virginia in search of the item. The
envoys soon reported that there was either none for sale, or that
prices were excessive—as high as $100 a sack. It was further
noted that railroad officials demanded abnormally high shipping
rates, or refused to haul the product altogether. Other items of
equal necessity were also found to be in such short supply that
illegal trade with the federal army and northern merchants
mushroomed dramatically. Lumber was freely exchanged with
Union-controlled New Orleans, and cotton was not only grown
in defiance of executive order, but certain individuals openly
favored making money from the practice. It seemed to be a
choice between starvation or military execution. The temptation
to participate in this kind of activity was surely encouraged by
the Union commander at New Orleans, Benjamin F. Butler, who
"gave assurances to planters that any sugar or cotton sent to
that city would be bought by the United States with specie."[50]

Repeatedly taxed by these and other infractions, Pettus responded by ordering that all cotton in danger of being seized by
the federals or traded to them be burned. A member of the
"Yazoo Rangers" noted that while some persons were able to
hide the staple, he destroyed 771 bales between June 26 and
July 3, 1862. Seemingly in opposition to the governor's stand,
certain planters and overseers simply abandoned cotton stores

---

[49] Davis to Pettus, June 19, 1862, in Rowland (ed.), *Jefferson Davis Constitutionalist*, IV, 282; William D. Somers to "Kind Friend," June 10, 1862, in William
D. Somers Papers, Duke University Library, Durham, N.C.; Entry for Summer,
1862, in Journal of Reverend James A. Lyon.

[50] L. J. Wilson to Pettus, July 1862, John H. Lenow to Pettus, July 4, 1862,
J. R. Fall to Pettus, July 11, 1862, Isaac Applewhite to Pettus, July 15, 1862, in
Governor's Correspondence, Vol. LVII; Gerald M. Capers, *Occupied City: New
Orleans Under the Federals, 1862–1865* (Lexington, Ky., 1965), 82.

to the enemy without raising a finger, or allowed slaves to flee into federal lines. Undoubtedly, the governor would have derived some satisfaction if he had known that the Yankees faced the same type of problems with officers who engaged in "*a speculating scheme*" when it came to cotton profits.[51]

As if the ordinary perils of wartime life were not enough, manifestations of disloyalty continued to increase. In particular, the northeastern portion of the state furnished much pro-Union sentiment, even to the point where nearly one hundred persons openly attended anti-Confederate rallies, while others collaborated with the enemy in various ways.[52]

Under such conditions Governor Pettus sought to command the faith of the people by bolstering his policies with coercion and an assortment of devices designed to tighten the conscription laws. Indignant cries of protest ensued, but there was little alternative. Requests for more security from bands of federals poured into the offices of state authorities. A Coffeeville resident noted that Union troops were "demoralizing the negro population" and granting amnesty to whites who joined their ranks. Nearly sixty men had already taken the Yankees up on the offer and had been mustered into the army at New Orleans. Nevertheless, Governor Pettus continued to see that as many individuals as were available entered the southern armed forces. The Canton *American Citizen*, commenting on the governor's actions and the growing shortage of manpower, gave a facetious summary of recent conscripts—noting that some were deaf, blind, or otherwise handicapped. "One had enlargement of the spleen; another, asthma; a third, rheumatism; a fourth, disease of the heart; a fifth, liver complaint; a sixth, chronic diarrhea."[53]

As the number of persons forcibly conscripted into military service rose, so did the level of desertions. Significant quantities

[51] H. M. Thompson to Pettus, July 3, 1862, E. L. Acee to Pettus, July 29, 1862, in Governor's Correspondence, Vol. LVII; Sam Stafford to Abby Stafford, August 5, 1862, in Abby E. Stafford Papers, Duke University Library, Durham, N.C.
[52] John H. Aughey, *Tupelo* (Lincoln, Neb., 1888), 79–80.
[53] W. Cooper to Pettus, August 9, 1862, in Governor's Correspondence, Vol. LVII; Canton *American Citizen*, August 8, 1862.

of Mississippians simply left their assigned units and returned home in the summer of 1862. And it was because of this that Pettus was ultimately forced to reverse his earlier policy of leniency toward deserters by ordering the arrest of anyone absent without leave from his assigned unit. The public was outraged. In Canton a rally was held and the residents demanded the impossible—a furlough for "all the militia in the field." Eventually Pettus was pressured into modifying his hard-line approach to the questions of dissension and disloyalty, proof enough that it had lacked wisdom and forethought. The major reason for this change of heart appears to have been the realization that, in the governor's eagerness to aid the Richmond government, he had sent too many conscripts into Confederate service. Learning that he did not have enough men to police his own state properly, Pettus appealed to General Earl Van Dorn to release Mississippians from his command so that they might be sent "where the people are calling." Additional troops from the Confederate manpower pool were also requested along with a reorganization of several state commands "for service on the river." [54]

Pettus next turned his attention once more to the matter of feeding his constituents. The salt situation had worsened, becoming critical by the fall of 1862. Large quantities of pork in northern Mississippi had already been lost because the preservative was not available. Jefferson Davis attempted as best he could to aid the beleaguered Governor Pettus by announcing that General Richard Taylor had been placed in charge of procuring salt from Louisiana mines. At this point, a source of salt was revealed at New Iberia, Louisiana, with the estimated cost of extracting it placed at approximately $75 per sack. Believing that anything was worth a try, Pettus requested one thousand

[54] Canton *American Citizen*, September 26, 1862; Pettus to Van Dorn, August 4, 1862, Pettus to Gideon J. Pillow, September 7, 1862, Pettus to W. C. Chambiss, September 3, 1862, Pettus to A. K. Farrar, September 6, 1862, in Governor's Correspondence, Vols. LVII, LVIII; Pettus to Van Dorn, September 17, 1862, in Earl Van Dorn Papers, Alabama Department of Archives and History, Montgomery, Alabama.

men to work the mine. When no word was received from President Davis regarding the matter, the governor issued another communiqué, forcefully urging that "vigorous action" be taken.[55] The appeal was eventually answered affirmatively.

From every corner of Mississippi came notices relating the scarcity of salt, and because of this a dramatic change in the tone of even the most loyal of constituents was in evidence. Requests for permission to exchange cotton with the federals for salt poured into the state executive mansion. Gradually Pettus began to weaken from his long-standing policy of no truck with the enemy and told Jefferson Davis that he was now willing to allow the exchange of cotton for salt. There was "no reason weighty enough against it to counterbalance the great utility and necessity" for doing so.[56]

When no confirmation of the new plan was forthcoming, Pettus once more, in unmistakable terms, notified the president that the bartering of cotton for salt was regarded "as a necessity." Although Davis soon reassured the governor that arrangements calculated to provide salt were underway and that the trade of which he had spoken might be interpreted as internal—thereby not in violation of existing laws—Pettus was not content to dally and went on to appoint his own personal agent to deal directly with Louisiana salt mine owners.[57]

Governor Pettus did not stop there; rather, ten days later he ordered four boats to Louisiana for the purpose of returning salt to Mississippi. When rebuked by Confederate Secretary of War George C. Randolph, to the effect that he was guilty of

[55] Pettus to Davis, September 6, 1862, in Governor's Correspondence, Vol. LXIII; Davis to Pettus, September 25, 1862, in Official Records, Ser. I, Vol. XVII, Part II, 713; Augus Chew to Pettus, September 16, 1862, Pettus to Davis, September 20, 1862, Pettus and Jones Hamilton to Davis, September 23, 1862, in Official Records, Ser. I, Vol. LII, Part II, 354–56.
[56] A. B. Longstreet to Pettus, October 3, 1862, C. F. Hanes to Pettus, October 11, 1862, G. W. Humphreys to Pettus, October 16, 1862, F. M. Vaughn to Pettus, October 19, 1862, in Governor's Correspondence, Vol. LVIII; Pettus to Davis, October 8, 1862, in Official Records, Ser. I, Vol. LII.
[57] Pettus to Davis, October 17, 1862, in Official Records, Ser. IV, Vol. II, 126; Pettus Executive Order, October 18, 1862, in Governor's Correspondence, Vol. LVIII.

violating laws pertaining to trade with the enemy, the governor retorted: "Our people must have salt." Indeed, anything that Pettus could do to aid his flagging region was perhaps justified. For, as the Mobile *Daily Tribune* noted, there were increasing numbers of people taking an oath of allegiance to any foreign government in order to avoid the hardships of war.[58]

Realizing full well the interrelationship between the public and private sectors of the war effort, it was neither strange nor surprising that Pettus acted as he did. Concessions and bold action were simultaneously called for, neither of which came cheap. Saving the state from outward destruction and internal demoralization was no easy matter. Although the ultimate test of strength would be found on future battlefields, the ominous present resembled a dark cloud that signaled a distant thunder of great magnitude. For the time being John Pettus had succeeded to some degree in keeping order amid the chaos of war. But the winter of 1862–63 would reveal something else again.

[58] Pettus to Randolph, October 28, 1862, in Governor's Correspondence, Vol. LX; Mobile *Daily Tribune*, October 21, 1862.

IX

Anguish and Compromise: The "Cold Gray Shadow"

THE LAST MONTHS of 1862 gave little cause for joy as far as Mississippi was concerned. Nevertheless, Governor John Pettus sustained the pretense of optimism and did what he could to encourage the fallen spirits of his people. When the Second Regiment of Volunteers voted to give him the company battle flag as a symbol of their loyalty to the state, the governor took the occasion to urge all persons onward because so many had "so nobly fought and bled."[1]

Since the spring of 1862 the federals had been operating quite freely in several parts of the state. In addition to military targets, some Union troops apparently did a great deal of needless damage to the property of private citizens. Near Columbus, for example, an officer in the Twelfth Indiana Volunteers wrote home that he was "ashamed to confess [that] our soldiers burnt pretty much all the fences and outhouses." Stealing was also rampant and some of the "officers winked at the thing," although they had orders to the contrary.[2]

This pillaging and looting had a demoralizing effect on many Mississippians. A Union soldier from Illinois, when in Oxford, noted the growing distaste for war in the Magnolia State. Viewing Mississippi as being "almost beyond the bounds of civiliza-

[1] Pettus to J. M. Stone, November 10, 1862, in John J. Pettus Papers.
[2] James Goodnow to Nancy Goodnow, December 1, 1862, in James H. Goodnow Papers, Library of Congress, Washington, D.C.

tion," he recorded the conversation of some captured state troops, who said: " 'We'ns dont [*sic*] go north to fight you'ns, why do you'ns come down here to fight we'ns?"[3]

Throughout all this, Governor Pettus labored long and hard in an effort to maintain maximum defense efficiency. However, it was not always the Yankees who hampered such preparations; rather, conflict between Confederate authorities and state officials led, on several occasions, to a disruption of cooperation within the Mississippi theater of operations. In this respect Pettus found that he had difficulty exercising control over Richmond personnel stationed within his state. When he issued a call for the impressment of slaves to work on fortification and salt mining projects, agents appointed for that purpose found planters unwilling to part with their chattel property. One commissioner discovered that this reluctance was partially due to the fact that Confederate officers had already "made the rounds" and collected large numbers of bondsmen. In the commissioner's assigned area of Lexington he was unable to "raise any negro men." An observer in Lee County gave two additional reasons for the limited success of slave impressment—the low amount of reimbursement to the owners and the fact that "swarms of negroes" were running away.[4]

The Mississippi governor likewise received little or no immediate assistance from Confederate authorities in his endeavors to provide nourishment for destitute families and to secure salt. Boats for the hauling of salt were hard to come by, while rail transportation was seriously impeded because state and central government officials competed for the use of rolling stock, occasionally even stealing the cars from each other. Yet when the public assessed blame for such adversity, it was Governor Pettus who reaped the whirlwind of dissatisfaction. The residents of

[3] Robert S. Finley to M. A. C., December 18, 1862, in Robert S. Finley Papers, University of North Carolina Library, Chapel Hill, N.C.

[4] Pettus to R. S. C. Foster, November 1, 1862, D. A. Holman to Pettus, November 1, 1862, J. A. Cason to Pettus, November 7, 1862, in Governor's Correspondence, Vol. LVIII; Entries for October 12, 13, 1862, in Samuel A. Agnew Diary.

Smith County were in an angry mood and demanded that something be done. Speculators in bread who had "proven themselves an even match for the rulers of France" needed to be dealt with by either Jackson or Richmond personnel. The story was much the same in Marion County where food was scarce because "shylocks and distillers" had cornered the market on grain.[5]

Even Pettus' unceasing struggle to secure precious salt achieved the same negative response: "salt for sale in very small quantities and at very high prices." So critical was this question that it evoked an almost universal outcry, one which was indirectly linked to the war effort on the home front. State Probate Judge I. W. Scarborough of Kosciusko expressed the prevailing opinion when he remarked that there was "danger of mutiny" in his community if salt could not be obtained. More punishing still was the fact that the state could not afford to purchase the preservative, even if sufficient quantities were made available. With a financial situation bordering on chaos and inflation running rampant, unheard-of prices were commonplace. Flour sold for $80 a barrel and a mere bushel of salt went for $100, when it could be found.[6]

Driven on by the alarming despair prevalent within the state, as noted earlier, Governor Pettus was left with no other alternative than to endorse the practice of allowing cotton to be traded for salt and other desperately needed commodities with the federals in occupied New Orleans. Not acting alone, he advised President Davis of his plans, who, in turn, consented to tolerate his cousin's contraband commerce. In reality, John

[5] Walter Goodman to John C. Pemberton, October 25, 1862, in Walter Goodman Papers, Confederate Citizens' File, National Archives, Washington, D.C.; John C. Pemberton Endorsement, November 1, 1862, John C. Pemberton to H. J. Raney, October 22, 1862, in Confederate Military Department Endorsements: Department of Mississippi and East Louisiana, 1862–1863, National Archives, Washington, D.C.; R. C. Safford to Pettus, November 3, 1862, C. M. Henderson to Pettus, November 8, 1862, R. O. Edwards to Pettus, December 3, 1862, in Governor's Correspondence, Vol. LVIII.

[6] H. O. Dixon to Pettus, November 4, 1862, Scarborough to Pettus, November 5, 1862, in Governor's Correspondence, Vol. LVIII. For the complete study of inflation and financial chaos during this period see Richard C. Todd, *Confederate Finance* (Athens, Ga., 1954).

Pettus did little more than place the official stamp of approval on what was already being practiced. His position was made abundantly clear in mid-November when he told his private secretary to inform anyone who inquired that he, the governor, had the "right and the power to exchange Cotton for Salt" and that he was "disposed to exercise this right to the amount of fifty thousand sacks."[7]

No sooner had Pettus agreed to traffic with the enemy for needed items and things had appeared brighter, than disaster befell the newly discovered Confederate source of salt. State salt agent D. S. Pattison, while on an inspection tour of Louisiana's New Iberia salt works, found that supply subject to increased federal harassment. Further, the southern troops deployed in defense of the place were of a low caliber and could not be made to stand and fight. With extraction at a near standstill, the price of salt rose to a minimum of $54 per small sack in the city of Jackson.[8]

Not easily daunted by news of deprivation and hardship, the grizzly governor granted salt contracts to a French privateer for several thousand sacks, to be procured at an exchange ratio of fifty bales of cotton per two hundred sacks of salt. Orders to insure safe passage through Confederate lines accompanied the agreement. Vigorous steps were also taken to guarantee that railroads would give first priority to salt destined for Mississippi, and President Davis was requested not to delay any assistance that he could render.[9] Time, however, was running out.

By late 1862 the clouds of war had descended upon Mississippi

[7] Edgar L. Erickson (ed.), "Hunting For Cotton In Dixie: From the Civil War Diary of Captain Charles E. Wilcox," *Journal of Southern History*, IV (November, 1938), 493–513; Robert S. Holzman, *Stormy Ben Butler* (New York, 1954), 94; Pettus to James H. Rives, November 17, 1862, in Governor's Correspondence, Vol. LVIII. One contemporary recalled that the Federals often drove a hard bargain, exchanging a bale of cotton for a sack of coffee.

[8] Pattison to Pettus, November 18, 1862, in Governor's Correspondence, Vol. LVIII; Jackson *Weekly Mississippian*, November 19, 1862.

[9] Pettus to A. Mernet, November 24, 26, 1862, Pettus to C. Steele, November 25, 1862, Pettus to F. W. Watch, n.d., 1862, W. M. Emanual to Pettus, November 3, 1862, Pettus to W. M. Emanual, November 26, 1862, in Governor's Correspondence, Vols. LVIII, LXIII.

with greater force than ever before. Yankee troops were able to roam fifty miles northward from the Gulf Coast. In many areas courts of every description had long since ceased to function, thus compounding the law enforcement problem. As the federals continued to penetrate the northern and southern portions of the state, reports of vandalism, desolation, speculation, and disloyalty reached the governor's ears daily. Many men did not stay to offer resistance to the northerners, but instead were busy evacuating their families from the state altogether. A Carrollton resident who witnessed such flight noted "large droves of negroes and strong able bodied men leaving to get out of the way of the Yankees." Particularly in the occupied northernmost reaches of the state, many individuals were "much excited" over the freeing of their slaves. Word of Lincoln's Emancipation Proclamation prompted constituents to attempt to have their counties represented in the U.S. Congress "at whatever cost," before the edict took effect. To do otherwise might result in the permanent loss of slave property.[10]

Loyal Mississippians, however, were still in abundance during these months and were not about to stand idly by while the state was sold out from within. Appalled by the shortcomings of their neighbors, some persons proposed remedies ranging from fasting vigilances to the drafting of men over sixty years of age. Others recommended disfranchising all who were disloyal. Governor Pettus was slightly more realistic than many of his well-intended followers. His study of the situation indicated that more force was necessary. On November 15, 1862, he wrote to Secretary of War Randolph requesting that as many men as possible be allowed to remain in the Magnolia State to aid its residents. Certain cavalry units were now needed at home. Pettus warned that if reinforcements were not sent, Mississippi

[10] J. S. McNeily, "War and Reconstruction In Mississippi, 1863–1890," in Dunbar Rowland (ed.), *Publications of the Mississippi Historical Society* (Oxford, Miss., 1918), Centenary Series, II, 270; J. H. Jones to Pettus, November 12, 1862, W. Cottman to Pettus November 15, 1862, in Governor's Correspondence, Vol. LVIII; Thomas W. Knox, *Camp-Fire and Cotton-Field: Southern Adventure In Time of War* (Cincinnati, 1865), 233.

would surely be overcome. Richmond authorities, however, were not eager to hurry to the governor's assistance. Past instances of non-cooperation on his part might have been a contributing factor, even though the weary Pettus insisted to the contrary. With no reinforcements in sight, the governor therefore went about the business of obstructing the rivers of the state so as to prevent their use by the invaders.[11]

Pettus' labors in the face of Gargantuan hardships were not without expressions of gratitude. The Jackson *Weekly Mississippian*, for instance, noted that he had proven himself capable of meeting earlier challenges, and predicted that the people would "again look to him with trust and confidence in this hour of danger." Although Mississippians had little real choice as to whether or not to follow executive guidance, certain of the governor's advisors urged that he bolster his position and share the burden of leadership by once more calling the legislature into special session.[12] Saddled with economic, civil, and military difficulties of overwhelming proportions he conceded, and summoned the lawmakers to Jackson for a meeting in mid-December.

During the interim Pettus dealt as best he could with those problems that would not await deliberation. The salt issue was still urgent and more agents were appointed to canvass the South in search of it. By now Pettus' problem was not as much one of access to salt, as it was a task of convincing railroad personnel that he had presidential permission to transport cotton to exchange for the precious commodity. But the railroad men were skeptical; speculators had tried numerous times to have their goods moved under false pretenses. Gradually, the proper authorities did arrive at the governor's point of view, but not

[11] Nattie Clayton to Pettus, November 18, 1862, Edward P. Jones to Pettus, November 20, 1862, Pettus to Randolph, November 15, 1862, A. J. Cochman to Pettus, October 27, 1862, Pettus Special Order Number 27, November 23, 1862, Pettus to J. V. Harris, November 28, 1962, in Governor's Correspondence Vols. LVIII, LXIII.

[12] Jackson *Weekly Mississippian*, November 26, 1862; C. Beckinwith to Pettus, November 23, 1862, Petition of Carrollton Town Meeting to Pettus, November 25, 1862, Reuben Davis to Pettus, November 26, 1862, in Governor's Correspondence, Vol. LVIII.

before he promised that none of the salt would fall into the wrong hands.[13]

As much as ever, desertion remained a festering dilemma. Conscripts, it appears, not only disliked their forced service, but found life in the army to be little short of starvation. Family men persisted in fleeing homeward to assist their often destitute kin. To make matters worse, counterfeit Confederate money was everywhere and communications were always less than adequate. Attempting to fight desertion, the governor tightened the conscription dragnet. So effective was the immediate result that several British subjects residing within the state soon found themselves in the ranks. Such things did not go unnoticed and a swift salvo of protest from the Acting British Consul at Mobile, Alabama, was soon on file.[14]

In spite of everything A.W.O.L. rates among Confederate troops remained high, and the same notion apparently infected large numbers of the state militia, whose ranks were also "discontented, half-mutinous." Conscription officer W. H. Varnado even discovered that "some of the conscripts is gone to the yankeys [sic], and many others talk of going." So alarming was the drain of manpower that the recently appointed Confederate commander in Mississippi, General John C. Pemberton, appealed to Pettus for permission to allow convicts in state prisons to enlist in the army.[15] The governor was not yet ready for such drastic measures.

On the positive side, the governor's information regarding the

[13] John C. Burdue to Pettus, December, 1862, Pettus to Thomas E. Nelson, Pettus to A. M. West, December 1, 1862, E. Emanuel to Pettus, M. L. Smith to Pettus, December 2, 1862, Pettus to J. R. S. Pitts, December 6, 1862, in Governor's Correspondence, Vols. LVIII, LXIII. See also Percy L. Rainwater (ed.), "Letters of James Lusk Alcorn," *Journal of Southern History*, III (May, 1937), 198–200.
[14] James Magee to Pettus, December 4, 1862, in Governor's Correspondence, Vol. LXIII. See also Milledge L. Bonham, *The British Consuls In the Confederacy* (New York, 1967), 16–17.
[15] Charles W. Ramsdell, *Behind the Lines In the Southern Confederacy*, ed. Wendell H. Stephenson (Baton Rouge, 1944), 55; Varnado to Pettus, December 8, 1862, Pemberton to Pettus, December 19, 1862, in Governor's Correspondence, Vol. LVIII.

war situation seemed brighter than many of the doleful military reports he had received in recent months. Far from wanting to avoid a direct confrontation with the federals, Pettus openly desired them to penetrate the Mississippi River to Vicksburg. At that juncture he still planned, as he had during the first stages of the war, to ambush and destroy them. And the Yankees obliged. Pettus would get his chance.

After their ill-fated attempt to capture Vicksburg in the summer of 1862, the Union army concentrated its thrust elsewhere. But in October of the same year, federal plans again called for the capture of that river city. Between those two dates comparatively little was done to bolster existing defenses. Instead, "the city had assumed a busy appearance; numerous stores were opened, and business, in a great measure, resumed its . . . activity." But when Union troops showed signs of returning, the picture of tranquility was supplanted by one entirely different. "The merchants are moving every thing out in the country—and families are moving out very rapidly—fearing an attack very soon." Defense construction was greatly hampered due to the fact that impressed Negroes were "running off home daily and their masters are not returning them."[16]

Union probing attacks on Vicksburg began in mid-November of 1862, and there was fighting in and around the city until the first of the year. At times the contest for the position reached heated proportions. An Alabama doctor witnessed one "desparate [sic] effort" to take a rifle pit, with federal forces charging one point thirteen times in an unsuccessful drive.[17]

For all his brave talk of ambushing the northerners, Governor Pettus soon resembled the proverbial lamb—and one with cold feet at that. In early December he and General James Phelan held a series of meetings to analyze the Mississippi war effort in general and the Vicksburg situation in particular. It was subsequently agreed that the two men should beseech President Davis

[16] Abrams, *Siege of Vicksburg*, 11; Sydney Champion to Matilda Champion, late 1862, in Sydney S. Champion Papers.
[17] Entry for December 29, 1862, in Joseph D. Alison Diary, University of North Carolina Library, Chapel Hill, N.C.

to come to the state, at least for a short period, in order to personally direct the course of the war. This would encourage the citizenry's confidence in both governments and manifest the need for a more vigorous dedication to the military program. Phelan relayed the request to Davis, stating that everything which had given "attractive coloring to the soldier's life" had now faded into a "cold, gray shadow with nine tenths of the army." To this Pettus added a further note of urgency when he reminded Davis that similar trips to the Army of Northern Virginia had served to advance its record. "A weak spirit" was afoot, said Pettus, and "something must be done to inspire confidence." Surely, the governor wrote his cousin, a visit by the president was just the thing to "greatly improve our situation."[18]

Davis was understandably troubled by this unhappy prognosis and by December 17 was in Jackson to personally survey the progress and strength of fortifications surrounding the city. A few days later Davis made a hurried journey to Grenada to review some 20,000 troops gathered there. The soldiers were elated and received him "with the greatest enthusiasm as he rode along the long line, halting in front of each regiment as he reached its center and returning its salute." On December 21, Davis conducted a tour of Vicksburg, then returned to Jackson, where he addressed the recently assembled state legislature. Admitting that the war had "assumed proportions more gigantic than . . . anticipated," the Confederate president called for maximum commitment in order to silence the "rumors of alarm and trepidation and despondency."[19]

While in the Mississippi capital, Davis held a series of meetings with Pettus. The conferences were more informal than formal, complete with persons wandering in and out of the governor's office at random. Having accomplished his mission, Davis

[18] Phelan to Pettus, December 8, 1862, Pettus to Davis, December, 1862, in Governor's Correspondence, Vol. LVIII; Phelan to Davis, December 9, 1862, in *Official Records*, Ser. I, Vol. LVIII, Part II, 790.
[19] Montgomery, *Reminiscences of a Mississippian*, 109; Jefferson Davis speech to Mississippi Legislature, December 26, 1862, in Moore (ed.), *Rebellion Record*, VI, 295–300.

departed for Richmond with full security precautions in effect.[20]

Meanwhile, members of the legislature had convened in Jackson. (The opening of the special session had been delayed for several days awaiting assembly of a quorum.) Governor Pettus' address to the lawmakers contained specific proposals for improving the conduct of the war and alleviating some of the pressing civilian demands. Since hostilities had increased in magnitude, "corresponding efforts" must be undertaken to counter those of the federals, said Pettus. A proposal to conscript the "entire white male population," up to the age of sixty, was submitted.[21]

Keenly aware of the growing shortage of southern troops, the governor made special reference to the hundreds of soldiers "absent without leave, or on expired furloughs, or recovered from disability" who had not returned to their units. In this instance, said Pettus, proper laws should be passed to insure that sheriffs and other officials "arrest and send to their commands all who owe service to the country and either neglect or refuse to perform it." By way of reinforcement, any citizen who failed to muster into service should be disfranchised. Such was only proper since local minutemen and the forty-six regiments under Confederate command had given good service. The governor reminded the assembly that the responsibility for defending Mississippi's "existence as a State" must fall equally on everyone.[22]

Turning his attention to other important matters, Pettus hit hard at the large planter class, insisting that efforts to enlist aid from that segment of the population had often failed. Attempts to induce slaveowners to dispatch their Negroes for work on fortification projects met only limited success, and in some quarters planters flatly "refused to contribute anything" to the war effort. A law for the mandatory impressment of slaves was necessary for the good of the state. Similarly, the legislators were reminded that poverty was widespread and provisions to care

[20] Russell, *My Diary North and South*, 299; Pettus to R. W. T. Daniel, December 28, 1862, in Governor's Correspondence, Vol. LXIII.
[21] Mississippi *Senate Journal*, Called Session (December, 1862), 4, 7.
[22] *Ibid.*, 7–11.

for the families of soldiers in the field were, thus far, "wholly inadequate." More money and legislation were also needed for transporting salt, foodstuffs, and war materials.

In an effort to curtail the evils of speculation and profiteering, Pettus advocated the enactment of price regulations aimed at stopping the deliberate hoarding of grain and its distillation into alcoholic spirits. If this sort of practice was permitted to go unchecked, the governor said, it would have the effect of transferring the "property of the country to the hands of the worst and least patriotic of our population." In the event the lawmakers passed favorably upon this list of priority items, then a few more months of hardship might ensue, but afterward, predicted Pettus, the "God who loves justice and rewards devotion, will bless our land with independence and peace."

In what might be described as record time, the legislators—displaying neither the tardiness nor disinterest so characteristic of them on earlier occasions—acted promptly on nearly all the governor's requests. Among those measures sanctioned were the allocation of $500,000 for the procurement of salt and authorization to impress "for public safety" any slaves between the ages of eighteen and fifty, as well as whatever horses, tools, or wagons might be deemed necessary. All military discharges were ordered revoked and sheriffs were directed to arrest all deserters and examine for authenticity all papers relating to leaves of absence or furloughs. A $5 fee (undoubtedly included as an added incentive) was to be paid for each deserter turned over to military officials. The manufacture of alcohol was prohibited, with a six-month jail sentence and a $5,000 fine to be levied against violators.[23]

Governor Pettus' optimistic view on the possible outcome of the war was not shared by all, for the legislature made arrangements to have public records moved from Jackson for safekeeping. Likewise, the solons proved to be slower and more cautious when it came to dealing with the state's military system. Instead

[23] Mississippi, *Laws of the State of Mississippi*, Called Session (December, 1862–January, 1863), 67, 79, 81–89, 95–96.

of strengthening laws relating to the armed forces, the legislators authorized the governor to use troops for service outside the state for limited periods only. Soldiers could be placed under Confederate command for only short, specified lengths of time, and the governor was permitted to exempt from service any person he thought deserving. When news of this last provision broke, the public clamor for exemptions ran high.[24]

Obviously stimulated by these events, a wave of renewed commitment to the war effort appeared in a number of places, some of which were unexpected. Convicts at the state penitentiary volunteered for military duty. The governor of Alabama announced that he would permit salt to be extracted from his state at minimum cost. Former salt speculators, infected by the germ of cooperation, decided to offer to secure the preservative for as little as $15 per bushel.[25] However, this sacrificial spirit was short-lived and failed to extend to other important segments of the war program.

Mississippi's relations with the Confederate government continued to be uncertain in several areas. Transportation—the use of railroad facilities in particular—remained a hotly contested matter, with the state and central powers often at odds. Typical of the problems faced were those pertaining to the transfer of men and supplies. One railroad official bitterly complained that although he was attempting to act in the state's best interest, Confederate authorities were invariably disregarding the priorities for food and salt set by Governor Pettus and would seize railroad cars designated for such uses.[26] Cases of flagrant bribery and corruption were likewise very much in evidence.

Confederate personnel also took a dim view of certain measures recently enacted by the state legislature. Specifically,

[24] James B. Ross to Pettus, Paul Maguader to Pettus, January 8, 1863, D. Harrison to Pettus, January 12, 1863, in Governor's Correspondence, Vol. LIX.
[25] Moses Jackson to Pettus, January 1, 1863, Gill Shorter to Pettus, January 3, 1863, George Wood to Pettus, January 9, 1863, W. A. Strong to Pettus, January 12, 1863, John A. Seward to Pettus, January 13, 1863, in Governor's Correspondence, Vol. LIX.
[26] D. M. Emanuel to Pettus, January 14, 1863, *ibid.*

those laws granting the governor draft exemption authority and dealing with the transfer of troops to Richmond jurisdiction for only short periods were held to be undesirable. Newly appointed Confederate Secretary of War James A. Seddon expressed his government's indignation on this point when he wrote John Pettus that the times were "too critical for any interference" with established military procedures.[27]

The new laws intended to strengthen and revitalize the conduct of the war in Mississippi failed to alter the quandary of soldiers in the field. Both the quality and quantity of food, for example, remained low. State food inspectors found rations "totally unfit" for human consumption. A field commander confided that his men were refusing to eat their supplies, "saying that they prefer to live."[28]

On the other hand, internal disloyalty and discontent also existed because of complications arising from the legislative changes in militia and conscription policies. A recruiting officer touring northern Mississippi to obtain replacements for the battered Twenty-Third Infantry Regiment was surprised to find "plenty of men who ought to be in service." These individuals had failed to report for duty because they wanted no part of the Confederate army, preferring the state militia and minuteman programs instead.[29]

Elsewhere, the situation was remarkably similar. State representative William L. Lewis found upon return to Louisville in late January, 1863, that his constituency was violently opposed to the new whiskey law. One man openly boasted that he would join the federal forces when they arrived because of the ruling, while others underscored their opposition by vowing to burn their corn before permitting Confederate or state personnel to have it. One factor handicapping the effectiveness of anti-distillation laws was the inability of the courts to function. "Criminal justice was administered laxly if at all, continuance

[27] Seddon to Pettus, January 10, 1863, *ibid.*
[28] Ben King et al. to Pettus, J. G. George to Pettus, January 19, 1863, *ibid.*
[29] J. B. Purnell to Pettus, January 20, 1863, *ibid.*

and change of venue were easily obtained, trials were held infrequently, and the fines which once seemed huge had become small through inflation." And indeed, by early 1863 inflation had caused the worth of the Confederate dollar to drop to only twenty cents in buying power.[30]

Despite the difficulties and dissatisfactions generated by the war and a lack of coordination among all parties, the state press was generally praiseworthy of Mississippi's chief executive. Especially revealing among contemporary accounts was one carried in the pages of the Jackson *Daily Southern Crisis* on January 28, 1863, which concluded that Pettus had "justly earned his title to an honorable distinction in history." The paper noted that Vicksburg, the very symbol of Mississippi's defiance, was well guarded because of the "unflinching firmness with which he wielded all his personal influence and executive authority . . . at all hazards and to the last extremity."

Governor Pettus had little time to rest on laurels of glowing acclaim, however, and was forced to devote considerable energy to impressing slaves for work on military fortifications. While requisitions for laborers arrived at the executive mansion in a steady stream, the applications proved to be more easily granted than filled. For although a number of planters acquiesced in the mandatory rental of their Negroes, many did not. Certain slaveowners disliked payments made in the form of inflated paper money and told impressment officials that they did not want their blacks used on hazardous war projects, preferring them to remain at home and plant crops. A Copiah County resident saw it a little differently. Declaring that he did not mind the state using his bondsmen, he nevertheless felt it necessary to decline to deliver them over because the more wealthy planters, with the greatest number of Negroes, were sending only one or two. An impressment official viewed the total situation as highly explosive. Voluntary compliance with the law was at a low ebb

---

[30] Lewis to Pettus, January 24, 1863, *ibid.*; Paul W. Gates, *Agriculture and the Civil War* (New York, 1965), 100; Wood, *Confederate Handbook*, 76.

and many planters who were sent notices to produce their slaves simply refused to do so.[31]

A number of large slaveholders took advantage of the governor's desperate straits and seized the opportunity to goad him into granting draft exemptions for both themselves and their overseers. Many of the latter, undoubtedly distressed over their liability for military service, saw no reason to aid the government in any way. Consequently, impressment official John C. Humphries disclosed that he could not find a single overseer to volunteer to supervise the work of slaves on Port Hudson fortifications.[32]

Conflict over slave impressment and draft exemptions was not the only drama of personal antagonism acted out during the early months of 1863. The never ending and often erratic struggle between Mississippi's military representatives and those from Richmond continued to rage, with Governor Pettus caught in an uneasy middle ground. As early as January, 1863, the governor had ordered all staff officers within the state placed on active duty and, at the same time, directed that "all white males between the ages of eighteen and fifty, . . . either permanently or temporarily residing in the State, to be included in the draft." Anyone who had seen prior service or had been discharged or otherwise exempted from military duty was to be included in said draft. Confederate officers, however, took the governor to mean that the men in question should be conscripted into *their* ranks. This misinterpretation angered Pettus immensely and when Richmond authorities resorted to the technique of overriding his furlough power or drafting state sol-

[31] F. Dillard to Pettus, February 18, 1863, John C. Humphries to Pettus, February 14, 1863, in Governor's Correspondence, Vols. LIX, LXIII. For a broader view of this entire problem see Harrison A. Trexler, "The Opposition of Planters to the Employment of Slaves as Laborers by the Confederacy," *Mississippi Valley Historical Review*, XXVII (1940–1941), 211–24.

[32] W. H. Middleton to Pettus, Robert F. Clark to Pettus, February 7, 1863, J. D. Kay to Pettus, February 9, 1863, Willie Lyons to Pettus, February 28, 1863, Humphries to Pettus, February 12, 1863, in Governor's Correspondence, Vols. LIX, LXIII.

diers on leave into Confederate units, the governor spoke out accordingly.[33]

Discontent with military service and conscription disrupted war preparations in a variety of other ways. In early February, Governor Pettus notified General Pemberton that there were a number of militarily eligible men in northern Mississippi, but that they were behind Union lines and opposed to the draft. Further, through a spokesman, Confederate commanders were told that many individuals desired to participate in military affairs, but under their own terms of organization—not wanting to be conscripted or placed in the infantry. At least one Confederate officer, however, did not believe this explanation, taking the view that they were simply deserters who would "resist any attempt to carry them back to the army."[34]

Meanwhile, large numbers of simple furlough appeals and pleas for draft exemptions continued to engulf John Pettus. The bulk of correspondence revealed that the privilege of freely submitting to service was uppermost in the minds of many. As one writer put it, the "idea of *volunteering* is a great attraction . . . , while the draft is perfectly odious." Others, such as the residents of Duck Hill, protested the thought of any duty whatsoever, believing that the continuous drain of men left their community subject to raids by "theving [sic] bands that are passing thrue [sic] . . . taking what Ever may please their fancy." Clearly, as a Port Gibson citizen analyzed, something must be done because the "Negroes are under no restraint at night." Hard pressed planters and farmers alike saw no reason to join the army when they already had their hands full preventing slaves from running off and trying to eke out a livelihood without money, tools, or food.[35]

[33] Pettus Order Number 271, January 19, 1863, Samuel Ellis to Pettus, February 6, 1863, Pettus to Pemberton, February 9, 1863, in Governor's Correspondence, Vol. LXIII.

[34] James Rives to J. R. Waddy, February 9, 1863, in Governor's Correspondence, Vol. LXIII; Howard Wilkinson to John C. Pemberton, January 17, 1863, in J. F. H. Claiborne Papers, National Archives.

[35] John C. Humphries to Pettus, February 13, 1863, Duck Hill Petition to Pettus, February 14, 1863, E. C. Patterson to Pettus, February 23, 1863, in

Elsewhere, speculation in foodstuffs and trade with the enemy, whether authorized or forbidden, increased sharply during the winter of 1862–63. Mississippi salt agent W. C. Turner reported to his superior that the product was available, but high prices made it impractical to procure. So worried were Governor Pettus and General Pemberton that they advocated the suspension of the writ of *habeas corpus* in the city of Jackson in order "to stop illicit trade." The impact of illegal trade and speculation forced the cost of living up in all sectors, public and private. The price of a calico dress ranged upward to $250 and the "price of a horse was counted by the thousands." Slaves, even those who were too young or too old to be of much real value, were sold at unbelievable prices. The cost of salt remained "stiff" and Pettus, in order to get any at all, had to readjust the cotton exchange ratio downward to one bale per twenty sacks to make such trade more attractive.[36]

By the late winter of 1863 unauthorized commercial activity stood at record level. Many of those who participated in this type of enterprise were the same individuals who had not given any military service. Governor Pettus was not alone in his efforts to smash contraband trade and often found the press by his side. The Natchez *Daily Courier* praised those who sold goods at reasonable rates and issued an unqualified condemnation of those who took their "pound of flesh." The governor issued stern warnings to speculators not to take him lightly.[37]

Neither did manifestations of disloyalty go unchecked whenever and wherever they were uncovered. A Presbyterian minister in Tupelo reported that he had witnessed rebels marching

Governor's Correspondence, Vol. LIX; Howard Wilkinson to Jacob Thompson, February 17, 1863, J. F. H. Claiborne to Jacob Thompson, March 15, 1863, in J. F. H. Claiborne Papers, National Archives.

[36] W. C. Turner to Pettus, February 24, March 14, 1863, W. A. Stuart to A. J. Caperton, March 12, 1863, Pettus to James Cangal, March 27, 1863, in Governor's Correspondence, Vol. LIX; Pemberton to Jefferson Davis, February 19, 1863, in *Official Records*, Ser. I, Vol. XXIV, Part III, 635; Fulkerson, *A Civilian's Recollection*, 111; David Dodge, "Domestic Economy In the Confederacy," *Atlantic Monthly*, LVIII (August, 1888), 232, 237.

[37] Natchez *Daily Courier*, March 21, 1863; Pettus to H. L. Lanman, March 31, 1863, in Governor's Correspondence, Vol. LX.

people out daily and shooting them "for the expression of senti-
ments adverse to the rebellion." Groups of deserters, draft-
dodgers, and bandits sometimes rode freely throughout the
countryside. So menacing were such vandals that in mid-March
Pettus had to order a detachment of troops to Itawamba, Marshall, Tippah, and Tishomingo counties for the express purpose
of contending with these unruly elements.[38]

The chronic problem of slave impressment, likewise, had not
disappeared by the early months of 1863. Some planters refused
to allow their Negroes to work on either state or Confederate
jobs, as the time for spring planting was near. Others, whose
slaves had already performed service, declined to let them be
used a second time, believing enough labor had been contributed. Impressment officers trying to procure bondsmen were
occasionally threatened with bodily harm. One, in fact, resigned
his post under the pretext that his life was in jeopardy.[39]

Planters would not adhere to the law because they feared that
their property would be mistreated. Several Holmes County citizens whose Negroes had been employed at Vicksburg informed
Governor Pettus that their slaves were treated "badly and
roughly" by overseers "using cudgels and sticks in chastesement
[sic]." Such methods produced runaways or flight to the federals. For his part, Governor Pettus accused Confederate personnel of illegal impressment procedures and, what was worse,
of not paying the owners. Moreover, the overseers employed to
superintend the labor of these bondsmen were "disregarded, the
negroes placed under the control of strangers, and in many cases
badly treated." In the future, the governor warned, good care
must be taken of impressed slaves so as to prevent "a feeling of
discontent."[40]

[38] John H. Aughey *The Iron Furnace: Slavery and Secession* (Philadelphia,
1863), 267; Pettus to W. L. Lowry, March 14, 1863, in Governor's Correspondence, Vol. LX.
[39] A. P. Anderson to Pettus, March 22, 1863, L. Andrews to Pettus, March
28, 1863, R. L. Adams to Pettus, March 19, 1863, in Governor's Correspondence,
Vol. LXIII.
[40] M. L. McGuire et al. to Pettus, March 23, 1863, James Rives to John Pember-

As Union activity gave promise of intensifying, so rose the number of Mississippians seeking to avoid the horrors of war. Frequent pleas for disbanding the state militia and petitions from troops in the field for wholesale furloughs were not uncommon. Pettus answered that such appeals were out of the question; to grant such favors would only endanger the southern cause. Many found the governor's answers unsatisfactory. The city of Canton became a gathering place for soldiers without leave from the army. In fact, public opinion actually encouraged such persons to remain at large. Sheriffs, who had the local task of arresting deserters, were either inefficient at the job or, because of intimidation, found it more convenient to collect taxes instead. A conscientious Simpson County law officer found his plight doubly difficult because deserters were hard to catch, and once apprehended their friends came "and Broke them out of jail."[41]

News of Mississippi's conscription and desertion problems soon reached Richmond. Although Pettus was instructed to redouble his energies to correct the situation, there was little the governor could do, except on paper. And as the spring of 1863 neared, it was somehow felt that a moment of truth and great decision was on its way.

---

ton, March 31, 1863, in Governor's Correspondence, Vol. LX; James H. Rives to John Pemberton, March 31, 1863, in *Official Records*, Ser. I, Vol. LII, Part II, 450.
  [41] P. T. Moore to Pettus, March 27, 1863, L. Curtis to Pettus, March 31, 1863, James Thompson to Pettus, March 31, 1863, in Governor's Correspondence, Vol. LX.

X

The Time of Reckoning: Vicksburg, Jackson, and After

WITH THE COMING OF SPRING, 1863, the problems of dissent, food shortages, and the drain of manpower resources approached crisis proportions in Mississippi. Promises to secure salt failed to materialize, and Governor John Pettus resorted more and more to the granting of contracts to foreigners rather than to Confederate citizens. Bands of army deserters, ranging on the average from twenty-five to thirty in number, became so bold as to harass the outskirts of Jackson. To the state's already pressing list of war miseries was added the fact that telegraph communications were disrupted almost daily. Parties of federals roamed the state concentrating on the sabotage of railway systems. So complete was their work that by early April the New Orleans, Jackson, and Great Northern Railroad was virtually out of commission.[1]

In many areas patriotism fell to its lowest ebb since the start of the war, especially when federal troops came on the scene. A Union soldier wrote that his Iowa unit "burnt every thing and took all the horses, mules and Niggers that we came across." On the other side, a member of the Twenty-eighth Mississippi Regiment compared the northern forces with the Goths and Vandals of the middle ages. The Union soldiers killed all the livestock

[1] Thomas D. Clark, *A Pioneer Southern Railroad From New Orleans to Cairo* (Chapel Hill, 1936), 115.

164

they could find, and what was worse, "all the women were ravished, the Yanks holding them whilst others were gratifying their hellish desires."[2]

Viewing such deplorable violence with dismay, contemporaries became disillusioned and blamed anyone in authority for their troubles. Reverend James Lyon of Columbus had some particularly harsh words along these lines when he wrote in his journal: "I . . . long realized with deep sorrow, the fact, that politics and the rains [sic] of government and the legislative and governmental interests of the state, had slipped almost exclusively into the hands of wicked unprincipled demagogues."[3]

Meanwhile, Confederate–state relations were still at odds over a variety of issues. Railroads not only refused to cooperate with each other, but delayed the transportation of Confederate supplies in favor of those of Mississippi. Governor Pettus took special pains to rebuke the Confederates for pressing state troops into the service of Richmond without his permission. Similarly, the Mississippi governor took a firm stand on the issues of forced slave labor and the confiscation of private property by Confederate personnel, demanding a fair price be paid for the assets of Mississippians. In case of dispute over the value of commodities taken by this means, the governor insisted that he alone had the authority to act as arbitrator. Undoubtedly, Pettus' position on this matter was heavily influenced by pressure brought to bear by large planters.[4]

State and Confederate personnel were not in disagreement on everything, however, and mutual ground for cooperation was often reached. Violators of state anti-distillation laws were prosecuted vigorously by both parties. Corn and copper were too

[2] Robert B. Hoadley to Elm Hoadley, May 29, 1863, in Robert B. Hoadley Papers, Duke University Library, Durham, N.C.; Sydney Champion to Matilda Champion, April 4, 1863, in Sydney S. Champion Papers.

[3] Entry for April, 1863, in Journal of Reverend James A. Lyon.

[4] John C. Pemberton to T. S. Williams, April 20, 1863, in John C. Pemberton Papers, Library of Congress, Washington, D.C.; Pettus to John C. Pemberton, April 13, 24, 1863, H. B. Lyons to Pettus, April 24, 1863, in Governor's Correspondence, Vol. LX.

desperately needed for the war effort to fall into home brewers' hands. A spirited crack-down on offenders became the strategy of Richmond and Jackson alike.[5]

If burning issues had brought Confederate and state authorities to loggerheads before, many of those past difficulties were soon to appear either petty in comparison or profoundly unwise. In either case, the reality of massive military danger which surfaced in the spring of 1863 brought home the naked truth that a lack of earlier cooperation was a costly blunder.

In early 1863 Vicksburg again became the focal point of the war effort in Mississippi. Governor Pettus, of course, had recognized the strategic value of the city since the early days of the secession movement. Such foresight appears commendable, especially since the federals themselves failed to comprehend the city's worth for some time. Previous attempts to capture that place in the spring and winter of 1862 had proved of no avail, but the situation had long since undergone change.

In the early stages of the war, Confederate Lieutenant-General Earl Van Dorn, a native Mississippian, was in charge of Vicksburg's defense. Pettus enjoyed an excellent working relationship with Van Dorn, and on one occasion presented him with a battle sword, which was proclaimed to have been "made in a stile [sic] worthy of yourself and the state . . . to flash defiance in the face of the enemies of Mississippi." When Van Dorn assumed his command in June, 1862, the flamboyant governor was on hand to jointly inspect Vicksburg's fortifications. But Van Dorn's tenure at Vicksburg was short-lived. Major General John Clifford Pemberton, introduced to Pettus as "an officer of great merit," took over responsibility for the station on October 1, 1862.[6]

With the fall of New Orleans, Fort Henry, Fort Donelson, Memphis, and other points along the Mississippi River, Vicks-

---

[5] James Rives to John Pemberton, April 22, 1863, Pemberton to Pettus, April 23, 1863, in *Official Records*, Ser. IV, Vol. XI, 510–11, 513.

[6] Pettus to Van Dorn, April 8, 1862, in Earl Van Dorn Papers; Davis to Pettus, September 20, 1862, in Rowland (ed.), *Jefferson Davis Constitutionalist*, V, 347.

burg took on added significance. Should Vicksburg succumb to the enemy, the Confederacy would be split in half and the prospects for southern independence were sure to be narrowed considerably.

Federal activity in the vicinity of Vicksburg during late 1862 and early 1863 was confined more to harrassment than to large-scale offensive. Work on the canal project was continued for a while, and Union gunboats did manage to run the gun batteries on occasion. But, for the most part, enemy troops were content to occupy other locations to the north and south, to ravage the countryside, and, once in a while, to free slaves for the purpose of enrolling them in the army. All things considered, residents of the river city felt secure and regarded the fortifications as "formidable."[7] This was destined for change, however.

In February and March the attitude of Vicksburg's inhabitants began to shift. The federal canal was still being dug, a naval expedition was on its way, and uncertain Union troop movements were noticed—all giving cause for alarm. Always in search of a focal point for fastening blame, constituents picked General Pemberton as a target for abuse. The Vicksburg *Daily Whig* confined its remarks to speculation as to his military ability. In view of the fact that Pemberton was a native of Philadelphia, Pennsylvania, the people were "naturally inclined to question his loyalty" to the southern cause. The knowledge that the officer who had surrendered New Orleans to the enemy (Mansfield Lovell) was also a former northerner undoubtedly contributed to much of the apprehension. Further, Pemberton was considered, among his peers, to be "a feeble and ineffectual general whose outstanding characteristic was doing things by half measures."[8]

Obviously distressed by this type of news, both Pemberton and Governor Pettus sprang into action. In April, Pemberton trans-

[7] Bell I. Wiley, *Southern Negroes, 1861–1865* (New Haven, 1938), 185; Entry for February, 1863, in Journal of James A. Lyon.
[8] Vicksburg *Daily Whig*, February 3, 1863; "A New Orleans Refugee" to Pettus, March 3, 1863, in Governor's Correspondence, Vol. LX; Hamilton Basso, *Beauregard The Great Creole* (New York, 1933), 217.

ferred his headquarters from Jackson to the very seat of discontent, while the governor and his Alabama brother conducted a personal tour of the area. As fate would have it, John Pettus was on hand when some of Union Admiral David D. Porter's gunboats and barges attempted to sail by the Vicksburg guns. A foolish commander of one of the vessels brazenly requested the surrender of the city. Pettus was surprised at first, but regained his composure and "unhesitatingly returned . . . [the] answer that he would defend Vicksburg until it was laid in ruins and then keep up the fight amid the ruins." Another contemporary, observing the same incident, recorded that the leather-lunged governor defiantly yelled to the Union officer that if he wanted the place he would have to "come and get it." At any rate, the governor was satisfied that the city was properly defended, and was praised for having made it into the "Gibraltar of the Western Hemisphere."[9]

Other persons, however, did not concur with the governor's sense of security, including his own brother, Edmund. Stationed with an Alabama regiment on duty at Vicksburg, Edmund was probably in a better position to obtain a truer picture of the situation than was his brother. In a letter to his wife, Edmund took note of the fact that he had "not been very favorably impressed with the spirit of the people." Aside from the army suffering from poor communications, there was also much evidence of "trading with the Yankees" and a preference on the part of many persons "to exercise their patriotism at home" by keeping "aloof from the struggle." Others of like thinking inferred that some military officers were more interested in attending parties than they were in fighting a war.[10]

Deep down, Governor Pettus may not have been so optimistic about things. Writing to Jefferson Davis, he spoke of Vicksburg as "a political necessity" in Lincoln's strategy. The federals sim-

[9] Jackson *Daily Mississippian*, April 16, 1863; William P. Chambers, "My Journal," in Dunbar Rowland (ed.), *Publications of the Mississippi Historical Society* (Oxford, Miss., 1925), V, 240.

[10] Edmund Pettus to Mary Pettus, April 12, 1863, in E. W. Pettus Papers; Jackson *Daily Mississippian*, April 24, 1863.

ply could not afford to abandon the idea of acquiring such a key position.[11]

As if apprehension for Vicksburg was not enough, Union commanders sent Colonel Benjamin H. Grierson on a diversionary and disruptive cavalry raid throughout the entire length of Mississippi in mid-April of 1863. Grierson's dashing maneuver, which ultimately ended in occupied Louisiana, was in part accomplished with the aid of information obtained from pro-Unionist Mississippians. Although little damage was done in terms of property, the Confederate war effort was thrown "off balance for a few days."[12] More importantly, the incident greatly added to the uneasiness already afoot.

Meanwhile, Edmund Pettus continued to survey the Vicksburg scene with much apprehension, believing that starvation could become a factor if Union forces ever decided to lay siege to the place. Nevertheless, "a day of blood" was predicted if the enemy elected to storm the city. Edmund's forecasting was cut short when he was captured by a Union patrol. But good fortune smiled his way and he made good his escape by hiding "behind a plank fence" during a rest stop on the way to a prisoner of war camp.[13]

With the pace of the war giving signs of quickening, Governor Pettus was in a flurry of activity. On May 2 Pemberton warned that Union forces were on the move in what was thought to be a spring offensive. Thinking that the capital might be in danger, Pemberton deemed it advisable to transfer state archives from the city. The governor was determined to stand his ground and requested that every resident of Jackson turn out with his slaves to help fortify the city by means of erecting rifle-pits, breastworks, and earthworks. Many citizens did what they were asked, but a few had to first be assured that they would be paid for the

[11] Pettus to Davis, April 16, 1863, in Governor's Correspondence, Vol. LX.
[12] D. Alexander Brown, *Grierson's Raid: A Cavalry Adventure of the Civil War* (Urbana, Ill., 1954), 8, 18.
[13] Edmund Pettus to Mary Pettus, April 22, May 12, 1863, in E. W. Pettus Papers; John Pemberton to John Pettus, May 1, 1863, Edmund Pettus to John Pettus, May 1, 1863, in Governor's Correspondence, Vol. LXIII.

services of their blacks. Most Jacksonians undoubtedly realized the urgency of the situation, for large numbers of whites were soon at work alongside their bondsmen. Others, who had recently dashed out in a vain attempt to stop Grierson's raiders, also volunteered for service on the firing line, in the event that they were needed.[14]

Endeavoring to warn the people of the deepening crisis, Pettus at the same time wished to make matters appear under control. And for good reason. For it appeared, judging from information reaching the Confederate State Department, that a sizable number of Mississippians were not waiting around to see what the Yankees had in store. Instead, they fled to Mobile and other cities in Alabama. In a press interview the governor displayed supreme confidence that the region was well guarded and that he and General Pemberton were working closely on all matters pertaining to the safety of the state. Nevertheless, the reporter sensed a note of hidden despair.[15]

In similar fashion Pettus dispatched propagandists and impressment officials throughout Mississippi to impress upon the population the necessity of a full commitment to the cause. His private secretary, sent on just such a mission to Noxubee County, indicated that although the people were aroused to a sense of danger, they were "divided as to what ought to be done." An impressment officer found the situation to be even more critical and notified his superior that it was "impossible" to obtain any slave laborers because "a good many of them . . . [had] been moved off to other states."[16]

Meanwhile, Pettus called for a closer working relationship with Richmond, contributing additional donations of horses, men, and supplies to the central government for Confederate

[14] Pemberton to Pettus, May 2, 9, 1863, C. C. Bennett to Pettus, May 5, 1863, John Adams to Pettus, May 6, 1863, in Governor's Correspondence, Vols. LXI, LXIII; Mary Ann Loughborough, *My Cave Life In Vicksburg With Letters of Trial and Travel* (New York, 1864), 25.
[15] Mobile *Daily Advertiser and Register*, May 2, 1863.
[16] James Rives to Pettus, May 2, 1863, A. L. Crumby to Pettus, May 2, 1863, in Governor's Correspondence, Vol. LXI.

use. Civil and military prisoners were evacuated from the state penitentiary at Jackson and sent to Alabama for safer keeping. Many Mississippians took matters in stride and followed their governor's leadership by organizing into local militia companies.[17] Others, however, were quite dissatisfied with the way the military picture looked and vented their wrath upon General Pemberton, a convenient symbol for abuse, who some believed would sell out the city of Vicksburg.

Governor Pettus, although displaying a more positive feeling, was nonetheless somewhat apprehensive. The "hour of trial is on us" he telegraphed Jefferson Davis. "We look to you for assistance. Let it be speedy." To this was added a ray of hope when Pettus noted that Mississippians up to the age of sixty were coming forth to volunteer their services and that he was leaving no stone unturned to see to it that any hostilities would be sustained at a high level of efficiency. Davis, in turn, assured the governor that reinforcements were ordered and that "every effort has been made to hasten them."[18]

On May 5 Pettus issued a lengthy patriotic proclamation designed to generate a united front against the enemy. "Let no man . . . withhold from the State his services. . . . Duty, interest . . . [and] safety demand every sacrifice necessary for the protection of our homes, our honor, liberty itself." The valiant war record of other years made it much more imperative that the state's honor, "the chivalry of her people, the glory of her daring deeds on foreign fields should [not] be tarnished and her streaming battle flag dragged in the dust by barbarian hordes." The people should form militia companies or volunteer for Confederate or state service, said Pettus. If they did not, he would personally find out who the cowards were and see to it that they

[17] John C. Pemberton, *Pemberton: Defender of Vicksburg* (Chapel Hill, 1942), 53, 104; Gill Shorter to Pettus, May 3, 1863, W. A. Banborn to John Adams, May 5, 1863, H. L. Brame to Pettus, May 7, 1863, Henry Martin to Pettus, May 8, 1863, C. A. Lewis to Pettus, May 9, 1863, John Grensham to Pettus, May 14, 1863, in Governor's Correspondence, Vol. LXI.

[18] Pettus to Davis, May 7, 8, 1863, in *Official Records*, Ser. I, Vol. LII, Part II, 464, 468; Davis to Pettus, May 9, 1863, in Governor's Correspondence, Vol. LXIII.

"hereafter wear the disgraceful badge of the dastardly traitor who refused to defend his home and his country."[19]

The governor's appeal met with only limited response. Deserters, draft-dodgers, and stragglers continued to be counted in large numbers. As a matter of fact, Pettus himself did not comply with the spirit of his proclamation, for he moved his family from Jackson to Enterprise in order to provide for their possible safety.[20] The Yankees were coming.

The Union army had developed a strategy which had the seizure of Vicksburg as its ultimate objective. Grierson's raid, as mentioned earlier, was part of the overall campaign plan to draw Confederate attention away from that area. Additional movements were also planned so as to further cloak the primary target from view. Basically, the federal design was to begin major operations at some point south of Vicksburg and then proceed in force toward Jackson, securing any southern strongholds along the way. With the state capital thus threatened, it was reasoned that either President Davis or the Confederate general in command of this theater of operations (Joseph Johnston) would order Pemberton to leave Vicksburg in order to aid the city of Jackson. Union commanders then projected that they would defeat Pemberton's force in the open, thereby avoiding the necessity of laying siege to Vicksburg. The Confederates, of course, had no way of knowing the strategy and acted accordingly.

On April 30, 1863, the Union plan began to unfold as U. S. Grant led an army across the Mississippi River south of New Carthage, Louisiana, and entered the Magnolia State. In rapid fashion the federals were in possession of Port Gibson and a few days later were about twenty-five miles from Raymond. There, Grant's forces rested for nearly a week, but were on the move again by May 8.[21]

The Confederate response was almost anticipated. Pemberton

[19] Natchez *Daily Courier*, May 9, 1863.
[20] W. Coltham to Pettus, May 10, 1863, Jones S. Hamilton to Pettus, May 9, 1863, in Governor's Correspondence, Vols. LXI, LXIII.
[21] Barron Deaderick, *Strategy In the Civil War* (Harrisburg, Pa., 1946), 99.

left Vicksburg in an effort to counter Grant's movements, but was unable to do so. Joseph E. Johnston, ill in Chattanooga, Tennessee, was then called upon to save the situation. While Johnston hurried toward the scene, federal forces occupied Raymond and marched on toward Jackson. Pemberton, however, was instructed not to go to the capital, but instead to proceed to a point west of the city and await further developments.[22] Other Union troops, under the command of Major General William Tecumseh Sherman, pushed on in the direction of the Mississippi capital.

News of the bluecoat advance swiftly reached the capital, which took on an air of intense excitement. A captive New York *Tribune* correspondent who had recently been released from Jackson's Marble-Yard Prison, viewed the scene with humor and interest, revealing that "a panic of the most decided kind existed among all classes of society." Every category of slaves seemed to enjoy the "quandry of their masters and mistresses." The city's newspaper packed up to carry out a "hegira to a safer quarter." The mayor called upon residents to remain calm and hammered out a proclamation to that effect. But it was duly recorded that he too was "a fugitive before the paste on his defiant pronunciamiento was fairly dry." "If the citizens were flying to arms," wrote the correspondent, "they must have concealed them somewhere in the country, and have been making haste in that direction to recover them." Another observer witnessed these events and labeled the occasion as a "terror-stricken flight of thousands" who went down the "roads that hot day, with everything . . . [they] could carry."[23]

Rather than fight and expose the city to the horrors of war, General Johnston withdrew his 15,000-man force and allowed Jackson to be occupied, offering only token opposition. The federals entered the city after a five-hour fight on May 14, 1863, sustaining a meager 43 dead and 251 wounded. Johnston's

[22] Robert S. Henry, *The Story of the Confederacy* (Indianapolis, 1931), 256–59.
[23] Junius Henri Browne, *Four Years In Secessia: Adventures Within and Beyond the Union Lines* (Hartford, 1865), 248–49; Thomas F. Gailor, *Some Memories* (Kingsport, Tenn., 1937), 11.

decision was due, at least in part, to the poor defensive preparations surrounding the city. A British military colonel and war
observer who arrived at the state capital a few days later told
of finding "a mild trench, which was dignified by the name of
the fortifications of Jackson." There were also piles of burnt
"stores and arms" and "great numbers of pikes and pikeheads"
which were, incredibly, supposed to serve as weapons. In any
event, Johnston's surrender of the capital with all its railroad and
munitions facilities was, in the words of one historian, "the greatest blunder of the Vicksburg campaign."[24]

During the advance on Jackson, Governor Pettus had left
town under the pretext of moving the state capital to Enterprise.
The defeat dealt a heavy blow to the morale of many Mississippians, and, as the governor's secretary confided to his chief, the
fall of Jackson had "thrown a damper over the spirits of the
people."[25]

Such despondency momentarily subsided when, on the afternoon of May 17, the federals withdrew from Jackson and moved
off toward Vicksburg. Before departing, they saw to it that
railroad tracks were torn up and that the state penitentiary,
munitions factories, gun foundries, and the Confederate House
Hotel were put to the torch.

Pettus returned to Jackson to find the town "badly sacked."
The governor praised the state cavalry for "dashing in" and
killing or capturing ten of the enemy. Although the total damage
to the city was placed at "from five to ten millions" of dollars,
somehow the executive mansion and the capitol had escaped
untouched. Nevertheless, many women had been robbed of their
jewelry, and an estimated 3,000 slaves had joined the federals
when they left.[26]

Other contemporaries recorded their assessment of the damage. Jackson, according to a Confederate, was "a beautiful place

[24] Walter Lord (ed.), *The Fremantle Diary: Being the Journal of Lieutenant Colonel James Lyon Fremantle, Coldstream Guards, On His Three Months In the Southern States* (Boston, 1954), 88; Bearss, *Decision In Mississippi*, 309.
[25] James Rives to Pettus, May 15, 1863, in Governor's Correspondence, Vol. LVI.
[26] Pettus Statement on Damages, May 18, 1863, *ibid.*

but the destroyed property and burnt houses show that the Yankees have been here." A Union soldier from Clinton, Iowa, gave a more complete and graphic account of his brief, but "fine old time" in Jackson. "Their [sic] was but little left in Jackson when we came along. What we did not take with us or give to the poor class of inhabitance [sic] was burned." Perhaps more revealing was the Yankee's tabulation of prices charged for goods at the time. Tea was $20 a pound; whiskey, $15 per bottle; flour, $125 a barrel; and coffee was "not to be had at any price."[27]

At least one Jacksonian, a certain Dr. Russell, did not elect to leave town when the federals came. Instead he sat on his veranda, "with a loaded double-barreled gun on his knees" and told the would-be pillagers who came to his home: "No man can die more than once. . . . There is nothing to prevent your going into this house, except that I shall kill the first two of you who move with this gun. Now then, gentlemen, walk in."[28] Dr. Russell's property was not bothered.

Other individuals, while deploring the destruction and loss of property, were more concerned about the behavior of slaves in that difficult hour. The Negroes "went around the streets displaying aggregate smiles of double-rowed ivory, and bending under a monstrous load of French mirrors, boots, shoes, pieces of calico, wash-stands and towels, hoop-skirts, bags of tobacco, parasols, [and] umbrellas."[29] To be sure, many Jacksonians who had sometimes not been particularly zealous in the war were converted by the federal onslaught into good and earnest rebels.

All things considered, the temporary setback at Jackson was more a demoralizing and disruptive factor than a military disaster. A soldier in the Thirty-fifth Alabama Regiment came close

[27] Rufus W. Cater to Cousins Lawrence and Fannie, June 1, 1863, Rufus W. Cater to Cousin Fannie, June 3, 1863, in Douglas J. Carter and Rufus W. Cater Correspondence, Library of Congress; Robert B. Hoadley to Cousin Elm, May 29, 1863, in Robert B. Hoadley Papers, Duke University Library.
[28] Lord (ed.), *Fremantle Diary*, 87.
[29] William D. McCain, *The Story of Jackson: A History of the Capital of Mississippi, 1821–1951* (Jackson, 1953), I, 198.

to the truth when he stated that the only reason Grant had for taking the capital was "for the enhancement of his own greatness, the *hallelujah* effect it would certainly produce in the military and civil domains of Abe Lincoln. In some ears it would sound like a very big thing for a Yankee army to occupy the capital of the great secession state of Mississippi, and home of the President of the Southern Confederacy." Yet, in the short run, Unionist troops might have even aided the Mississippi war cause. For "Jacksonians never loved Rebel soldiers so well before, as they did after they had had some experience with blue-coated Yankees."[30]

From Jackson the center of war quickly shifted westward. Pemberton's command, badly outnumbered, was ordered back to Vicksburg. Grant's army pressed its Confederate opposition hard, forcing Pemberton to fight a retreating action most of the way. A battle at Champion's Hill on May 17 resulted in 6,000 southern casualties. The following day the Confederates narrowly avoided disaster when they found themselves with their backs to the Big Black River. With a bit of luck they crossed the river on a steamboat converted into a pontoon bridge. A few of the southerners, however, did not choose to return to Vicksburg. Instead, they "stacked arms and were lying in the grass in the shade," waiting to surrender.[31] By May 20, Pemberton's forces were back inside the river stronghold, safe for the time being. What Grant had hoped to avoid—siege—now had become a necessity.

Meanwhile, Governor Pettus did what little he could for the good of the effort. Faced with the extreme seriousness of the hour he announced that those convicts not already transferred to Alabama who were willing to serve could go free if they joined the southern army. Response to a plea to enlist in the ranks was

---

[30] Albert T. Goodloe, *Confederate Echoes: A Voice from the South in the Days of Secession and of the Southern Confederacy* (Nashville, 1907), 275–76, 282.

[31] Fletcher Pratt, *The Battles That Changed History* (Garden City, N.Y., 1956), 311–12; Benjamin P. Thomas (ed.), *Three Years With Grant As Recalled by War Correspondent Sylvanus Cadwallader* (New York, 1956), 85.

not as productive as it should have been, because several intolerably shortsighted local commanders had furloughed far too many state troops and permitted others to be used to harvest corn crops. Telegraphing President Davis on May 21, Pettus emphasized the necessity of sending reinforcements, declaring that it might be too late to reach Vicksburg unless such troops were "strong enough to fight their way in."[32]

Unknown to Pettus, some reinforcements had already arrived. These units, however, were numerically small. A sergeant attached to the Twenty-ninth Georgia Volunteer Infantry took a dim view of recent developments, noting on May 15: "My opinion is be it worthless or not is that Vicksburg is now lost." Even so, Pettus tried to put his house in order, and before long was appealing to Richmond for money to start rebuilding his burned city.[33]

As the struggle for the important river city settled down to become one of protracted stalemate, federal army operations were hampered by a variety of unexpected developments. Word of the favorable Union position reached northern communities and in short order "floods of visitors began to pour in" on Grant's camp, including civilian, political, and military figures. Desertion also troubled the enemy, with "quite a number" leaving their units rather than "salute negro officers."[34]

Elsewhere, General Joseph Johnston feverishly attempted to assemble an army strong enough to effect a breakthrough to Vicksburg. However, the gathering of men and supplies was slow and he often went "begging vainly" for support. Accentuating the crisis at hand, Johnston and Pettus issued a joint proc-

[32] C. H. Manship to Pettus, May 23, 1863, J. Gholson to Pettus, May 21, 1863, in Governor's Correspondence, Vols. LXI, LXIII; Pettus to Davis, May 21, 1863, in *Official Records*, Ser. I, Vol. LII, Part II, 476. See also Kenneth P. Williams, *Lincoln Finds A General: A Military Study of the Civil War* (New York, 1956), IV, 398.

[33] Bell I. Wiley (ed.), *Confederate Letters of John W. Hagan* (Athens, Ga., 1954), 16–17; James A. Seddon to Jefferson Davis, May 31, 1863, in James A. Seddon Letters, Duke University Library, Durham, N.C.

[34] Ulysses S. Grant, *Personal Memoirs of U. S. Grant*, ed. E. B. Long (New York, 1952), 282; Goodloe, *Confederate Echoes*, 270.

lamation calling upon Mississippians "to rally to that army which is to fight the battle on which your liberties, your homes and property depend" and demonstrate "to our soldiers the assurance that they fight for a people worthy of their protection." The manifesto reached the citizenry, produced a favorable reaction, and caused the Natchez *Daily Courier* to wishfully predict that within a few weeks the "vandals" would be driven into retreat.[35]

Governor Pettus ordered state forces into Confederate commands without hesitation. Yet, defense preparations were impeded considerably for want of slave labor. Even when Negroes could be found for impressment purposes, the well-worn path of argument as to how much an owner should be compensated was often traversed. Undoubtedly, it was this dismal outlook that prompted the governor to move his family from Enterprise to Macon.[36]

As the enemy campaign directed at Vicksburg grew stronger during late May and early June, Confederate commanders in the entire area were given further cause for alarm. On May 21, United States Lieutenant Commander John G. Walker successfully led a force of five vessels against a southern naval yard at Yazoo City—destroying all such war material in the vicinity. A few days later Port Hudson, Louisiana, another link in the dwindling Confederate chain of strongholds protecting the Mississippi River, was surrounded by a northern force under the generalship of Nathaniel Banks.[37]

Things looked better at Vicksburg, at least on the surface. For even though the city was almost totally surrounded, its geographic position high on the bluffs overlooking the river afforded an excellent natural defense advantage. Union gunboats found

[35] Alexander, *Military Memoirs of A Confederate*, 364; Natchez *Daily Courier*, June 3, 1863.
[36] E. K. Hicks to Pettus, June 8, 1863, Mary Polka to Pettus, June 5, 1863, in Governor's Correspondence, Vol. LXIII; Goodloe, *Confederate Echoes*, 270–71.
[37] John D. Milligan, *Gunboats Down the Mississippi* (Annapolis, Md., 1965), 165–66; Edward Cunningham, *The Port Hudson Campaign, 1862–1863* (Baton Rouge, 1963), xi.

it difficult to bombard the city and could not elevate their guns enough to cause any damage until adjustments were made. Moreover, the defenders had an army of about 31,000 men with a firm resolve to hold their ground. A contributing factor here might have been the rumor that the Yankees intended to use black soldiers against the people of the state.[38]

While the beleaguered city outwardly reflected composure, the facts ran contrary to the image. The jails of the town were "filled with thieves and malefactors of every kind" who were described as being "filthy, ragged, coarse-featured, vile-spoken, and every way disgusting." More disturbing still was the fact that several of the Confederate officers serving there harbored a profound dislike for the commanding general. "They all said harsh, ill natured things, made ill-turned jests in regard to Gen. Pemberton," went one report of May 30.[39]

More relevant to the situation were those issues pertaining to the siege and their long-range implications. Since Grant's encirclement of Vicksburg, it was almost impossible for supplies or personnel to enter the city. Fear was manifested in high places that the defenders would not have "munitions enough for a long fight." Pemberton, it seems, had neglected to take maximum precautions against a prolonged confrontation and, prior to the coming of the Union army, had undercut his own position by quarrelling with railroad authorities. Not only inefficient, the general was further known to be a trivial man who, "in the very thickest of the campaign," spent too much time issuing orders "prescribing the manner in which communications should be folded and addressed, and gravely assuring us that none others would be considered."[40]

[38] Wilbur F. Crummer, *With Grant At Fort Donelson, Shiloh and Vicksburg* (Oakpark, Ill., 1915), 92; John Fiske, *The Mississippi Valley In the Civil War* (2nd ed.; Boston, 1928), 181; Quarles, *The Negro In the Civil War,* 220–22; Charles A. Dana, *Recollections of the Civil War, With the Leaders at Washington and in the Field in the Sixties* (New York, 1902), 86–87.
[39] Browne, *Four Years In Secessia,* 241; Entry for May 30, 1863, in William A. Drennan Diary.
[40] Frank E. Vandiver, *The Civil War Diary of General Josiah Gorgas* (University, Ala., 1947), 40; Robert C. Black, III, *The Railroads of the Confederacy* (Chapel

More troops arrived daily to supplement enemy resources. Rather than leading large-scale assaults against the southern defenses, the federals resorted to mortar and siege gun bombardment. In turn, the Confederates constructed appropriate shelters and civilians took to cave dwelling as a means of protection. Although the almost continuous day-to-day shelling did surprisingly little damage, everyone shared "the general fear of a sudden and frightful death." Although one individual found the rain of artillery fire humorous—being "highly amused" to see all the people jumping about trying to avoid the shells—the situation was serious. Disease added to the miseries of the place, and with the reality of siege it was not long before food began to run low. Sustenance was nearby, but the Confederates lacked both the labor to gather it or the ability to get it through the lines. Rationing was instituted, and rats, "mule-meat, and even dog-meat, became luxuries" in a little while. A song describing the dilemma went in part: "Old Grant is starving us out, our grub is fast wasting away; Pemb' don't know what he's about, and he hasn't for many a day." Morale was bound to wane and to supplement a lenten diet "men in blue and gray fraternized with one another, exchanging Yankee bread for Rebel tobacco."[41]

In the civilian sector things were not much better. A small bag of salt cost $45 and a turkey was $50. Boredom was often the order of the day, and men offered to "give any price for a drink of whiskey"—anything "for extra excitement." General Pemberton was not indifferent to these conditions nor to charges of his incompetence. In a two-fold attempt to rally the flagging spirits of his men and to counter his critics' accusation that he would

---

Hill, 1952), 194; J. H. Jones, "The Rank and File At Vicksburg," in Franklin L. Riley (ed.), *Publications of the Mississippi Historical Society* (Oxford, Miss., 1903), VII, 18–19.

[41] Loughborough, *My Cave Life in Vicksburg*, 78, 106, 113; J. T. Trowbridge, *The South: A Tour of Its Battlefields and Ruined Cities* (Hartford, 1866), 358; Entry for May 25, 1863, in Samuel A. Whyte Diary, University of North Carolina Library, Chapel Hill; Cunningham, *Doctors In Gray*, 172; Willard A. Heaps and Porter W. Heaps, *The Singing Sixties: The Spirit of Civil War Days Drawn from the Music of the Times* (Norman, Okla., 1960), 327; James A. Rawley, *Turning Points of the Civil War* (Lincoln, Neb., 1966), 160–61.

sell Vicksburg, he replied: "I will sell Vicksburg! When the last pound of beef and bacon and flour—the last grain of corn, the last cow and the last man shall perish in the trenches, then and only then will I sell Vicksburg."[42]

Outside the confines of the encircled city, Confederate and state authorities made every effort to send relief, but often with small results. Governor Pettus frequently urged President Davis to furnish additional manpower, believing that the river stronghold must "be held at every sacrifice." But the governor received little good news other than glowing tributes for his own labor.[43]

Even in the light of increasing adversity a few individuals, notably from the press, managed to maintain an optimistic posture. Atlanta papers reported that "Yankee dead" were "rotting" on the Vicksburg battlefield and that "the slaughter of the Yankees" was in excess of "any other battle of the war." Through the pages of the Jackson *Daily Mississippian* local people were informed that the defenders were "in good health" and "fine spirits," eager to be led against "the Vandal hordes of old Abe." The paper assured it readers, "The idea of surrendering never enters the head of any of them."[44]

Other contemporaries, especially the unprincipled ones, believed not a word of the superlative accounts directed at them and seized the opportunity to desert their units in the field. A Natchez conscription officer wrote of growing opposition to the entire war and expressed astonishment at the large number of non-furloughed troops in evidence. Sadly, "no way [could] be found to *force* them back into service."[45] Likely prospects for the military sometimes found it expedient to band together to resist draft personnel, and, in turn, were guilty of banditry.

John Pettus handled the situation as best he could, but with

[42] Entry for June 1, 1863, in William A. Drennan Diary; Natchez *Daily Courier*, May 31, 1863.
[43] Pettus et al. to Davis, June 10, 1863, in *Official Records*, Ser., I, Vol. LII, Part II, 493–94; James A. Seddon to Pettus, June 12, 1863, in Governor's Correspondence, Vol. LX.
[44] Atlanta *Daily Southern Confederacy*, May 28, 1863; Jackson *Daily Mississippian*, June 12, 16, 17, 1863.
[45] Lewis Pipes to Pettus, June 28, 1863, in Governor's Correspondence, Vol. LXI.

dwindling resources his motions lacked meaning. On one occasion he did order the confiscation of weapons from a privately organized militia company that planned to leave the state for Virginia.[46] Yet, considering the fact that nearly all of northern Mississippi was raid ridden, the southern part was occupied, and the federals had a stranglehold on Vicksburg, any action at all on his part was worth mentioning.

During June, 1863, the military atmosphere in Mississippi was one of utter depression. Although Vicksburg was not yet in enemy hands, many believed it was only a matter of time before it would be. Grant's army was in complete mastery of the situation, receiving a steady flow of fresh troops. The Union general even added insult to injury by obtaining supplies from neighboring plantations owned by President Davis and his brother Joseph. Nevertheless, even with all advantages in their favor, the northern soldiers were not always the most contented people. Local environment contributed to the discomfort of one Iowa sergeant who wrote that the "mosquitoes are becoming intolerable." Meals of "stewed beans and fritters" bothered a Yankee hospital steward, who longed for his wife to send him "a peace [sic] of the pie in the letter that you are going to write tonight."[47]

As June dragged on, the Rebels inside Vicksburg more than ever doubted the ability of John Pemberton, referring to him as being "wholly incapable to act as Gen. of an army." Jefferson Davis also garnered his share of negative comment, with a Mississippi soldier insisting that the president had "shamefully neglected us in every particular."[48] The end was drawing near.

In other quarters, Joseph Johnston was busy trying to assemble an impossible 50,000 troops in order to attempt an eleventh-hour link-up with Pemberton. Aware of these activities, Grant sent

[46] French, Two Wars, 138.
[47] Carl Sandburg, Storm Over the Land: A Profile of the Civil War (New York, 1939), 187; Entry for July 1, 1863, in John Hughes Diary, Library of Congress, Washington, D.C.; Silas W. Browing to Sarah Browing, June 28, 1863, in Silas W. Browing Papers, Library of Congress, Washington, D.C.
[48] Entry for June 1, 1863, in W. W. Lord, "Journal of the Siege of Vicksburg," Library of Congress, Washington, D.C.; Sydney Champion to Matilda Champion, June 25, 1863, in Sydney S. Champion Papers.

Sherman to harass Johnston's preparations and make menacing moves toward the Mississippi capital. This maneuver sapped the rebel commander's limited resources and created additional discomfort by forcing the Confederates to deal with a steady stream of refugees.[49]

The new Union thrust toward Jackson led the governor to conclude that the main object of the expedition was to capture *him*. In something less than a display of absolute valiantry, Petus fled the city nightly to a camp on the opposite side of the Pearl River near Jackson. Apparently, the pressures of the moment got the better of him, for he soon left the city altogether. Much to the displeasure of Richmond reinforcements, "who had come well nigh a thousand miles to assist that government," they arrived only to find the "Governor's family gone, his mansion deserted, the entire machinery of his government removed, and ... [themselves] left, without the assistance, support, countenance, or even the presence of its head."[50]

Johnston's army unable to move, the last vestige of hope for Vicksburg vanished. General Pemberton's emphatic pronouncement that he was "determined to die in the trenches rather than surrender" amounted to mere empty rhetoric. The Gibraltar of the Western Hemisphere capitulated on July 4, 1863. The fall of Vicksburg, coupled with the near simultaneous check sustained by Robert E. Lee's forces at Gettysburg, compounded southern misery.

Surrender procedures at Vicksburg were conducted with ceremony and dispatch. One observer noted that the federal forces "acted splendidly" and neither jeered nor taunted those who turned in their arms. However, as the rebels were abandoning their weapons a gun accidentally discharged, killing a bystander —the last to die on that battlefield. After processing, most of the Confederate troops were paroled and allowed to return

[49] Grant, *Personal Memoirs*, 290; Bruce Catton, *Grant Moves South* (Boston, 1960), 460–61; Mary E. Massey, *Refugee Life In the Confederacy* (Baton Rouge, 1964), 88.
[50] French, *Two Wars*, 183; D. W. Yandell to John M. Johnson, June 17, 1863, in Rowland (ed.), *Jefferson Davis Constitutionalist*, VI, 3.

home. A few were sent to New Orleans before being released because they announced that they would not abide by the terms of release. A small number of southerners, it is interesting to note, even joined the Union army at that time.[51]

Although the losses sustained at Vicksburg dealt a powerful blow to both the morale of Mississippi in particular and the South in general, President Davis did not learn the sad news of what happened along the Mississippi River for several days. On July 8 he was still trying to locate the confused and troubled Governor Pettus, telegraphing: "What is the state of affairs at Vicksburg?" For that matter, General Johnston still had not heard anything official from Vicksburg by July 11. Before long Pettus did regain some semblance of composure and was once again analyzing military matters. After finally receiving Davis' dispatch of July 8, the governor replied that Vicksburg had fallen and acknowledged that Port Hudson gave signs of doing so. In sum, he wrote, the "affairs [in] Mississippi look gloomy."[52]

Yet, Governor Pettus was not ready to concede defeat. Since 30,000 or so Confederate and state troops had surrendered at Vicksburg, the federals, as was their custom, released them under a loyalty pledge and the promise not to participate in the war again. Nevertheless, Pettus proposed to Jefferson Davis that the paroled men be requested to rearm and fight once more. By this method "Mississippi *may yet be saved.*" The southern president declined the recommendation and expressed "painful disappointment" with military developments, but indicated that he preferred to prepare the remainder of the state for defense so as to rally "public opinion."[53]

---

[51] Loughborough, *My Cave Life In Vicksburg*, 139; Jones, "The Rank and File At Vicksburg," 30; Garner, *Reconstruction In Mississippi*, 53.

[52] Davis to Pettus, July 8, 1863, in Governor's Correspondence, Vol. LXII; Johnston to Jefferson Davis, July 11, 1863, in Jefferson Davis Papers, Duke University Library; Pettus to Davis, July 14, 1863, in *Official Records*, Ser. I, Vol. LII, Part II, 507.

[53] H. C. Clarke (ed.), *The Confederate State Almanac and Repository of Useful Knowledge for 1865, Compiled and Published by H. C. Clark* (Mobile, 1865), 79; Pettus to Davis, July 9, 1863, Davis to Pettus, July 11, 1863, in Governor's Correspondence, Vols. LXI, LXIII.

Meanwhile, the federals had focused their attention on Jackson. As a Massachusetts soldier put it, "we are going to bag Johnston or get whipped Grant says." Six miles of Confederate lines spread available manpower so thin that a direct, large-scale assault would have certainly succeeded. Unaware of this weakness General Sherman was content to bombard the city in a fashion not unlike that employed at Vicksburg. "The weather," he later recalled, "was fearfully hot, but we continued to press the siege day and night, using our artillery pretty freely."[54]

Inside the capital, opinions were mixed. Talk had it that the city was properly defended. But one soldier who was critical in this respect noted that "the old men at home are all generals now. Our soldiers have all come to the conclusion that they have no friends out of the army except the ladies." The Yankees were not long in determining that the defenses of Jackson were something less than formidable. An Illinois captain summed it up fairly well when he wrote that the fortifications were more imaginary than real. Breastworks, for example, contained "sham" or "wooden guns" only.[55]

Realizing the fruitlessness of continued defensive warfare and the possibility of being trapped into another Vicksburg, Joseph Johnston ordered the evacuation of the city. During the night of July 16 his entire army, undetected, withdrew and headed for Enterprise, the temporary capital of the state. While marching toward the new objective large numbers of men simply deserted and left for home. Believing that Johnston had made a wrong decision, one of the men in his command probably reduced the overall feeling of the moment to words when he said: "I am truly tyerd [sic] of this unholy war."[56]

Yankee troops occupied Jackson on the morning of July 17.

[54] William F. Draper to Father, July 12, 1863, in William F. Draper Letters, Library of Congress, Washington, D.C.; William T. Sherman, *Memoirs of General W. T. Sherman* (New York, 1892), I, 359.
[55] Douglas Cater to Cousin Fannie, June 24, 1863, in Douglas J. Cater and Rufus W. Cater Papers; Entry for July, 1863, in Wimer Bedford Diary, Library of Congress, Washington D.C.
[56] Taylor (ed.), *Reluctant Rebel*, 122; Wiley (ed.), *Confederate Letters of John W. Hagan*, 28.

The following evening the governor's mansion was the scene of a large victory party. A general, noticed to be missing next morning, was found "asleep beneath the table, so freely had the wine flowed." Union forces, however, did follow the rebels for a short period, then, because "it was so hot and water so scarce [*sic*]," they stopped and were content to tear up ten miles of railroad track. At the same time prominent Mississippi Unionists appeared in Jackson and began to chart plans for peace and a new state government.[57] But the war was not over and more fighting lay ahead.

At first glance the surrenders of Vicksburg and Jackson gave every indication of complete disaster. Although this turn of events was unwelcome, the reality of the matter was that the Mississippi River had long since ceased to be of major use in obtaining food and war supplies from the trans-Mississippi region. The now complete loss of unimpeded access to the river was more of a propaganda disappointment to the South than a military and economic blow.

A more important consideration relates to the southern side of the Mississippi campaign. Strategy and defense maneuvers often proved to be unimaginative, hesitant, and erratic. Aside from the lack of complete unity between Confederate and state authorities, Richmond officials often failed to coordinate campaign philosophy. Notable among the difficulties generated by these circumstances were the well-known differences of opinion held by Jefferson Davis and Joseph Johnston and the failure of the central government to achieve a unified command system in this theater of operations until it was too late.

In November, 1862, Johnston was made supreme commander of a six-state area which included Mississippi. He was a capable man, but "his authority was never clearly defined."[58] Moreover, the general's orders to subordinates were occasionally contra-

---

[57] Shelby Foote, *The Civil War: A Narrative* (New York, 1963), II, 621; Robert Hoadley to Cousin Elm, July 30, 1863, in Robert B. Hoadley Papers; Garner, *Reconstruction In Mississippi*, 51–53.
[58] Frank E. Vandiver, *Rebel Brass: The Confederate Command System* (Baton Rouge, 1956), 58–59.

dicted by the president or otherwise complicated by members of the War Department. Apart from the fact that he was ill at the moment when Grant began his thrust toward Vicksburg via Jackson, Johnston was still able to arrive in time to grasp the meaning of the situation and was in a position to have salvaged at least the bulk of the rebel forces that were ultimately blundered away.

As Grant's plan became evident, Johnston ordered Pemberton to evacuate the city if possible and save his army. But the president had already intervened and issued instructions that Vicksburg be held at all cost. Pemberton, caught in the middle, followed Davis' lead and soon became pinned down in a siege.[59] Johnston, with no viable alternative, made the best of an impossible situation by attempting to raise an army out of thin air, with which to relieve his beleaguered subordinate.

Fundamentally, Joseph Johnston and Jefferson Davis differed widely on the way wars and campaigns ought to be conducted. Johnston advocated a policy of large-scale coordinated assault, while Davis preferred defensive techniques, especially in reference to Vicksburg. By this stage of the conflict it was numbers and armies that mattered most, not cities. Unfortunately for Johnston, in the words of one historian, "too much of [his] career consists of the things he would have done, if circumstances had only been different."[60]

Surprisingly enough, the only real villain to emerge from the Mississippi campaign and the protracted struggle for Vicksburg was John Pemberton. Although an individual given to courage and self-reliance, such attributes had a habit of cancelling each other when it came to making decisions. Both his motives and dedication to the southern cause were often the subject of inquiry, with an almost universal contemporary condemnation

[59] Frank E. Vandiver, "Jefferson Davis and Unified Army Command," *Louisiana Historical Quarterly*, XXXVIII (1955), 33–34.
[60] Joseph E. Johnston, *Narrative of Military Operations Directed During the Late War Between the States* (Bloomington, Ind., 1959), 216; Ross H. Moore, "The Vicksburg Campaign of 1863," *Journal of Mississippi History*, I (July, 1939), 167.

resulting.[61] However, it was not Pemberton's treason in generous-
ly bestowing such a prize upon the enemy that really mattered;
rather, it was what the federals were in a position to ultimately
take that counted. The chief error that Vicksburg's defender committed was that of surrendering the city on the day that he did.
In the last analysis, no matter what course he had elected to
follow, his posture in the history books probably would not have
changed much. Time and circumstance had him cornered in
more ways than the Union army.

While the Mississippi campaign was to be debated long into
the future, contemporary Mississippians were far more concerned with the realities of the day than with trying to affix
abstract blame for what happened. The war was over for many,
but for those who desired to continue the struggle the task of
once more putting together a war machine was complicated as
never before.

By the end of July, 1863, a huge portion of the Magnolia State
was in enemy hands. Subsequent calls to the colors proved all
but useless, yielding a mere 176 volunteers.[62] With the fall of
Jackson, military necessity dictated that the governor transfer
the seat of government several times during the next few months.
Although hard pressed, John Pettus was determined to resist
the federals to the last extremity. Events had taken a decisive
turn and the ultimate verdict of destiny could not be far behind.

[61] Joseph B. Mitchell, *Decisive Battles of the Civil War* (New York, 1955), 139.
[62] Gill Shorter to Pettus, July 6, 1863, in Governor's Correspondence, Vol. LXI;
Joseph Johnston to Pettus, July 13, 1863, in *Official Records*, Ser. I, Vol. XXIV,
Part I, 201.

XI

From "Utter Destruction" to Exile

THE MILITARY FABRIC OF MISSISSIPPI during the summer of 1863 was one of profound deterioration. All points of strategic or propaganda value had vanished. Vicksburg, Jackson, the Gulf Coast, and northern and western Mississippi were occupied. There was little hope of reclaiming any of those areas since the manpower reserves were near total exhaustion.

In an attempt to come to grips with these developments the Confederate Congress strengthened existing conscription policies, especially with reference to substitutions (President Davis had already extended the age limits). Specifically, a new law stated that any individual who elected to furnish a substitute was to be held responsible for duty in the event the services of the substitute were "lost to the Government from any cause other than the casualties of war."[1] Jefferson Davis knew full well that the effective southern forces must be added to as promptly as possible.

The new policy was pressed into use in unoccupied Mississippi, but the same old story of noncooperation was still in evidence. Conflict between Confederate authorities and Governor John Pettus was due to a number of reasons. Colonel T. P. August, inspecting officer for the Richmond Bureau of Conscrip-

---

[1] Confederate Conscription Notice, July 21, 1863, in Governor's Correspondence, Vol. LXI.

tion, visited the temporary capital at Enterprise. After examining the state adjutant general's military files, August found that collaboration was nearly impossible because the records were "so very meager that I could not ascertain the number of regiments, [or] batteries . . . furnished by the State." With his own military resources at a premium and several companies well below minimum fighting strength, Pettus was in no mood to help the implementation of Richmond's hard-line measures. The governor felt that if Confederate officials would relax their stand instead of strengthening it, he would be able, through state personnel, to raise men from regions where the Richmond officials could not "get out the conscripts."² President Davis concurred.

The governor's approach did meet with some initial success. Within two weeks, two regiments and three battalions as well as several unattached companies—fearing Confederate conscription—volunteered for state service. Unfortunately, Confederate officers had not been informed of the president's agreement with the governor and insisted upon forcibly drafting state units into central government ranks. Such procedures, Pettus complained, only brought "total demoralization," and "for the good of the cause" enlistees must be allowed to remain in state service. Davis reassured his anxious cousin that no further interference would occur.³

The Davis–Pettus understanding was not only confusing, but invoked a good deal of displeasure from certain Confederate officers. Brigadier General Gideon J. Pillow questioned the wisdom of the move and grumbled bitterly to the secretary of war that it was downright impossible to determine which organizations belonged to whom. Cavalry units were particularly hard to distinguish, as the countryside was "full of floating companies . . . without having been mustered or received by the State authorities; all claiming to be parts of the State force." The

² August to G. W. Lay, August 10, 1863, Pettus to Jefferson Davis, August 11, 1863, in *Official Records*, Ser. IV, Vol. II, 707, 762.
³ Pettus to Davis, August 25, 1863, Davis to Pettus, August 28, 1863, in Governor's Correspondence, Vol. LXI.

entire program, Pillow contended, was deliberately designed for the purpose of "taking shelter from conscription." A spokesman for the governor denied this charge, asserting that it was not the intention of the state to undermine the policies of Richmond.[4]

Amid these unsettled times Governor Pettus managed to make room for consultations with Alabama's chief executive. At a meeting in Demopolis joint cooperation was pledged between the two neighboring states, but nothing substantive emerged. Undoubtedly, the strain of office had begun to tell, for the Mississippian appeared tired and weak.[5]

Throughout September and October, conscription continued to be a thorny question, so Pettus sent advisor James Rives into the field for a firsthand look. After close investigation, Rives wrote to his superior that a number of companies were embroiled in the same old controversy and concluded that such strife would "result in no good to the service." Another observer noted that a large number of men were taking advantage of the Pettus–Davis understanding by "loitering about under the pretence of raising Cavalry Companies."[6]

In view of this, and prompted by Joseph Johnston, the governor temporarily acquiesced on the issue of conscription by ordering one thousand troops enrolled in Confederate ranks. President Davis, also concerned about the draft dilemma, made a hurried trip to Mississippi and held a series of discussions with Pettus at Lauderdale Springs. The prime topic of conversation was, of course, the festering military situation. It was subsequently agreed that the state's military system would undergo reorganization, whereby any "unattached companies" would be surrendered to Richmond control. A compromise was struck, to the effect that units or groups turned over by this method would not be broken up and placed in new commands under

[4] Pillow to James Seddon, August 26, 1863, James Rives to Gideon Pillow, August 25, 1863, in *Official Records*, Ser. IV, Vol. II, 759–60.
[5] Edmund Pettus to Mary Pettus, August 14, 1863, in E. W. Pettus Papers.
[6] Rives to Pettus, September 3, 1863, James Drane to Pettus, September 27, 1863, in Governor's Correspondence, Vol. LXI.

new officers. No sooner had the meetings ended, however, when Pettus took great liberty with the guidelines and rescinded his earlier decision to send General Johnston one thousand men. The explanation given for this action was that these troops might be split into new organizations.[7]

By the autumn of 1863 disenchantment with the war had grown to serious proportions, even in the unoccupied portions of the Magnolia State. A friend of the governor voiced the sad conclusion that the federals would occupy "the most of Mississippi" in a short while. Even stronger words were expressed by another contemporary who advocated complete surrender and the adoption of the Union oath policy as a way of ending the fruitless struggle. But the fiery governor refused to capitulate and set about on the vain mission of obstructing the state's rivers in order to hamper federal operations. In reality, Pettus was not in a position to do much of anything. When he was forced into Alabama to avoid a Yankee patrol, a newspaper editor asked: "Who's the Governor of the State of Mississippi in Alabama?"[8] At this stage, Pettus might just as well have been the governor of a desert island. His control over the affairs in his own state was more imaginary than real—a paper kingdom.

Pettus' term of office was due to expire in early November of 1863. Since state law did not permit his reelection a third successive time, he became a political "lame duck," unable to implement any bold new programs, even if they might have had any chance for success. Elections were duly held in October, and General Charles Clark was overwhelmingly chosen to replace Pettus. Of the large number of candidates in the field, Clark—described as a moderate—was the front-runner with 16,428 votes. His two nearest rivals, Absalom W. West and Reuben Davis (both close associates of Pettus), ran a poor sec-

[7] James Rives to Johnston, October 15, 1863, Pettus to S. J. Gholson, October 30, 1863, *ibid.*

[8] Robert Kells to Pettus, September 14, 1863, W. L. Nugent to Pettus, September 27, 1863, in Governor's Correspondence, Vol. LXI; Pettus to Joseph E. Johnston, October 15, 1863, in *Official Records*, Ser. I, Vol. LII, Part II, 544; Natchez *Daily Courier*, October 20, 1863.

ond and third, polling 4,863 and 2,009 ballots, respectively.[9]

The legislature convened for a regular session in Macon during early November. Governor Pettus addressed the gathering and brought the lawmakers up to date on existing affairs of state, not failing to make appropriate recommendations for continuing armed resistance. High on the list of topics was disloyalty. While admitting that some individuals had taken the oath of allegiance to the United States, Pettus optimistically reassured his listeners that the "great heart of the people of Mississippi . . . [had re-mained] as true to the cause . . . as hopeful and buoyant as when the contest first began." He bolstered this contention with statistics relating to military enlistments and war production.[10]

Next, Pettus elaborated upon the slave question. The solons were urged to take action to prevent Negroes from falling into enemy hands, so as to prevent their use by the federals. Many bondsmen freed by Union troops were guilty of pillaging neigh-borhoods and murdering people in their homes. Evidently, Washington's policy was also one of using Negro troops "to per-fect the destruction and demoralization of the country which the Federal army may occupy." For this reason and this reason alone, the governor said, he had stood in the way of transferring state forces to Confederate command.

Knowing that this discourse would be his final one as Missis-sippi's chief executive, Pettus uttered his last official words in bombastic and patriotic fashion. It was necessary for the people of Mississippi, he said, to "spend what we have in manly resis-tance [rather] than permit it to become the prey of plundering invaders." Since the "known purpose" of the Yankees was to "lay waste our land and confiscate whatever escapes the ravages of war . . . [and] reduce this people to a condition far worse than European serfdom," there was no alternative other than fighting to the bitter end. Monetary considerations should not "stand in the way of the amplest preparations of men and

---

[9] Mississippi *House Journal* (November, 1863), 112–14. Statistics differ slightly in the Mississippi *Senate Journal* (November, 1863), 113.

[10] Mississippi *Senate Journal* (November, 1863), 89–100.

means." There could be "no half-way house of rest in this revolution," affirmed the governor. "Independence or death" were the only avenues available. A prayer was offered, beseeching the "God who favors the just cause" to guide the lawmakers in the difficult times ahead.

Upon the conclusion of his message, Pettus left the legislature which he had known and worked with for two full decades never to return to its chambers. An era was rapidly drawing to a close. In his final official act as governor, Pettus cancelled outstanding salt contracts, ordered the state's money to be returned to the treasury, and exchanged political office for the battlefield.[11]

John Pettus bestowed upon the new chief executive a legacy punctuated with compromise, defeat, and disloyalty. The die that had been cast in the fire of secession and tempered in the heat and flame of war now formed a steel noose around the state. The problems that Charles Clark had to contend with were the same as those of his predecessor, only worse. Although the reins of state government were not surrendered to the federals until May 22, 1865, little meaningful remained for the new governor to do but to prolong the agony and the inevitable. By 1864, the "whole of Mississippi . . . [was] beyond aid from Richmond."[12] Without such assistance the alternatives were few and the measures of great consequence none.

Upon leaving office John Pettus elected to remain within Mississippi. Although there had been talk during the spring of the year that he would seek a Confederate senate seat, any movement along those lines failed to materialize—Pettus had too many enemies. Instead, he joined his family for a brief rest period and went into hiding in the central part of the state. Union troops were always on the lookout for him; however, they only managed to carry off some of his slaves.[13]

---

[11] Pettus to W. C. Turner, November 9, 1863, in Governor's Correspondence, Vol. LXI.

[12] Nathaniel W. Stephenson, *The Day of the Confederacy: A Chronicle of the Embattled South* (New Haven, 1920), 115.

[13] Walker, *Vicksburg*, 209; Edmund Pettus to Mary Pettus, March 11, 1864, in E. W. Pettus Papers.

During the summer of 1864 the former governor concluded that he must, once again, come to the aid of his state. He did so in humble fashion by enrolling as a private in Company B of the First Mississippi Infantry, better known as the "Copiah Guards," which was under command of Colonel H. W. Foote. No record exists for that company's activities, but it was known that Pettus did receive an appointment as a major in the same organization on August 8. A month later he became a colonel and was placed in command of manpower centers at Grenada and Macon.[14]

Before long Pettus was writing to Governor Clark and freely tendering his advice on the conduct of the war. Pettus indicated that if he were still governor he would utilize roving militia companies for the protection of counties along the Mississippi River, where the federals were operating at will. Such commands would remain on detached service in order to safeguard the region "from utter destruction by negroes and Yankees." Clark promptly reminded Pettus that the direct responsibility for the area in question, at this particular time, belonged to General Nathan Bedford Forrest, and the former chief executive was instructed to operate as he saw fit, after first consulting Forrest.[15]

Meanwhile, the war in Mississippi went on. But by the end of the year the total submission of the state was so near complete that General Sherman was able to report that he had laid "a swath of desolation fifty miles broad across the State of Mississippi, which the present generation will not forget."[16]

Ex-governor Pettus continued to traverse the state in an effort to rally the flagging hopes of the people and was said to have unsuccessfully tried to raise his own regiment of five hundred men. Few details are known of his activities from the winter of 1864 until April, 1865, at which time he was stationed near Canton.

[14] State of Mississippi, *Register of Commissions, Army of Mississippi, 1861–1865*, Ser. L, Vol. A, 135, Mississippi Department of Archives and History; Rowland, *Official and Statistical Register*, 935.
[15] Pettus to Clark, August 29, 1864, Clark to Pettus, September 1, 1864, in Governor's Correspondence, Vol. LXVI.
[16] Lloyd Lewis, *Sherman: Fighting Prophet* (3rd. ed.; New York, 1960), 333.

Pettus took the news of Robert E. Lee's Virginia surrender hard. From Canton he made his way to Bolivar County Judge W. L. Harris' home. There, on September 4, 1865, Pettus signed the United States loyalty oath.[17]

Within a week the former governor was back at his home in Kemper County. On September 10 he dispatched a letter requesting personal amnesty and parole to President Andrew Johnson. The communication took special note of the president's interest in the "reconciliation of the two sections" of the nation.[18] When no action was taken on the application, Pettus went into hiding in neighboring Arkansas, where he had relatives and friends. An associate, T. N. T. Roberts, accompanied him into this self-imposed exile, as did a former slave called Pleas. Pleas apparently had been so thoroughly frightened into believing that the bluecoats were worse than the devil himself that he went of his own accord.[19]

For some time after the assassination of Abraham Lincoln, a rumor circulated throughout the nation that a conspiracy of southern leaders had been responsible for his death. While no evidence exists that John Pettus was ever named in that charge, both he and his family believed that he would be. According to a daughter, Willie Pettus Lapsby, her father felt certain that his arrest was imminent and therefore suggested the possibility of migrating with Jefferson Davis and others to Mexico together and "there perfect their plans for their future." Such plans included the resumption of the war on a guerilla basis.[20] This, of course, failed to materialize and the former governor went to Arkansas instead.

[17] S. S. Angevine to James R. Chalmers, August 20, 1864, in *Official Records*, Ser. I, Vol. XXXIX, Part II, 789; Yazoo City *Sentinel*, October 20, 1910; Pettus Loyalty Oath, September 4, 1865, in John Jones Pettus Amnesty Papers, Group No. 94, National Archives and Record Service, Washington, D.C.
[18] Pettus to Johnson, September 10, 1865, in John Jones Pettus Amnesty Papers. William Sharkey, provisional governor of Mississippi, attached a note to the same letter indicating his personal approval of the application.
[19] Boyd, "Personal Interview with ex-slave Joe Pettus."
[20] Willie Pettus Lapsby to John L. Power, December 10, 1897, in John L. Power Papers, Mississippi Department of Archives and History. For reference to

Once in Arkansas, Pettus took up residence on a small plantation in Pulaski County owned by a distant relative, John M. Jones. Although he grew a long, full beard, the federals were able to learn of his general whereabouts and on different occasions unsuccessfully sought him out. Once, they even hired Indian trackers to aid in the search, forcing Pettus to seek refuge in a swamp for several days. So cleverly did he disappear from view that his brother Edmund was unable to communicate with him and consequently had to assume the burden of caring for John's wife and children.[21]

In early 1866 a number of persons attempted to intercede with federal officials on John Pettus' behalf. Notable among these individuals was brother Edmund. On January 13, 1866, he wrote to Washington appealing his brother's case. Edmund declared that although John had used "all his powers to aid the Confederates," he had done so "in an open and manly way."[22]

When nothing transpired regarding the amnesty question, John returned to Mississippi and once more signed the oath of allegiance to the United States. Moreover, he wrote a second letter to President Johnson outlining his limbo status and underscored the fact that he preferred to "remain a citizen of the United States" instead of "seeking a house in a foreign land among strangers." The new governor of Mississippi, Benjamin G. Humphreys, also attested to Pettus' "truth and integrity" by signing the same communication.[23]

While this series of events was unfolding the ex-governor visited his wife and family at Scooba. Daughter Willie noted that her father seemed "bent and changed" by his recent ordeal. Yet, the Washington government was not ready to grant him

---

the assassination conspiracy see Richard N. Current, *Old Thad Stevens: A Story of Ambition* (Madison, Wisc., 1942), 208–209, 212.

[21] Clarksdale *Register*, October 14, 1910; Little Rock *Arkansas Gazette*, October 9, 1938; Edmund Pettus to John A. Winston, December 24, 1865, in E. W. Pettus Papers.

[22] Edmund Pettus to Lewis E. Parsons, January 13, 1866, in John Jones Pettus Amnesty Papers.

[23] Pettus Loyalty Oath, February 8, 1866, Pettus to Johnson, February 8, 1866, Humphreys to Johnson, February 19, 1866, *ibid.*

forgiveness. A final petition was made on his behalf in the spring of 1866, at which time it was noted that the family wanted him home because of his "very delicate health."[24]

Meanwhile, with no relief in sight, John returned to Arkansas where he continued to periodically outwit and outrun those who would bring him to the bar of Reconstruction justice. But the turbulent years of war and then of constant flight ultimately took their toll. In early 1867 John Pettus died—an outcast in his own land. All sources concur that the cause of death was pneumonia; however, the exact time of demise remains in doubt —either January 26 or February 6.[25] At any rate, Pettus was buried in a cornfield on the Jones plantation. This property was eventually acquired by Thomas H. Allen of Memphis, Tennessee, who on January 1, 1886, sold it to Robert A. Little of Little Rock for $10,000.[26]

In June, 1888, while surveying the far corners of his plantation, Little discovered a grave marked only by "a few rude posts." An inquiry established that the grave belonged to John Pettus. Not wishing to have the remains continue to reside on his estate, believing a field to be no proper resting place for a person of Pettus' significance, Little ordered the metal casket transferred to Flat Bayou Burial Ground near Wabbaseka, Arkansas. This was accomplished and the episode all but forgotten.[27]

Interest in the governor's grave was revived in the late 1920s when the Memphis *Commercial Appeal* carried a story which contended that Dr. M. A. Shelton of Wabbaseka knew the exact

[24] Willie Pettus Lapsby to John Power, December 10, 1897, in John L. Power Papers; R. W. Lewis to James Speed, April 23, 1866, in John Jones Pettus Amnesty Papers.
[25] Edmund Pettus states that his brother's death occurred on February 6, 1867. See Mrs. Louis Raymond to John Power, in John L. Power Papers. Other sources insist that John died on January 26, 1867. See Little Rock *Arkansas Gazette*, October 9, 1938; Pocahontas H. Stacy, *The Pettus Family*, ed. A. B. Rudd (Washington, D.C., 1957), 18.
[26] General Index to Deeds, 1884–1896, Deed Records, Vol. XXVIII, Lonoke County Courthouse, Lonoke, Ark. The author acknowledges the generous assistance provided by Circuit Clerk Garland Bain in this matter.
[27] *Daily Arkansas Gazette*, June 10, 1888.

site of Pettus' interment. The article stated that the grave had never been properly marked.[28] News of the discovery soon reached Mississippi, and on January 20, 1928, Representative David C. Langston of Lee County introduced a bill into the Mississippi house of representatives calling for the appropriation of $1,000 for the purpose of returning the former governor's remains to his home state. Three days later the measure was passed by a vote of 108 to 12. The state senate, by the margin of 43 to 1, followed suit on the matter.

Although preparations for the transfer were made, along with planned celebrations and other appropriate ceremonies, such endeavors proved to be of no avail. First, Pettus' granddaughter, Caroline Weedon, refused to sanction the disinterment, believing that the state that had afforded him refuge should continue to possess his bones. Secondly, Mississippi Governor Theodore G. Bilbo vetoed the bill providing funds for the return. For, as he viewed it, the measure was clearly "discretionary and should have included provisions allowing for the removal of the body of former Governor [John J.] McRae from its grave in British Honduras."[29]

The author visited Flat Bayou Burial Ground in the summer of 1968 and his investigation revealed no clear evidence that Governor Pettus' grave is in that location. However, two senior citizens of Wabbaseka, Dave Bogy and Edward Townsend, consulted at closely separated intervals, insisted that the burial site is indeed there. Both indicated the position of the grave to be in the extreme western portion of the cemetery, beneath an old oak tree. Be this as it may, such is often the price of contrasting fortune in periods of great thunder, and perhaps the missing grave stands as an excellent reminder of that kind of history John Jones Pettus passed through.

[28] Memphis *Commercial Appeal*, January 29, 1928.
[29] Little Rock *Arkansas Gazette*, October 9, 1938; Jackson *Daily Clarion-Ledger*, February 16, 1928.

Epilogue

THE CIVIL WAR was not over for either Mississippi or the embattled Confederacy when John Jones Pettus left office as governor of his state. It had gone too far for that, and perhaps the temperament of a people in the process of being overwhelmed militarily would not have let it end. (In reference to certain social and cultural attitudes, it has never really ended at all.) However, by late 1863 Mississippi was no longer in a position to play a decisive role in determining the ultimate destiny that would be concluded at Appomattox courthouse in April, 1865.

Pettus' tenure in various elective offices within his state not only coincided with the first cycles of the secession movement, but witnessed the virtual collapse of efforts calculated to achieve permanent southern independence. To gauge the significance of this man in terms of the negative and rather dusty "lost cause" philosophy is neither fair nor accurate and does not quite get at the heart of the matter. The rendering of balanced judgment can only be achieved by means of an understanding of the interaction of the various groups and forces present during the war years.

On occasion, John Pettus has been evaluated somewhat unkindly. Yet, considering the fact that so many contemporaries went on record in one fashion or another, it is not unnatural that conflicting interpretations should appear. Those persons who participated in the mainstream of events during the period might understandably have been more emotional than objective. On the other hand, historians should have done more to uncloud the picture.

In any case, Pettus' lifework, when examined within the context of the unsettled 1850s and 1860s, emerges as a thing of value, not only for the political and military fabric of Mississippi, but for the larger spectrum of the Confederate side of the Civil War drama. If nothing else, many of his activities demonstrate that he did not fit the stereotype commonly attached to southern gov-

ernors during this crucial period of history. Unfortunately, the
time has not yet arrived when students of the Civil War fail to
accept such personages as governors Joseph E. Brown of Georgia, John Milton of Florida, and Zebulon B. Vance of North
Carolina as being representative of southern state executive
leadership from 1860 to 1865. The latter individuals, often re-
membered for their notorious defiance of Richmond authority
and lack of cooperation, probably contributed heavily to the
generalization that gubernatorial guidance was sadly lacking
and too often tainted by self-indulgent states-rights attitudes.
A thorough analysis of the southern Civil War governors needs to
be conducted. By concentrating on the chief executive officer
of each of the Confederate states, a clearer picture of the unfolding of events is likely to emerge along with substantive
change in historical interpretation.

John Pettus' career, unlike those of certain other men who
held public station during the era, manifested support for a
unified course of action on behalf of the South. For without unity
what chance would there have been in the secession movement,
let alone war? If not a military expert—and they were few and
far between—Pettus proved capable of analyzing such developments with great accuracy. By far the most fundamental program for which Pettus labored was that of southern nationalism.
His support of the Nashville convention of 1850, the proposed
Atlanta convention of 1860, greater commercial intercourse
among the slaveholding states, and an enlarged system of roads
and railroads appears to reinforce this conviction.

Another point needs further elaboration, namely, that which
pertains to the motives of the man. Pettus was, after all, a politician. If judged according to principle as much as result, he
must be considered a success. When first elected governor in
late 1859, he commanded 75 percent of the electorate. Even
the most cursory inspection of the language employed during
the campaign could leave little doubt as to what his long-range
objectives were. At a time when cool and clear heads were
needed with which to pursue the arts of peace and compromise,

John Pettus waxed bold and aggressive. He and others like him fed on the raw fruit of passion and uncertainty. Such attitudes, once taken to logical conclusion, produced a situation with only the most limited of alternatives. Assuming as he did his state's championship in the secession movement, it is only just that part of the responsibility for the horrible consequences which followed be placed on his shoulders. Electing to flow with, if not lead, a tide nourished by emotion instead of attempting to pour oil on troubled waters, he contributed in no small way toward bringing on the ravages of war.

In all fairness, however, one should not overlook the fact that Pettus did not go about his plans for disunion unmindful of the possible outcome. But the public clamor for withdrawal from the Union soon left him with little choice other than the course dictated by election mandate. Although fully committed to secession, and often failing to temper his radicalism with the advice offered by men of more moderate persuasion, he chose to hear and believe only that which he wanted to. On several occasions he gave credence to military and political evaluations that amounted to little more than mere wishful thinking. Once hostilities began he sometimes allowed himself to rely upon political doctrines rather than military realities. This policy frequently undercut his effectiveness and left him open to the charge of being too slow. Even so, he was not telepathic, but did grasp the meaning of inflation, a cotton embargo, offensive warfare, and the impact of a federal blockade.

In the election contest of 1861, Pettus commanded nearly 90 percent of the popular vote. As the war magnified in intensity, the people made known their fears and needs and he left no stone unturned in trying to ease their suffering. Yet, his efforts were not enough and at times lacked gusto. Moreover, there are numerous instances on record where he chose to argue political issues at the expense of more germaine problems. Rather than inform his constituents that he did not have the authority to correct an adverse situation, he might have acted on his own, even if it meant exceeding his constitutional prerogatives. The times were certainly critical enough to warrant more positive leadership. The supreme irony of it all seems to have been that the very doctrine which began the secession movement in the first place—limited governmental authority—made Pettus a prisoner in his own camp.

If criticism for Mississippi's failure to make a better showing in the war must be a factor, it would appear that responsibility should rest jointly upon the governor and Confederate authorities. The fall of Jackson and that of Vicksburg amply illustrate this point.

Along similar lines, Mississippi's legislature must also be held accountable for the circumstances of the times. The legislature was often sluggish in attending to military matters, even when the governor repeatedly tried to impress upon its members the necessity for swift and positive action. The lawmakers failed to adjust to the economic demands of the hour and elected not to transfer into the hands of a single man the powers necessary to deal with contingencies at hand. By the time the legislators had acted meaningfully, the war had reached such volume that regardless of what transpired, the course of history could hardly have been altered.

Although rurally oriented, John Pettus was the true champion of almost all his people. Conversely, he was often uncommon in that he was able to divorce himself from political considerations when the need arose. Decisions pertaining to the state Military Board, militia laws, enforcement of conscription policies, the acquisition of salt, and the production of cotton proved unpopular but necessary. Intellectually and spiritually he remained strong. The weight of leadership might have proven more tolerable had it not been for an unyielding legislature and the persistence of pro-Union sentiment within the state. Whigs and other anti-secessionists compounded a difficult situation and never really vanished. In giving too much freedom and taking too little responsibility, Pettus was unable to eliminate such attitudes. In keeping within the paradox of contemporary ideology, it would appear that Mississippi's war effort, in part, "died of democracy."[1]

Although the governor was theoretically the leader of his state, the burden for the eventual outcome of events must simultaneously reside with the state legislature, Confederate officials, and the people—all of whom found themselves, at one time or another, working at cross-purposes. Singularly, the people grew tired of war, and resistance to it—direct or indirect —grew more manifest as conditions became more desperate. Few men are miracle workers. Given monumental handicaps to overcome, John Pettus probably proved on occasion to be both too imaginative and too slow to be entirely effective. Under the circumstances, what is most amazing is that the struggle for Mississippi's independence lasted as long as it did.

[1] David Potter, "Died of Democracy," in David Donald (ed.), *Why the North Won the Civil War* (Baton Rouge, 1960), 79.

Genealogical Note

THE PETTUS FAMILY of America possesses a colorful ancestry that is traceable as far back as fifteenth-century England. Beyond that point the family tree becomes obscure and its genealogical roots reveal a variety of related names, such as Pettis, Pethawe, Pethowe, Pethous, and Petyous. In any event, the "Pettus" cognomen probably had its origin in the ancient Greek word "petros," meaning stone.[1] A derivation of the same term appears to have eventually made its way into the French language and then entered the English vocabulary as a linguistic byproduct of the Norman conquest. In Christian circles, words pertaining to the stem "pet" have long enjoyed wide popularity because of an identification with the *New Testament* apostle Peter.

As far as available records indicate, the Pettus surname first became distinct around 1450, with the birth of Thomas Pettus in Norwich, England. A grandson and namesake of the latter is likewise of more than passing significance. This Thomas Pettus was not only the owner of a large estate (Rockheath Hall), but succeeded in establishing a future family precedent for public service when he became sheriff, and later mayor, of the Norwich community. Thomas Pettus' son, Sir John Pettus, furthered the tradition of his forebears by also serving as mayor of Norwich and then ascending to a seat in Parliament in 1601.[2] While serving in that august body, Sir John invested in the London Company's commercial venture that ultimately culminated in the founding of Jamestown, Virginia.

An adventurous, one-time soldier-of-fortune in European religious wars and cousin of Sir John, Thomas Pettus, immigrated to Virginia during 1638 and occupied 2,000 acres of land belonging to his uncle. This founder of the American branch of the

---

[1] Stacy, *The Pettus Family*, i; "Historical and Biographical Sketch of the Pettus Family," Weedon Collection.

[2] "The Pettus Line," Typescript prepared by Charles J. Colcock, in E. W. Pettus Papers. See also Hiram K. Douglas, *My Southern Families* (Dorset, England, 1967), 120.

Pettus clan soon became a conspicuous figure in the affairs of that colony, respectively serving as a captain (later colonel) in the local militia and as a member of the Virginia Governor's Council (1646–60).[3] The family coat of arms, denoting military fortitude, honor, generosity, and elevation of mind, was at last planted in the New World.

Throughout the same period members of the Pettus family in England found themselves embroiled in the civil war that swept that nation during the 1640s. Many of them remained loyal to King Charles I, and when the monarch's forces collapsed certain Pettus names were among those included on the prison rolls of the victorious Oliver Cromwell administration. Such unfortunate circumstances undoubtedly account for the accelerated migration of other members of the Pettus clan to America during the next few years. Before long, persons of related lineage were dispersed throughout several Virginia counties, where they became plantation owners and intermarried with such other notable households of the future as the Henrys, Winstons, Taylors, and Madisons.[4]

During the American War of Independence the Virginia Pettuses were staunch patriots and contributed to the colonial cause in both word and deed. One of their number, Samuel Overton Pettus, distinguished himself in two Virginia regiments (Second and Ninth), but had the misfortune of being captured at the battle of Germantown. Another descendant served under George Washington, but, while holding the latter's leadership in the highest regard, often complained of his use of profanity and the "freedom with which 'The Father of his Country' used the English language."[5]

[3] Charles Colcock to Edmund W. Pettus, April 4, 1903 in Weedon Collection; "Pettus Family Notebook" (Typescript in E. W. Pettus Papers), n.d.; Robert A. Stewart (ed.), *Genealogy of Members: Sons of the Revolution in the State of Virginia* (Richmond, 1939), 321; George C. Greer, *Early Virginia Immigrants, 1623–1666* (Baltimore, 1960), 258.

[4] "Notes on Family Genealogy" (Typescript in Weedon Collection), n.d.; William Sclater to E. W. Pettus, April 22, 1903, in Weedon Collection; *Arkansas Gazette*, August 12, 1934.

[5] Virginia House of Delegates Resolution, November 9, 1791; Edmund W. Pettus to Mrs. A. P. Hall, August 20, 1902, in Weedon Collection.

Both before and after the revolutionary conflict, Pettus families prospered on American soil. Typical was the case of Dabney Pettus, a resident of Charlotte County and great-grandson of the original Thomas Pettus. Dabney was not only a planter but the owner of eleven slaves. One of his eight children is of singular significance—John. John and his wife Barbara (a cousin), also slaveholders, had a son who was named in honor of the grandfather.[6] This individual, because of future residence, is genealogically known as John Pettus of Fluvanna County. In turn, he was to become the father of the subject of this study—John Jones Pettus.

[6] Dabney Pettus Will, March 3, 1770, "Pettus Family Bible Records."

Bibliography

PRIMARY SOURCES

MANUSCRIPTS AND PUBLIC DOCUMENTS

Alabama Department of Archives and History, Montgomery
Andrew B. Moore Papers.
Edmund Winston Pettus Papers.
Earl Van Dorn Papers.

Library of Congress, Washington, D.C.
Jasper N. Barritt Papers.
Wimer Bedford Diary.
Judah P. Benjamin Diary.
Silas W. Browing Papers.
William R. Cannon Papers.
Douglas J. Cater and Rufus W. Cater Correspondence.
Confederate Justice Department: District Court Northern Division Mississippi, Minutes Book, 1861–1865.
J. F. H. Claiborne Papers.
John C. Crittenden Papers.
Earl Van Dorn Letters and Telegrams.
William F. Draper Letters.
James H. Goodnow Papers.
William J. Hardee Correspondence.
John Hughes Diary.
Mortimer D. Leggett Papers.
W. W. Lord, "Journal of The Siege of Vicksburg."
John C. Pemberton Papers.

Lonoke County Courthouse, Lonoke, Arkansas
Deed Records.
General Index to Deeds.

Mississippi Department of Archives and History, Jackson
James Lusk Alcorn Diary.
James Lusk Alcorn Papers.
Luther S. Baechel Diary.
Compiled Service Records of Confederates Who Served In Organizations From Mississippi: 28th Cavalry (Microfilm Copy).
Correspondence of Governor John Jones Pettus, 1859–1863, Governor's Records, Series E, Vols. XLIX–LXIII.
William A. Drennan Diary.

1850 Population Census Schedules, Kemper County, Mississippi (Microfilm Copy).

1860 Population Census Schedules, Hinds County, Mississippi (Microfilm Copy).

1860 Population Census Schedules, Kemper County, Mississippi (Microfilm Copy).

Samuel A. French Papers.

Governor's Executive Journal: Governors Foote, Pettus, and McRae, 1852–1857.

Governor's Executive Journal: Governors McRae, Pettus, Clark, and Humphreys, 1856–1866.

Governor's Executive Journal: Governors McRae, McWillie, Pettus, Clark, Humphreys, and Ames, 1857–1870.

James A. Lyon Journal.

Minutes of the Military Board of the State of Mississippi, Series L, Vol. LXXV.

Mississippi State Planning Commission. *A Summary of Statistical Data Relating to the Growth and Distribution of Mississippi Population*, 1939 (Typescript).

Personal Tax Rolls, Kemper County, Mississippi, 1843 (Microfilm Copy).

John Jones Pettus Papers.

Pittman, Anna. "The Pettus Family," n.d. (Typescript).

John L. Power Papers.

Records of the Secretary of State of the State of Mississippi. Series F, Vols. LVIII, LXI, LXV, LXXV.

Stacy, Pocahontas Hutchinson. "The Pettus Family of Virginia," 1940 (Typescript).

State of Mississippi. *Communications From the Hon. Peter B. Starke as Commissioner to Virginia to His Excellency J. J. Pettus, With Accompanying Documents.* Jackson: Ethelbert Barksdale Printers, 1860.

———. *The Constitution of the State of Mississippi*, 1832.

———. *Journal of the House of Representatives of the State of Mississippi.* Called Session, July, 1861.

———. *Journals of the House of Representatives of the State of Mississippi.* Regular Sessions, 1844, 1846, 1861, 1863, 1928.

———. *Journals of the Senate of the State of Mississippi.* Called Sessions, January, 1857; November, 1860; January, 1861; July, 1861; December, 1862.

———. *Journals of the Senate of the State of Mississippi.* Regular Sessions, 1848, 1850, 1852, 1854, 1856, 1858, 1859, 1863, 1928.

———. *Journal of the State Convention and Ordinances and Resolutions* (1861).

———. *Laws of the State of Mississippi.* Regular Sessions, 1850, 1858, 1859–1862.

———. *Register of Commissions, Army of Mississippi, 1861–1865.* Series L, Vol. A.

James H. Stuart Diary.
Swift, Charles J. "James Lusk Alcorn" in James Lusk Alcorn Papers.

National Archives, Washington, D.C.
Amnesty Papers, Group No. 94.
Company Muster Roll: Company B, Colonel Foote's First Mississippi Infantry.
J. F. H. Claiborne Papers, in C.S.A. Private Citizens' File.
Walter Goodman Papers, in C.S.A. Private Citizens' File.
Robert Kells Papers, in C.S.A. Private Citizens' File.
Letters, Orders and Circulars Received by Brigadier General James Chalmers.
Letters and Telegrams In Relation to Illicit Trade With the Enemy: Department of Mississippi and East Louisiana, 1862–1863.
Military Department Endorsements: Department of Mississippi and East Louisiana, 1861–1865.
Telegrams Received by C.S.A. Secretary of War, 1861–1865.
Telegrams Sent by C.S.A. Secretary of War, 1861–1865.

Perkins Library, Duke University, Durham.
Amos B. Browning Scrapbook.
Sydney S. Champion Papers.
Jefferson Davis Papers.
William C. Doub Papers.
Oren E. Farr Papers.
Robert B. Hoadley Papers.
Miscellaneous Confederate Army Letters, 1863–1865.
James A. Seddon Letters.
William D. Somers Papers.
Abby E. Stafford Papers.
Joseph D. Stapp Papers.
Benjamin L. C. Wailes Diary.
John B. Webber Diary.

Southern Historical Collection, University of North Carolina, Chapel Hill.
Samuel A. Agnew Diary.
James Lusk Alcorn Papers.
Joseph D. Alison Diary.
Everard G. Baker Diary.
Boidrick, Annie L. "A Recollection of Thirty Years Ago," 1893 (Typescript).
Brandon, William L. "Military Reminiscences of General William L. Brandon," in J. F. H. Claiborne Papers.
J. F. H. Claiborne Papers.
Robert S. Finley Papers.

"Memoranda by D. C. Glenn on Secession Convention," in J. F. H. Claiborne Papers.
Power (ed.), J. L. "Proceedings and Debates of the Mississippi State Convention of 1861," in J. F. H. Claiborne Papers.
"Speech of A. M. Clayton Before the Secession Convention," in J. F. H. Claiborne Papers.
Samuel A. Whyte Diary.
U.S.S. *Oneida* Diary.

Government Documents
Scott, R. N., et al. *War of the Rebellion: A Compilation of the Official Records of the Union and Confederate Armies.* 129 Vols. Washington: Government Printing Office, 1891.
U. S. War Department. *List of Staff Officers of the Confederate States Army, 1861–1865.* Washington: Government Printing Office, 1891.

NEWSPAPERS

Aberdeen (Miss.) *Monroe Democrat,* 1851.
Aberdeen (Miss.) *Weekly Conservative,* 1855.
Atlanta (Ga.) *Daily Southern Confederacy,* 1863.
Augusta (Ga.) *Daily Chronicle and Sentinel,* 1860.
Brandon (Miss.) *Herald of the South,* 1859.
Canton (Miss.) *American Citizen,* 1860–63, 1865.
Charleston (S.C.) *Daily Courier,* 1859.
Charleston (S.C.) *Mercury,* 1860.
Chattanooga (Tenn.) *Rebel,* 1862.
Clarksdale (Miss.) *Register,* 1910.
DeKalb (Miss.) *Democrat,* 1859.
Fayette (Miss.) *Gazette,* 1862.
Fayette (Miss.) *Jefferson Journal,* 1857.
Fayette (Miss.) *Watch Tower,* 1856.
Fernandina (Fla.) *East Floridian,* 1860.
Hazlehurst (Miss.) *Copiah County News,* 1861.
Hinds County (Miss.) *Gazette,* 1865, 1860, 1862.
Jackson (Miss.)*Clarion,* 1878.
Jackson (Miss.) *Clarion-Ledger,* 1968.
Jackson (Miss.) *Daily Clarion-Ledger,* 1928.
Jackson (Miss.) *Daily Mississippian,* 1861–63.
Jackson (Miss.) *Daily News,* 1952.
Jackson (Miss.) *Daily Southern Crisis,* 1863.
Jackson (Miss.) *Semi-Weekly Mississippian,* 1850, 1859–63.
Jackson (Miss.) *Times,* 1878.
Jackson (Miss.) *Weekly Mississippian,* 1859–63.
Little Rock (Ark.) *Arkansas Gazette,* 1934, 1938.
Little Rock (Ark.) *Daily Arkansas Gazette,* 1888.
Macon (Miss.) *Beacon,* 1862.

Memphis (Tenn.) *Commercial Appeal*, 1928.
Memphis (Tenn.) *Daily Appeal*, 1863.
Mobile (Ala.) *Daily Advertiser and Register*, 1863.
Mobile (Ala.) *Daily Tribune*, 1862.
Monticello (Miss.) *Journal*, 1859.
Natchez (Miss.) *Mississippi Free Trader*, 1857, 1859–63.
Natchez (Miss.) *Daily Courier*, 1860–61, 1863.
Natchez (Miss.) *Weekly Courier*, 1850, 1859–63.
New Orleans (La.) *Bee*, 1860–61.
New Orleans (La.) *Daily Delta*, 1860.
New Orleans (La.) *Daily Picayune*, 1860.
New York *News*, 1863.
New York *Times*, 1860.
New York *Tribune*, 1861.
Okolona (Miss.) *Prairie News*, 1859.
Oxford (Miss.) *Intelligencer*, 1861.
Paulding (Miss.) *Eastern Clarion*, 1860–63.
Pontotoc (Miss.) *Examiner*, 1857.
Port Gibson (Miss.) *Daily Southern Reveille*, 1859.
Richmond (Va.) *Enquirer*, 1860.
Richmond (Va.) *Whig and Public Advertiser*, 1860.
Vicksburg (Miss.) *Daily Whig*, 1860–63.
Vicksburg (Miss.) *Republican*, 1835, 1861.
Vicksburg (Miss.) *Sun*, 1859–60
Vicksburg (Miss.) *Weekly Whig*, 1854, 1859–60.
Woodville (Miss.) *Republican*, 1835, 1861.
Yazoo City (Miss.) *Democrat*, 1854, 1859.
Yazoo City (Miss.) *Sentinel*, 1910.
Yazoo City (Miss.) *Weekly Whig*, 1854.

BOOKS

Abrams, Alexander S. *A Full and Detailed History of the Siege of Vicksburg*. Atlanta: Intelligencer Steam Press, 1863.
Alexander, Edward P. *Military Memoirs of a Confederate: A Critical Narrative*. Bloomington, Ind.: Indiana University Press, 1962.
Archer, Richard T. *Speech of Richard T. Archer, August 10, 1860, at Port Gibson, Mississippi*. Port Gibson, Miss.: Southern Reveille Job Office Press, 1860.
Aughey, John H. *The Iron Furnace: Slavery and Secession*. Philadelphia: William S. and Alfred Martien, 1863.
———. *Tupelo*. Lincoln, Neb.: State Journal Company, 1888.
Beaumont, Mrs. B. *Twelve Years of My Life: An Autobiography*. Philadelphia: T. B. Peterson and Brothers, 1887.
Boyd, Samuel S. *Speech of Hon. Samuel S. Boyd, Delivered at the Great Union Festival Held at Jackson, Mississippi, On the 10th Day of October, 1851*. Natchez: Book and Job Office of the Natchez Courier, 1851.

14 BIBLIOGRAPHY

Browne, Junius Henri. *Four Years In Secessia: Adventures Within and Beyond the Union Lines.* Hartford: O. D. Case and Company, 1865.

Brownlow, W. G. *Sketches of the Rise, Progress, and Decline of Secession.* 2nd. ed. New York: Dacapo Press, 1968.

Chesnut, Mary Boykin. *A Diary From Dixie.* Edited by Ben A. Williams. Boston: Houghton Mifflin Company, 1949.

Claiborne, J. F. H. *Life and Correspondence of John A. Quitman.* 2 vols. New York: Harper and Brothers, 1860.

Clarke, H. C. (ed.). *The Confederate States Almanac and Repository of Useful Knowledge for 1865, Compiled and Published by H. C. Clarke.* Mobile: Printed for the Author, 1865.

Cluskey, M. W. (ed.). *The Political Text-Book, 1858.* Philadelphia: James B. Smith and Company, 1860.

Crummer, Wilbur F. *With Grant At Fort Donelson, Shiloh and Vicksburg.* Oakpark, Ill.: E. C. Crummer and Company, 1915.

Cumming, Kate. *Kate: The Journal of a Confederate Nurse.* Edited by Richard B. Harwell. Baton Rouge: Louisiana State University Press, 1959.

Dana, Charles A. *Recollections of the Civil War, With the Leaders at Washington and in the Field in the Sixties.* New York: D. Appleton Company, 1902.

Davis Jefferson. *A Short History of the Confederate States of America.* New York: Belford Company, 1890.

————. *The Rise and Fall of the Confederate Government.* 2 vols. 2nd. ed. New York: Thomas Yoseloff Company, 1958.

Davis, Reuben. *Recollections of Mississippi and Mississippians.* Boston: Houghton Mifflin Company, 1890.

Davis, Varina Howell. *Jefferson Davis: Ex-President of the Confederate States of America.* 2 vols. New York: Bedford Company, 1890.

Dawson, Sarah Morgan. *A Confederate Girl's Diary.* Edited by James I. Robertson. 2nd. ed. Bloomington, Ind.: Indiana University Press, 1960.

Duncan, Thomas D. *Recollections of Thomas D. Duncan, A Confederate Soldier.* Nashville: McQuiddy Printing Company, 1922.

Dumond, Dwight L. (ed.). *Southern Editorials on Secession.* New York: Century Company, 1931.

Eggleston, George C. *A Rebel's Recollections.* 5th ed. Bloomington, Ind. Indiana University Press, 1959.

Farrar, C. C. S. *The War: Its Causes and Consequences.* Memphis: Blalock and Company, 1864.

Foote, Henry Stuart. *War of the Rebellion: Or Scylla and Charybdis. Consisting of Observations Upon the Causes, Course and Consequences of the Late Civil War in the United States.* New York: Harper and Brothers, 1866.

French, Samuel G. *Two Wars: An Autobiography of General Samuel G. French.* Nashville: Confederate Veteran Publishers, 1901.

Fulkerson, Horace S. *A Civilian's Recollections of the War Between the*

States. Edited by Percy L. Rainwater. 2nd ed. Baton Rouge: Otto Claitor Printer, 1939.
————. *Random Recollections of Early Days in Mississippi*. Vicksburg: Vicksburg Printing and Publishing Company, 1885.
Gailor, Thomas F. *Some Memories*. Kingsport, Tenn. Southern Publishers, 1937.
Goodloe, Albert T. *Confederate Echoes: A Voice from the South in the Days of Secession and of the Southern Confederacy*. Nashville: Smith and Lamar Company, 1907.
Grant, Ulysses S. *Personal Memoirs of U. S. Grant*. Edited by E. B. Long. New York: World Publishing Company, 1952.
Greeley, Horace. *The American Conflict: A History of the Great Rebellion In the United States of America, 1860–1864*. 2 vols. Hartford: O. D. Case and Company, 1864.
Henry, R. H. *Editors I Have Known*. New Orleans: E. S. Upton Printing Company, 1922.
Hunter, John, et al. *Memorials of the Life and Character of Willy P. Harris*. Jackson: Clarion Printing Company, 1892.
Johnston, Joseph E. *Narrative of Military Operations Directed During the Late War Between the States*. Bloomington, Ind.: Indiana University Press, 1959.
Jones, J. B. *A Rebel War Clerk's Diary At the Confederate States Capital*. 2 vols. Philadelphia: J. B. Lippincott and Company, 1866.
Knox, Thomas W. *Camp-Fire and Cotton-Field: Southern Adventure In Time of War*. Cincinnati: Jones Brothers and Company, 1865.
Lord, Walter (ed.). *The Fremantle Diary: Being the Journal of Lieutenant Colonel James Arthur Lyon Fremantle, Coldstream Guards, On His Three Months In the Southern States*. Boston: Little, Brown, and Company, 1954.
Loughborough, Mary Ann. *My Cave Life In Vicksburg With Letters of Trial and Travel*. New York: D. Appleton and Company, 1864.
McKim, Randolph H. *A Soldier's Recollections: Leaves from the Diary of a Young Confederate*. New York: Longmans, Green and Company, 1910.
Montgomery, Frank A. *Reminiscences of a Mississippian in Peace and War*. Cincinnati: Robert Clarke Company, 1901.
Moore, Frank (ed.). *The Rebellion Record: A Diary of American Events*. 11 vols. New York: D. Van Nostrand Company, 1862–71.
Olmsted, Frederick Law. *A Journal in the Back Country in the Winter of 1853–1854*. 2 vols. New York: G. P. Putnam's Sons, 1907.
Pollard, Edward A. *The Lost Cause: A New Southern History of the War of the Confederates*. New York: E. B. Treat and Company, 1866.
Richardson, James D. (ed.). *A Compilation of the Messages and Papers of the Confederacy*. 2 vols. Nashville: United States Publishing Company, 1905.
Rowland, Dunbar (ed.). *Jefferson Davis, Constitutionalist: His Letters,*

Papers and Speeches. 6 vols. New York: J. J. Little and Ives Company, 1923.

————. *Roll of Mississippi Confederate Soldiers.* 10 vols. Jackson: Printed for the Mississippi Archives, 1915.

Russell, William Howard. *My Diary North and South.* New York: Harper and Brothers, 1863.

————. *Pictures of Southern Life, Social, Political and Military.* New York: James G. Gregory Company, 1861.

Scarborough, William K. (ed.). *The Diary of Edmund Ruffin.* Baton Rouge: Louisiana State University Press, 1972.

Sherman, William T. *Memoirs of General W. T. Sherman.* 2 vols. New York: Charles L. Webster Company, 1892.

Stone, Kate. *Brokenburn: The Journal of Kate Stone, 1861–1868.* Edited by John Q. Anderson. Baton Rouge: Louisiana State University Press, 1955.

Taylor, F. Jay (ed.). *Reluctant Rebel: The Secret Diary of Robert Patrick, 1861–1865.* Baton Rouge: Louisiana State University Press, 1959.

Taylor, Richard. *Destruction and Reconstruction: Personal Experiences of the Late War.* Edited by Richard B. Harwell. New York: Longmans, Green and Company, 1955.

Thomas, Benjamin P. (ed.). *Three Years With Grant As Recalled by War Correspondent Sylvanus Cadwallader.* New York: Alfred A. Knopf, 1956.

Thrasher, John B. *Slavery A Divine Institution: A Speech Made Before the Breckinridge and Lane Club, November 5th, 1860.* Port Gibson, Miss.: Southern Reveille Job Office Press, 1861.

Trowbridge, J. T. *The South: A Tour of Its Battlefields and Ruined Cities.* Hartford: L. Stebbing Company, 1866.

Vandiver, Frank E. *The Civil War Diary of General Josiah Gorgas.* University, Ala.: University of Alabama Press, 1947.

Wiley, Bell I. (ed.). *Confederate Letters of John W. Hagan.* Athens, Ga.: University of Georgia Press, 1954.

MISCELLANEOUS SOURCES

Boyd, Mrs. G. C. Personal interview with ex-slave Joe Pettus. DeKalb, Miss., 1936 (Typescript).

————. Personal interview with John Jackson. DeKalb, Miss., 1937 (Typescript).

William Pettus Weedon Collection, Privately held, 200 items, Denver.

Secondary Sources

MONOGRAPHS AND SPECIAL STUDIES

Ambler, Charles H. *Sectionalism in Virginia from 1776 to 1861.* Chicago: University of Chicago Press, 1970.
Angle, Paul M., and Earl S. Miers. *The Tragic Years, 1860–1865.* 2 vols. New York: Simon and Schuster, 1960.
Barnes, Gilbert H. *The Anti-Slavery Impulse, 1830–1844.* New York: American Historical Association, 1933.
Bartlett, Napier. *Military Record of Louisiana.* Baton Rouge: Louisiana State University Press, 1964.
Basso, Hamilton. *Beauregard The Great Creole.* New York: Charles Scribner's Sons, 1933.
Bearss, Edwin C. *Decision In Mississippi: Mississippi's Important Role in the War Between the States.* Jackson: Mississippi Commission on the War Between the States, 1962.
Bernard, Mother M. *The Story of the Sisters of Mercy in Mississippi, 1860–1930.* New York: P. J. Kennedy and Sons, 1931.
Bettersworth, John K. *Confederate Mississippi: The People and Policies of a Cotton State in Wartime.* Baton Rouge: Louisiana State University Press, 1943.
Black, Robert C., III. *The Railroads of the Confederacy.* Chapel Hill: University of North Carolina Press, 1952.
Boatner, Mark. *The Civil War Dictionary.* New York: David McKay Company, 1959.
Boney, F. N. *John Letcher of Virginia.* Tuscaloosa, Ala.: University of Alabama Press, 1966.
Bonham, Milledge L. *The British Consuls In the Confederacy.* New York: AMS Press, 1967.
Boykin, James H. *North Carolina In 1861.* New York: Bookman Associates, 1961.
Bradford, Gamaliel. *Confederate Portraits.* Freeport, N.Y.: Books for Libraries Press, 1914.
Bradlee, Francis B. C. *Blockade Running During the Civil War and the Effect of Land and Water Transportation on the Confederacy.* Salem, Mass.: The Essex Institute, 1925.
Bragg, Jefferson Davis. *Louisiana In the Confederacy.* Baton Rouge: Louisiana State University Press, 1941.
Brewer, William. *Alabama: Her History, Resources, War Record, and Public Men From 1540 to 1872.* Montgomery: Barrett and Brown Company, 1872.
Brown, D. Alexander. *Grierson's Raid: A Cavalry Adventure of the Civil War.* Urbana, Ill.: University of Illinois Press, 1954.
Burnham, W. Dean. *Presidential Ballots, 1836–1892.* Baltimore: Johns Hopkins University Press, 1955.

Cain J. B. *Methodism In the Mississippi Conference, 1846–1870.* Jackson: Mississippi Conference Historical Society, 1939.

Campbell, Mary E. R. *The Attitude of Tennesseans Toward the Union, 1847–1861.* New York: Vantage Press, 1961.

Capers, Gerald M. *John C. Calhoun—Opportunist: A Reappraisal.* Gainesville, Fla.: University of Florida Press, 1960.

———. *Occupied City: New Orleans Under the Federals, 1862–1865.* Lexington, Ky.: University of Kentucky Press, 1965.

Capers, Henry D. *The Life and Times of C. G. Memminger.* Richmond: Everett Waddey Company, 1893.

Carroll, Thomas B. *Historical Sketches of Oktibbeha County.* Gulfport, Miss.: The Dixie Press, 1931.

Catton, Bruce. *Grant Moves South.* Boston: Little, Brown and Company, 1860.

Cauthen, Charles E. *South Carolina Goes to War, 1860–1865.* Chapel Hill: University of North Carolina Press, 1950.

Clark, Thomas D. *A Pioneer Southern Railroad From New Orleans to Cairo.* Chapel Hill: University of North Carolina Press, 1936.

Cotterill, R. S. *The Old South: The Geographic, Economic, Social, Political and Cultural Expansion, Institutions and Nationalism of the Ante-Bellum South.* Glendale, Calif.: Arthur H. Clark Company, 1937.

Coulter, E. Merton. *The Confederate States of America, 1861–1865.* Baton Rouge: Louisiana State University Press, 1950.

Craven, Avery O. *The Growth of Southern Nationalism, 1848–1861.* Baton Rouge: Louisiana State University Press, 1953.

Crenshaw, Ollinger. *The Slave States in the Presidential Election of 1860.* Baltimore: Johns Hopkins University Press, 1945.

Cunningham, Edward. *The Port Hudson Campaign, 1862–1863.* Baton Rouge: Louisiana State University Press, 1963.

Cunningham, H. H. *Doctors In Gray: The Confederate Medical Service.* Baton Rouge: Louisiana State University Press, 1958.

Current, Richard N. *Old Thad Stevens: A Story of Ambition.* Madison, Wisc.: University of Wisconsin Press, 1942.

Davis, William W. *The Civil War and Reconstruction In Florida.* 2nd ed. Gainesville, Fla.: University of Florida Press, 1964.

Deaderick, Barron. *Strategy In the Civil War.* Harrisburg, Pa.: Military Service Publishing Company, 1946.

Denman, Clarence P. *The Secession Movement In Alabama.* Montgomery: Alabama State Department of Archives and History, 1933.

Dodd, William E. *Jefferson Davis.* New York: Russell and Russell, 1907.

———. *Robert J. Walker, Imperialist.* Chicago: Chicago Literary Club, 1914.

———. *The Cotton Kingdom: A Chronicle of the Old South.* New Haven: Yale University Press, 1919.

Dorman, Lewy. *Party Politics in Alabama From 1850 Through 1860* Wetumpka, Ala.: Wetumpka Printing Company, 1935.

Dorris, Jonathan T. *Pardon and Amnesty Under Lincoln and Johnson: The*

Restoration of the Confederates to their Rights and Privileges, 1861–1898. Chapel Hill: University of North Carolina Press, 1953.

Douglas, Hiram K. *My Southern Families.* Dorset, England: The Blackmore Press, 1967.

Dowdey, Clifford. *The Land They Fought For: The Story of the South as the Confederacy, 1832–1865.* New York: Doubleday and Company, 1955.

DuBois, W. E. B. *Black Reconstruction In America.* New York: Russell and Russell, 1962.

Dumond, Dwight L. *The Secession Movement, 1860–1861.* New York: Macmillan Company, 1931.

Dunham, Chester F. *The Attitude of the Northern Clergy Toward the South, 1860–1865.* Toledo: Gray Company Publishers, 1942.

Eaton, Clement. *A History of the Old South.* New York: Macmillan Company, 1949.

———. *A History of the Southern Confederacy.* New York: Macmillan Company, 1958.

———. *The Growth of Southern Civilization, 1790–1860.* New York: Harper and Brothers, 1961.

Ethridge, George H., and Walter N. Taylor (eds.). *Mississippi, A History.* Hopkinsville, Ky.: Historical Record Association, 1939.

Fiske, John. *The Mississippi Valley In the Civil War.* 2nd ed. Boston: Houghton Mifflin Company, 1928.

Fleming, Walter L. *Civil War and Reconstruction in Alabama.* New York: Columbia University Press, 1905.

Foote, Shelby. *The Civil War: A Narrative.* 2 vols. New York: Random House, 1963.

Franklin, John H. *The Militant South: 1800–1861.* Cambridge: Harvard University Press, 1956.

Fulton, John. *Memoirs of Frederick A. P. Bernard.* New York: Macmillan Company, 1896.

Garner, James W. *Reconstruction In Mississippi.* New York: Macmillan Company, 1901.

Gates, Paul W. *Agriculture and the Civil War.* New York: Alfred A. Knopf, 1965.

Gentry, Claude. *Private John Allen, Gentleman—Statesman—Sage—Prophet.* Decatur, Ga.: Bowen Press, 1951.

Goff, Richard D. *Confederate Supply.* Durham: Duke University Press, 1969.

Gray, Wood. *The Hidden Civil War: The Story of the Copperheads.* New York: The Viking Press, 1964.

Greer, George C. *Early Virginia Immigrants, 1623–1666.* Baltimore: Genealogical Publishing Company, 1960.

Hale, Will T., and Dixon L. Merritt. *A History of Tennessee and Tennesseans.* Chicago: Lewis Publishing Company, 1913.

Hamilton, Holman. *Prologue to Conflict: The Crisis and Compromise of 1850.* Lexington, Ky.: University of Kentucky Press, 1964.

Hartje, Robert G. *Van Dorn: The Life and Times of a Confederate General.* Nashville: Vanderbilt University Press, 1967.
Heaps, Willard A., and Porter W. Heaps. *The Singing Sixties: The Spirit of Civil War Days Drawn from the Music of the Times.* Norman, Okla.: University of Oklahoma Press, 1960.
Hendrick, Burton J. *Statesmen of the Lost Cause: Jefferson Davis and His Cabinet.* New York: Literary Guild of America, 1939.
Henry, Robert S. *The Story of the Confederacy.* Indianapolis: Bobbs-Merrill Company, 1931.
Hesseltine, William B. *Civil War Prisons: A Study In War Psychology.* New York: Frederick Ungar Publishing Company, 1964.
Holzman, Robert S. *Stormy Ben Butler.* New York: G. P. Putnam's Sons, 1914.
Howe, Daniel W. *Political History of Secession to the Beginning of the American Civil War.* New York: G. P. Putnam's Sons, 1914.
Howerton, Huey B., et al. *Yesterday's Constitution Today.* Edited by Edward H. Hobbs. University, Miss.: University of Mississippi Press, 1960.
Hunter, Martha T. *A Memoir of Robert M. T. Hunter.* Washington, D.C.: Neale Publishing Company, 1903.
Johnson, Thomas C. *The Life and Letters of Benjamin Morgan Palmer.* Richmond: Presbyterian Committee of Publications, 1906.
Jones, Archer. *Confederate Strategy From Shiloh to Vicksburg.* Baton Rouge: Louisiana State University Press, 1961.
King, Spencer B. *Ebb Tide: As Seen Through the Diary of Josephine Clay Habersham.* Athens, Ga.: University of Georgia Press, 1958.
Klingberg, Frank W. *The Southern Claims Commissions.* Berkeley: University of California Press, 1955.
Leavell, Z. T., and T. J. Bailey. *A Complete History of Mississippi Baptists From the Earliest Times.* 2 vols. Jackson: Mississippi Baptist Publishing Company, 1904.
Lee, Charles R. *The Confederate Constitutions.* Chapel Hill: University of North Carolina Press, 1963.
Lewis, Lloyd. *Sherman: Fighting Prophet.* 3rd ed. New York: Harcourt, Brace and World, 1960.
Livermore, Thomas L. *Numbers and Losses In the Civil War In America, 1861–1865.* Bloomington, Ind.: Indiana University Press, 1957.
Long, E. B., and Barbara Long. *The Civil War Day by Day, An Almanac, 1861–1865.* New York: Doubleday, 1971.
Lonn, Ella. *Desertion During the Civil War.* New York: Century Company, 1928.
———. *Salt As A Factor In the Confederacy.* New York: Walter Neale Publishers, 1933.
Lowry, Robert, and William H. McCardle. *A History of Mississippi.* Jackson: R. H. Henry and Company, 1891.
Lynch, James D. *The Bench and Bar of Mississippi.* New York: E. J. Hale and Son, 1881.
McCain, William D. *The Story of Jackson: A History of the Capital of*

Mississippi, 1821–1951. 2 vols. Jackson: J. F. Hyer Publishing Company, 1953.

McElroy, Robert M. *Jefferson Davis: The Unreal and the Real*. 2 vols. New York: Harper and Brothers, 1937.

Marshall, Theodora B., and Gladys C. Evans. *They Found It In Natchez*. New Orleans: Pelican Publishing Company, 1939.

Massey, Mary E. *Refugee Life In the Confederacy*. Baton Rouge: Louisiana State University Press, 1964.

May, John A., and Joan R. Faunt. *South Carolina Secedes*. Columbia, S.C.: University of South Carolina Press, 1960.

Mayes, Edward. *Lucius Q. C. Lamar: His Life, Times and Speeches*. 2nd ed. Nashville: Barbee and Smith Company, 1896.

Miles, Edwin A. *Jacksonian Democracy In Mississippi*. Chapel Hill: University of North Carolina Press, 1960.

Milligan, John D. *Gunboats Down the Mississippi*. Annapolis: U.S. Naval Institute, 1965.

Mitchell, Joseph B. *Decisive Battles of the Civil War*. New York: G. P. Putnam's Sons, 1955.

Moore, Albert B. *Conscription and Conflict In the Confederacy*. New York: Macmillan Company, 1924.

Nevins, Allan. *The Emergence of Lincoln*. 2 vols. New York: Charles Scribner's Sons, 1950.

———. *The Statesmanship of the Civil War*. New York: Macmillan Company, 1953.

Overdyke, W. Darrell. *The Know-Nothing Party in the South*. Baton Rouge: Louisiana State University Press, 1950.

Parks, Joseph H. *John Bell of Tennessee*. Baton Rouge: Louisiana State University Press, 1950.

Pemberton, John C. *Pemberton: Defender of Vicksburg*. Chapel Hill: University of North Carolina Press, 1942.

Pereyra, Lillian A. *James Lusk Alcorn, Persistent Whig*. Baton Rouge: Louisiana State University Press, 1966.

Phillips, Ulrich B. *Life and Labor in the Old South*. Boston: Little, Brown and Company, 1929.

Pratt, Fletcher. *The Battles That Changed History*. Garden City, N.Y.: Doubleday Company, 1956.

Quarles, Benjamin. *The Negro in the Civil War*. New York: Russell and Russell, 1968.

Rainwater, Percy L. *Mississippi: Storm Center of Secession, 1856–1861*. Baton Rouge: Otto Claitor Publisher, 1938.

Ramsdell, Charles W. *Behind the Lines In the Confederacy*. Edited by Wendell H. Stephenson. Baton Rouge: Louisiana State University Press, 1944.

Ranck, James B. *Albert Gallatin Brown: Radical Southern Nationalist*. New York: D. Appelton-Century Company, 1937.

Rawley, James A. *Turning Points of the Civil War*. Lincoln, Neb.: University of Nebraska Press, 1966.

Rhodes, James Ford. *History of the Civil War, 1861–1865.* Edited by E. B. Long. New York: Frederick Ungar Publishing Company, 1961.

——. *History of the United States from the Compromise of 1850 to the McKinley–Bryan Campaign of 1896.* 8 vols. 2nd ed. New York: Macmillan Company, 1920.

Ringold, May S. *The Role of the State Legislatures In the Confederacy.* Athens, Ga.: University of Georgia Press, 1966.

Robinson, William M., Jr. *Justice In Grey: A History of the Judicial System of the Confederate States of America.* Cambridge: Harvard University Press, 1940.

Rowland, Dunbar. *Encyclopedia of Mississippi History.* 2 vols. Madison, Wisc.: S. J. Clarke Company, 1925.

——. *History of Mississippi: The Heart of the South.* 4 vols. Jackson, S. J. Clarke Company, 1925.

——. *The Official and Statistical Register of the State of Mississippi.* Nashville: Brandon Printing Company, 1908.

Sandburg, Carl. *Storm Over the Land: A Profile of the Civil War.* New York: Harcourt, Brace and World, 1939.

Schultz, Harold S. *Nationalism and Sectionalism in South Carolina, 1852–1860.* Durham: Duke University Press, 1950.

Schwab, John C. *The Confederate States of America, 1861–1865: A Financial and Industrial History of the South During the Civil War.* New York: Charles Scribner's Sons, 1901.

Seitz, Don Carlos. *Braxton Bragg.* Columbia, S.C.: The State Company, 1924.

Shanks, Henry T. *The Secession Movement in Virginia, 1847–1861.* Richmond: Garrett and Massie, 1934.

Shenton, James P. *Robert John Walker: A Politician from Jackson to Lincoln.* New York: Columbia University Press, 1961.

Sillers, Florence W. *History of Bolivar County, Mississippi.* Jackson, Miss.: Hederman Brothers, 1948.

Silver, James W. *A Life for the Confederacy: As Recorded In the Pocket Diaries of Private Robert A. Moore.* Jackson, Tenn: McCowat-Mercer Press, 1959.

——. *Confederate Morale and Church Propaganda.* Tuscaloosa, Ala.: Confederate Publishing Company, 1957.

Simkins, Francis B., and James W. Patton. *The Women of the Confederacy.* New York: Garrett and Massie, 1936.

Sitterson, Joseph C. *The Secession Movement in North Carolina.* Chapel Hill: University of North Carolina Press, 1939.

Smith, Edward C. *The Borderland In the Civil War.* New York: Macmillan Company, 1927.

Stacy, Pocahontas Hutchinson. *The Pettus Family.* Edited by A. R. Rudd. Washington, D.C.: Privately Printed, 1957.

Stampp, Kenneth M. *And the War Came: The North and the Secession Crisis, 1860–1861.* Baton Rouge: Louisiana State University Press, 1950.

Steiner, Paul E. *Disease In the Civil War: Natural Biological Warfare In 1861–1865.* Springfield, Ill.: Charles L. Thomas, Publisher, 1968.

Stephenson, Nathaniel W. *The Day of the Confederacy: A Chronicle of the Embattled South.* New Haven: Yale University Press, 1920.

Stewart, Robert A. (ed.). *Genealogy of Members: Sons of the Revolution in the State of Virginia.* Richmond: Mitchell and Hotchkiss Printers, 1939.

Strode, Hudson. *Jefferson Davis: American Patriot, 1808–1861.* New York: Harcourt, Brace and Company, 1955.

Sydnor, Charles S. *A Gentleman of the Old Natchez Region: Benjamin L. C. Wailes.* Durham: Duke University Press, 1938.

————. *Slavery in Mississippi.* New York: American Historical Association, 1933.

Talley, Robert. *One Hundred Years of the Commercial Appeal: The Story of the Greatest Romance In American Journalism, 1840–1940.* Memphis: Memphis Publishing Company, 1940.

Tatum, Georgia Lee. *Disloyalty In the Confederacy.* Chapel Hill: University of North Carolina Press, 1934.

Thomas, Benjamin P. *Abraham Lincoln: A Biography.* New York: Alfred A. Knopf Company, 1952.

Todd, Richard C. *Confederate Finance.* Athens, Ga.: University of Georgia Press, 1954.

Vandiver, Frank E. *Ploughshares Into Swords: Josiah Gorgas and Confederate Ordnance.* Austin: University of Texas Press, 1952.

————. *Rebel Brass: The Confederate Command System.* Baton Rouge: Louisiana State University Press, 1956.

Walker, Peter F. *Vicksburg: A People At War, 1860–1865.* Chapel Hill: University of North Carolina Press, 1960.

Warner, Ezra J. *Generals In Gray: Lives of the Confederate Commanders.* Baton Rouge: Louisiana State University Press, 1959.

Weaver, Herbert. *Mississippi Farmers, 1850–1860.* Nashville: Vanderbilt University Press, 1945.

Wender, Herbert. *Southern Commercial Conventions, 1837–1859.* Baltimore: Johns Hopkins University Press, 1930.

White, Laura A. *Robert Barnwell Rhett: Father of Secession.* New York: American Historical Association, 1931.

Wiley, Bell I. *The Life of Johnny Reb: The Common Soldier of the Confederacy.* New York: Bobbs–Merrill Company, 1962.

————. *Southern Negroes, 1861–1865.* New Haven: Yale University Press, 1938.

Williams, Kenneth P. *Lincoln Finds A General: A Military Study of the Civil War.* 4 vols. New York: Macmillan Company, 1956.

Winston, Robert W. *High Stakes and Hair Trigger: The Life of Jefferson Davis.* New York: Henry Holt Company, 1930.

Wise, Barton H. *The Life of Henry A. Wise of Virginia, 1806–1876.* New York: Macmillan Company, 1899.

Wood, Robert C. *Confederate Handbook: A Compilation of Important Data and Other Interesting and Valuable Matters Relating to the War Between the States, 1861–1865.* New Orleans: Graham Press, 1900.

Wooster, Ralph A. *The People In Power: Courthouse and Statehouse in the Lower South, 1850–1860.* Knoxville: University of Tennessee Press, 1969.

————. *The Secession Conventions of the South.* Princeton: Princeton University Press, 1962.

Yearns, Wilfred B. *The Confederate Congress.* Athens, Ga.: University of Georgia Press. 1960.

Zorn, Walter L. *The Descendants of the Presidents of the United States of America.* 2nd ed. Monroe, Mich.: Privately Printed, 1955.

PERIODICAL ARTICLES

Anderson, John Q. "Dr. James Green Carson Ante-Bellum Planter of Mississippi and Louisiana," *Journal of Mississippi History,* XVIII (October, 1956), 243–67.

Barnard, Frederick A. P. "Autobiographical Sketch of Dr. F. A. P. Barnard," *Publications of the Mississippi Historical Society.* 14 vols Edited by Franklin L. Riley (Oxford, Miss.: Printed for the Society, 1912), XII, 104–21.

Bonham, Milledge L. "Financial and Economic Disturbance in New Orleans On the Eve of Secession," *Louisiana Historical Quarterly,* XIII (January, 1930), 32–36.

————. "Louisiana's Seizure of the Federal Arsenal at Baton Rouge, January, 1861," *Proceedings of the Historical Society of East and West Baton Rouge,* VIII (1917–18), 47–55.

Boudurant, Alexander L. "Did Jones County Secede?" *Publications of the Mississippi Historical Society.* 14 vols. Edited by Franklin L. Riley (Oxford, Miss.: Printed for the Society, 1898), I, 104–106.

Bowman, Robert. "Yazoo County In the Civil War," *Publications of the Mississippi Historical Society.* 14 vols. Edited by Franklin L. Riley (Oxford, Miss.: Printed for the Society, 1903), VII, 57–73.

Cabaniss, Francis A., and James A. Cabaniss, "Religion In Mississippi Since 1860," *Journal of Mississippi History,* IX (October, 1947), 195–218.

Caldwell, Joshua W. "John Bell of Tennessee: A Chapter of Political History," *American Historical Review,* IV (July, 1899), 652–64.

Cappleman, Josie F. "Local Incidents of the War Between the States," *Publications of the Mississippi Historical Society.* 14 vols. Edited by Franklin L. Riley (Oxford, Miss.: Printed for the Society, 1901), IV, 79–87.

Cauthen, Charles E. "South Carolina's Decision to Lead the Secession Movement," *North Carolina Historical Review,* XVIII (July, 1949), 360–72.

Chambers, William P. "My Journal," *Publications of the Mississippi His-*

torical Society. 5 vols. Edited by Dunbar Rowland (Jackson: Printed for the Society, 1925), Centenary Series, V, 227–386.

Cole, Arthur C. "The South and the Right of Secession in the Early Fifties," *Mississippi Valley Historical Review,* I (December, 1914), 376–99.

DeBow, J. D. B., "Journal of the War," *DeBow's Review,* XXXII (May–August, 1862), 319–31.

Deupree, J. G. "The Noxubee Squadron of the First Mississippi Cavalry, C. S. A., 1861–1865," *Publications of the Mississippi Historical Society.* 5 vols. Edited by Dunbar Rowland (Oxford, Miss.: Printed for the Society, 1918), Centenary Series, II, 9–143.

Dodge, David. "Domestic Economy In the Confederacy," *Atlantic Monthly,* LVIII (August, 1886), 229–42.

Drake, Winbourne M. "The Mississippi Constitutional Convention of 1832," *Journal of Southern History,* XXIII (August, 1957), 354–70.

"Edmund Winston Pettus," *Dictionary of American Biography,* 21 vols. Edited by Allen Johnson and Dumas Malone (New York: Charles Scribner's Sons, 1928–37), XIV, 519–20.

"Edmund Winston Pettus," *The New Century Cyclopedia of Names.* 3 vols. Edited by Clarence L. Barnhart (New York: Appleton–Century–Crofts, 1954), III, 3157.

Erickson, Edgar L. (ed.). "Hunting for Cotton In Dixie: From the Civil War Diary of Captain Charles E. Wilcox," *Journal of Southern History,* IV (November, 1938), 493–513.

Fleming, Walter L. "Jefferson Davis' First Marriage," *Publications of the Mississippi Historical Society.* 14 vols. Edited by Franklin L. Riley (Oxford, Miss.: Printed for the Society, 1912), XII, 21–36.

Garner, James W. "The First Struggle Over Secession in Mississippi," *Publications of the Mississippi Historical Society.* 14 vols. Edited by Franklin L. Riley (Oxford, Miss.: Printed for the Society, 1901), IV, 89–104.

———. "The State Government of Mississippi During the Civil War," *Political Science Quarterly,* XVI (June, 1901), 283–302.

Gonzales, John E. "Henry Stuart Foote: A Forgotten Unionist of the Fifties," *The Southern Quarterly,* I (January, 1963), 129–39.

Grenshaw, Ollinger, "Christopher G. Memminger's Mission to Virginia, 1860," *Journal of Southern History,* VIII (August, 1942), 334–49.

Gunn, Jack W. "Mississippi in 1860 As Reflected in the Activities of the Governor's Office," *Journal of Mississippi History,* XXII (July, 1960), 179–92.

Halsell, Willie D. "The Friendship of L. Q. C. Lamar and Jefferson Davis," *Journal of Mississippi History,* VI (July, 1944), 131–44.

Harris, Wiley P. "Autobiography of Wiley P. Harris," in Dunbar Rowland, *Courts, Judges and Lawyers of Mississippi, 1798–1935* (Jackson: Hederman Brothers Press, 1935), I, 270–329.

Haskell, Fritz (ed.). "Diary of Colonel William Camm, 1861 to 1865," *Journal of the Illinois State Historical Society,* XVIII (October, 1925), 793–969.

Hearon, Cleo. "Mississippi and the Compromise of 1850," *Publications of the Mississippi Historical Society*. 14 vols. Edited by Franklin L. Riley (Oxford, Miss.: Printed for the Society, 1914), XIV, 7–227.

———. "Nullification In Mississippi," *Publications of the Mississippi Historical Society*. 14 vols. Edited by Franklin L. Riley (Oxford, Miss.: Printed for the Society, 1912), XII, 37–71.

Hooker, Charles E. "Mississippi," *Confederate Military History*. 12 vols. Edited by Clement A. Evans (Atlanta: Confederate Publishing Company, 1899), VII, 3–515.

James, Alfred P. "General Joseph Eggleston Johnston, Storm Center of the Confederate Army," *Mississippi Valley Historical Review*, XIV (December, 1927), 342–59.

Johnson, Frank. "The Vicksburg Campaign," *Publications of the Mississippi Historical Society*. 14 vols. Edited by Franklin L. Riley (Oxford, Miss.: Printed for the Society, 1909), X, 63–90.

Johnston, Joseph E. "Jefferson Davis and the Mississippi Campaign," *Battles and Leaders of the Civil War*. 4 vols. Edited by Robert U. Johnson and Clarence C. Buell (New York: Century Company, 1887–88), III, 472–82.

Jones, J. H. "The Rank and File at Vicksburg," in Franklin L. Riley (ed.) *Publications of the Mississippi Historical Society* (Oxford, Miss.: Printed for the Society, 1903), VII, 17–31.

Kelley, Donald B. "Harper's Ferry: Prelude to Crisis in Mississippi," *Journal of Mississippi History*, XXVII (November, 1965), 351–72.

Lang, Herbert H. "J. F. H. Claiborne At 'Laurel Wood' Plantation, 1853–1870," *Journal of Mississippi History*, XVIII (January, 1956), 1–17.

Leavell, Z. T. "The Ante-Bellum Historical Society of Mississippi," *Publications of the Mississippi Historical Society*. 14 vols. Edited by Franklin L. Riley (Oxford, Miss.: Printed for the Society, 1904), VIII, 227–37.

McFarland, Baxter. "A Forgotten Expedition to Pensacola In January, 1861," *Publications of the Mississippi Historical Society*. 14 vols. Edited by Franklin L. Riley (Oxford, Miss.: Printed for the Society, 1906), IX, 15–23.

McNeily, J. S. "War and Reconstruction In Mississippi, 1863–1890," *Publications of the Mississippi Historical Society*. 5 vols. Edited by Dunbar Rowland (Oxford, Miss.: Printed for the Society, 1918), Centenary Series, II, 165–535.

Montgomery, Goode. "Alleged Secessions of Jones County," *Publications of the Mississippi Historical Society*. 14 vols. Edited by Franklin L. Riley (Oxford, Miss.: Printed for the Society, 1904), VIII, 13–22.

Moore, Glover. "Separation From the Union, 1854–1861," *A History of Mississippi*, 2 vols. Edited by Richard A. McLemore (Hattiesburg, Miss., 1973).

Moore, J. Quitman. "The Attitude of the South," *DeBow's Review*, XXIX (July, 1860), 25–31.

Moore, John H. "Mississippi's Ante-Bellum Textile Industry," *Journal of Mississippi History*, XVI (April, 1954), 81–98.

Moore, Ross H. "The Vicksburg Campaign of 1863," *Journal of Mississippi History*, I (July, 1939), 151–68.

Odom, Van D. "The Political Career of Thomas Overton Moore, Secession Governor of Louisiana," *Louisiana Historical Quarterly*, XXVI (October, 1943), 975–1054.

Owsley, Frank L. "The Fundamental Cause of the Civil War: Egocentric Sectionalism," *Journal of Southern History*, VII (August, 1941), 3–18.

Parks, Joseph H. "A Confederate Trade Center Under Federal Occupation: Memphis, 1862 to 1865," *Journal of Southern History*, VII (1941), 289–314.

———. "John Bell and the Compromise of 1850," *Journal of Southern History*, IX (August, 1943), 328–56.

Patridge, I. M. "The Press of Mississippi—Historical Sketch," *DeBow's Review*, XXIX (October, 1860), 500–509.

Perkins, Howard C. "A Neglected Phase of the Movement for Southern Unity, 1847–1852," *Journal of Southern History*, XII (May, 1946), 153–203.

Peterson, Owen. "Ethelbert Barksdale in the Democratic National Convention of 1860," *Journal of Mississippi History*, XIV (October, 1952), 257–78.

Pike, Albert. "Dixie," In Albert Bushnell Hart (ed.), *Welding of the Nation, 1845–1900* (New York: Macmillan Company, 1901), 277–78.

Porter, David D. "The Opening of the Lower Mississippi," *Battles and Leaders of the Civil War*. 4 vols. Edited by Robert U. Johnson and Clarence C. Buell (New York: Century Company, 1887–88), II, 22–56.

Potter, David. "Died of Democracy," *Why the North Won the Civil War*. Edited by David Donald (Baton Rouge: Louisiana State University Press, 1960), 79–90.

Price, Beulah M. D'Olive (ed.). "Excerpts From the Diary of Walter Alexander Overton, 1860–1862," *Journal of Mississippi History*, XVII (July, 1955), 191–204.

"Proceedings of the Southern Convention Held At Vicksburg, Mississippi," *DeBow's Review*, XXVII (July, 1859), 94–103.

Rainwater, Percy L. "An Analysis of the Secession Controversy in Mississippi, 1854–1861," *Mississippi Valley Historical Review*, XXIV (June, 1937), 35–42.

——— (ed.). "The Autobiography of Benjamin Grubb Humphreys, August 26, 1808–December 20, 1882," *Mississippi Valley Historical Review*, XXI (September, 1934), 231–55.

——— (ed). "Letters of James Lusk Alcorn," *Journal of Southern History*, III (May, 1937), 196–209.

———. "Notes On Southern Personalities," *Journal of Southern History*, IV (May, 1938), 209–27.

Riley, Franklin L. "Life of Col. J. F. H. Claiborne," *Publications of the Mississippi Historical Society*. 14 vols. Edited by Franklin L. Riley (Oxford, Miss.: Printed for the Society, 1903), VII, 217–44.

Ringold, May S. "James Lusk Alcorn," *Journal of Mississippi History*, XXV (January, 1963), 1–14.

Silver, James W. (ed.). "The Breakdown of Morale in Central Mississippi in 1864: Letters of Judge Robert S. Hudson," *Journal of Mississippi History*, XVI (April, 1954), 99–120.

"Southern Rights Association of Virginia," *DeBow's Review*, XXVIII (February, 1860), 173–82.

Stover, John F. "Colonel Henry S. McComb, Mississippi Railroad Adventurer," *Journal of Mississippi History*, XVII (July, 1955), 177–90.

Sydnor, Charles S. "Historical Activities in Mississippi in the Nineteenth Century," *Journal of Southern History*, III (May, 1937), 139–60.

Trexler, Harrison A. "The Opposition of Planters to the Employment of Slaves as Laborers by the Confederacy," *Mississippi Valley Historical Review*, XXVII (1940–41), 211–24.

Vandiver, Frank E. "Jefferson Davis and Unified Army Command," *Louisiana Historical Quarterly*, XXXVIII (1955), 26–38.

Venable, Austin L. "The Conflict Between the Douglas and Yancey Forces in the Charleston Convention," *Journal of Southern History*, VIII (May, 1942), 226–41.

Weathersby, W. H. "A History of Mississippi College," *Publications of the Mississippi Historical Society*. 5 vols. Edited by Dunbar Rowland (Oxford, Miss.: Printed for the Society, 1925), Centenary Series, V, 184–220.

Wheaton, C. C. "The Secession of Louisiana, January 26, 1861," *Proceedings of the Historical Society of East and West Baton Rouge*, VLLI (1917–18), 55–60.

Whittington, G. P. "Thomas O. Moore: Governor of Louisiana, 1860–1864," *Louisiana Historical Quarterly*, XIII (January, 1930), 5–31.

Woods, Thomas H. "A Sketch of the Mississippi Secession Convention of 1861—Its Membership and Work," *Publications of the Mississippi Historical Society*. 14 vols. Edited by Franklin L. Riley (Oxford, Miss.: Printed for the Society, 1902), VI, 91–104.

UNPUBLISHED SOURCES

Rawson, Donald M. "Party Politics in Mississippi, 1850–1860." Unpublished Ph.D. dissertation, Vanderbilt University, 1964.

Adams, Horace. "Military Operations In and Around Jackson, Mississippi, During the Civil War." Unpublished Master's thesis, University of Mississippi, 1950.

Wade, John C. "Charles Clark, Confederate General and Mississippi Governor." Unpublished Master's thesis, University of Mississippi, 1949.

Index